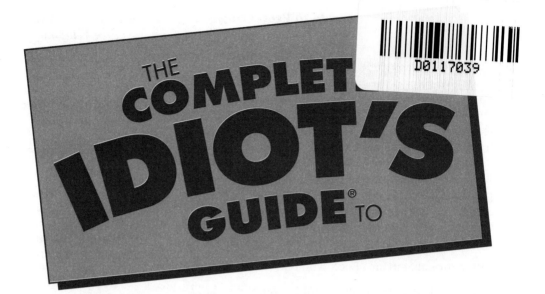

THE COMPLETE IDIOT'S GUIDE® TO

Protecting Yourself Online

by Preston Gralla

A Division of Macmillan Computer Publishing
201 W. 103rd Street, Indianapolis, IN 46290

Trademarks

Warning and Disclaimer

Executive Editor
Greg Wiegand

Acquisitions Editor
Stephanie McComb

Development Editor
Gregory Harris

Technical Editor
John Ray

Managing Editor
Thomas F. Hayes

Project Editor
Leah C. Kirkpatrick

Copy Editor
Kelli Brooks

Indexer
William Meyers

Proofreaders
Jeanne Clark
Ryan Walsh

Interior Design
Nathan Clement

Cover Design
Michael Freeland

Illustrator
Judd Winick

Copy Writer
Eric Borgert

Layout Technicians
Lisa England
Tricia Flodder

Contents at a Glance

Contents

Part 3 Snoopers Everywhere: How to Keep Your Email Private   77

About the Author

Preston Gralla is the author of 11 books, including the best-selling *How the Internet Works* and *The Complete Idiot's Guide to Online Shopping*. He has written about the Internet and computer technology for many magazines and newspapers, including *USA Today, PC Magazine,* the *Los Angeles Times, Boston Magazine,* and *PC/Computing,* and has won several writing and editing awards, including one for the best feature article in a computer magazine from the Computer Press Association. As a well-known Internet expert, he appears frequently on TV and radio shows such as *CBS This Morning, MSNBC,* and ZDTV's *Call for Help.* He is the executive editor of the ZDNet Software Library at www.hotfiles.com, and was the founding managing editor of *PC Week* and a founding editor of *PC/Computing.* Gralla lives in Cambridge, Massachusetts, with his wife, Lydia, children, Gabriel and Mia, and a rabbit named Polichinelle. He also writes the free *Gralla's Internet Insider* email newsletter. To subscribe to it for free, send email to preston@gralla.com with the words SUBSCRIBE NETINSIDER on the subject line.

Acknowledgments

This book, as any, is the work of many people. I'd like to thank Stephanie McComb, acquisitions editor, for making this book happen, and development editor Gregory Harris for whipping it into shape. Many thanks also go to John Ray, tech editor extraordinaire, who made sure that my facts were accurate and that I wasn't missing anything important. Thanks also to project editor Leah Kirkpatrick, copy editor Kelli Brooks, and the production staff.

And, as always, thanks to my agent, Stuart Krichevsky, my wife, Lydia, and my kids, Gabriel and Mia.

Tell Us What You Think!

As the reader of this book, *you* are our most important critic and commentator. We value your opinion and want to know what we're doing right, what we could do better, what areas you'd like to see us publish in, and any other words of wisdom you're willing to pass our way.

As a Publisher for Que, I welcome your comments. You can fax, email, or write me directly to let me know what you did or didn't like about this book—as well as what we can do to make our books stronger.

Please note that I cannot help you with technical problems related to the topic of this book, and that due to the high volume of mail I receive, I might not be able to reply to every message.

When you write, please be sure to include this book's title and author as well as your name and phone or fax number. I will carefully review your comments and share them with the author and editors who worked on the book.

Fax: (317) 581-4666

Email: gwiegand@mcp.com

Mail: Greg Wiegand
          Que Corporation
          201 West 103rd Street
          Indianapolis, IN 46290 USA

Introduction

Recently, someone pointed out to the head of one of the world's largest computer companies, Scott McNealy of Sun Microsystems, that a new Internet technology his company was developing could lead to a massive invasion of people's privacy. His terse response: "You have zero privacy now. Get over it."

This book is devoted to showing you just how wrong he is. Yes, it's true that your privacy and security can be endangered when you use the Web. But as I'll show you, you can do much more than merely try and "get over it." You can fight back, take control of your online life, and make sure that you're safe and secure whenever you use the Internet or online services.

There's been nothing in the history of humankind like the Internet—nothing else can give you access to such a vast amount of information; nothing else lets you communicate in so many ways with so many other people whether they be down the street or on the other side of the globe; nothing else gives you such power over the way you shop, the way you live, the way you work, and the way you have fun.

And nothing else can allow your privacy to be invaded or security threatened so easily. Sure, you already know it's the greatest information-gathering resource ever invented—but that also means it's an easy way to gather information about *you*. And in many ways, it's also easy to threaten your security.

This book teaches you all the essentials about staying safe when you go online. Whether you're worried about details of your private life being gathered, scared that your email can be intercepted and read, or concerned that your Web surfing habits are being watched, I teach you how to fight back. If you're worried about being scammed and spammed, no problem. I show you what you can do. Whether the issue be fear of viruses, worries about the safety of your kids when they log on, concern that your credit card number will be stolen when you buy at a Web store, or anything else related to privacy and security, I teach you how you can be safe and secure whenever you get onto the Internet or an online service such as America Online.

Here's some more good news: Staying safe and protecting your privacy on the Internet need not be a chore. It doesn't have to get in the way of enjoying the Internet or gaining access to its vast resources. I show you easy, simple things you can do to protect yourself and your family, no matter what you do online or how you use the Internet.

I've been using the Internet since before the days when the World Wide Web was invented, so I've been concerned with these kinds of security and privacy issues for quite a while. Over the years, I've gathered scores and scores of ways to keep myself, and my family, safe and secure no matter what we do on the Internet. And as part of my job as Executive Editor of the ZDNet Web site at www.zdnet.com, I am constantly getting email from people wanting advice on how to fight viruses or keep their email secure. I've offered them advice over the years on what to do, and now I'm passing all that on to you.

So check out this book, follow my advice, and you'll never have to worry again when you head online.

How to Use This Book

I've organized this book into nine parts. I start off teaching you about the basics of Internet privacy and security, so that you fully understand how the Internet works, why it can be used to gather information about you, and why it can be such an unsecure place. Next, you see how you can put up your first line of cyberdefense with your Internet service provider. We move on from there to learn about how to protect yourself and your privacy when using email, when on the Web, or when chatting or participating in public discussion groups. There's a section devoted to keeping your children and family safe and another showing you how to stay safe when shopping online. You also learn how to protect yourself against viruses. In the last part of the book, you get tips and advice on how to protect your PC—and how you can use the Internet to track down privacy-related information.

In Part 1, "The Basics of Internet Privacy and Security," you learn all the basics of Internet privacy and security. You get an understanding of how the Internet works and why it's such an unsecure place. And you get a rundown of all the dangers to your privacy and security whenever you connect.

Part 2, "Putting Up Your First Line of CyberDefense," shows you the first steps to take to ensure that you're safe when you go online and that no one snoops on you. You see how to remove your name from Web databases so that no one can gather information about you, what you can do to make sure that your Internet service provider (ISP) doesn't invade your privacy, and how to create hacker-proof passwords, so they can't be stolen. You also learn how to protect yourself against online scams.

In Part 3, "Snoopers Everywhere: How to Keep Your Email Private," you learn about all the dangers of email—everything from your private messages being read by others to getting viruses from files attached to email to how you can be targeted by scammers and junk emailers, called spammers. But you do more than just learn about the dangers—I give you easy-to-follow advice on how you can keep your email private and make sure you aren't targeted by junk mailers.

Part 4, "Protecting Your Privacy and Security on the World Wide Web," covers all the dangers posed by the most popular part of the Internet—the Web. There are many of them. Your surfing habits can be traced, put into databases, and sold to the highest bidder. Cookies—little bits of information—can be put on your hard disk without you knowing about it, and so everything you do on a site can be tracked. Registration forms can be used to gather huge amounts of personal information about you. And Web sites can look inside your browser and find out a surprising amount of information about you. This section of the book shows how you can fight against all that, so that your privacy need not be invaded.

In Part 5, "Protecting Yourself in Chat Areas and Usenet Newsgroups," you see the dangers posed by chatting and joining public discussions—and what you can do to make sure that you're never a victim. Personal profiles can be built about you based on what you say online, and in this section, you learn how to make sure you're never profiled.

Part 6, "Protecting Your Children and Family Online," covers the very serious issue of how to keep your children safe when they surf the Web, chat, send or receive email, or do anything else on the Internet or online services. You can see that some simple steps will keep your kids safe and secure. I have two children of my own who are online all the time, and I give advice about what I've learned in my years of teaching them how to use the Internet safely.

In Part 7, "Let's Go CyberShopping: How to Buy Online Safely," you learn all about how to stay safe when using the Internet to buy. There are great deals to be had on the Internet, and it offers convenience and a wealth of goods to buy. In this section, you see the steps to take to make sure your credit card information isn't stolen or privacy invaded. You see how to check out a site to make sure that it's one you can trust. And you learn how to make sure that when you buy at auction sites, you never get burned. (By the way, for more information on how to buy online, you might want to check out my book *The Complete Idiot's Guide to Shopping Online*.)

Part 8, "Protecting Yourself Against Viruses, Trojan Horses, and Other Nasty Creatures," shows you how to make sure that your computer is never infected by a virus or other program that can do damage. You might be surprised at just how easy it is fight against viruses and other malicious programs.

Part 9, "Protecting Your PC and Other Privacy Issues," covers issues beyond the Internet. You see how you can password-protect your computer so that no one else can use it and snoop on you. You find out that even when you delete a file, someone can still read it—but I show you how to make sure that when you delete it, it can *never* be read. You also see how you can use the Internet to get information about privacy and security issues of all kinds, not just those related to your online life.

Finally, there is a glossary, "Speak Like a Geek," that defines computer and technical terms that you might be confused about.

Extras

To help you understand the online jungle, this book also gives you extra secrets, inside tips, and bits of information that will help you get the most out of your money. You'll find them in these boxes:

Check This Out!

The Check This Out sections throughout the book point out things that are noteworthy, stuff to be leery of, great tips—basically, they are full of information that adds to your understanding of security or give insightful background.

Techno Talk

Techno Talk boxes highlight terms, methods, or brainy stuff that you don't necessarily need to know, but that definitely helps you make more sense out of security and privacy.

Notes

The Note boxes are used as a catchall to pass along cross-references pointing you to other sections of the book, to provide interesting facts, or for anything else you should take a look at.

Part 1

The Basics of Internet Privacy and Security

There are hackers and crackers out there. There are people who want to snoop on your email and flood your email box with junk mail. They want to con you out of your money, invade your privacy, steal your identity, get your credit card number, find out your Social Security number, and put viruses on your hard disk. They want to find out why your Aunt Mary spent two months away from home just before she was married, they want to tie you up with rope and tickle your feet, they want to…

Oops, sorry, got carried away there. Forget about Aunt Mary and your feet. But the truth is, there are people and businesses who want to get information about you, impinge on your security, and invade your privacy when you're online. Luckily, there's a lot you can do to fight back. But before you learn how to fight back, you'll have to first understand the basics of Internet privacy and security. That's what you'll learn in this part. You'll learn how the Internet works, you'll find out why it can be so easily used to invade your privacy and impinge on your security, you'll learn why shopping online can cause problems, and you'll find out about viruses and what dangers there are to kids online.

So come on along. You'll learn about all that and more…and no one will tickle your feet, I promise.

Oooh...

Chapter 1

Understanding the Internet and Online Security

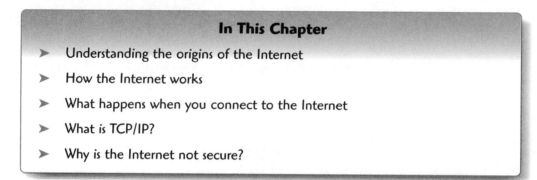

In This Chapter

➤ Understanding the origins of the Internet

➤ How the Internet works

➤ What happens when you connect to the Internet

➤ What is TCP/IP?

➤ Why is the Internet not secure?

Surprise! If you visit the Internet, someone might be watching you. The very thing that makes the Internet a great, freewheeling place to talk to others, find information, do business, and generally have a great time is the same thing that makes it a place to take precautions with your security and privacy.

In this chapter, you'll take a look at the Internet and online security. You'll see how the Internet had its origins in the days of the Cold War and bell bottoms and look at how the basic design of the Internet makes it a place that can be insecure.

What Do the Brady Bunch, Disco, the Internet, and World War III Have in Common?

Why is the Internet an insecure place? To understand that, let's look at how the Internet was born. Step with me for a minute into my Wayback Machine and let's go back in time a decade or two, which, in the computing world, is practically the beginning of recorded history.

In the late 1960s and early- to mid-1970s, the military and computer scientists had some problems. These were big problems, ones that posed even greater challenges to the future of Western Civilization than did disco, bell bottoms, smiley faces, and the Brady Bunch—although those were pretty big problems as well. Anyway, the two basic problems that the military and computer scientists faced were these:

➤ How can computer scientists and military researchers better share information and computing resources with each other?

➤ What are we going to do if World War III breaks out? How can we build a network that can survive the Bomb?

You're probably thinking that if World War III broke out, the last thing you'd worry about is getting a bunch of computers to talk to each other. Instead, you'd like to know something more basic like, "Will I live past 2 p.m. tomorrow afternoon?" Me, too. But you're probably not in the military and probably aren't a computer scientist. They're paid to think differently than us. And if you're going to keep the U.S. mail and income taxes going, you need a computer network.

Making things even more complicated was that, in those days, people were using all kinds of different computers. People at one university used one kind of computer, a computer scientist used another, the military used yet others. They had to figure out a way to get them all to talk to one another. Considering that computer scientists sometimes didn't talk to their colleagues down the hall, this was no small feat.

Techno Talk

What's a Communications Protocol?

For computers to talk to one another, they have to agree on a kind of common language. A common language that lets computers talk to one another is called a communications protocol. There are many different kinds of communications protocols, including several that govern how computers talk to one another over the Internet.

They came up with a pretty smart plan, though. There were two parts to the plan:

➤ Come up with a common way for different kinds of computers to talk to one another—communications protocols that allow computers to exchange information with one another.

The protocols they came up with even allowed someone with a computer in one part of the country to use the resources of a much larger computer in another part of the country.

➤ Develop a system that allows computers to communicate with each other from anywhere in the country, even if wires are cut between them.

They did this by developing a technique that was smart enough to reroute messages over a different set of wires from one computer to another if anything went wrong between them. In fact, they created a system that allowed hundreds or thousands of computers across the country to be joined in a giant network.

The computers in the network were smart enough to know the fastest route for a message to be sent and continually checked for the fastest ways for messages to be sent. If a wire or computer got zapped by a nuclear blast in Ohio, the message could be sent by way of Wisconsin.

Eventually, what the computer scientists and Defense Department came up with became what we call the Internet today.

Techno Talk

What's a Computer Network?

When computers are connected to each other and communicate with each other, they're called a network. Many workplaces have networks of computers hooked up to one another in what's called a *local area network*—a network of computers just for that company. But there are other networks as well. The biggest is the Internet, which is a network of networks—a whole lot of networks connected together across the whole planet.

You're probably thinking, what does this have to do with Internet privacy and security? Plenty, as it turns out. Back in those let-it-all-hang-out days of the '60s and '70s, no one thought that malicious people might use the computer network for nefarious purposes. In fact, the entire network was specifically designed to be as open as possible. How else could researchers share information? How else could a scientist in one part of the country control a computer located two thousand miles away? Back then, people who used computer networks were a small, relatively close-knit group of people, and they never imagined that the network they were working on would one day span the globe and include many, many millions of people. It was kind of like an old-fashioned neighborhood where no one ever locked their front doors because they all knew each other. Try that today, and you'll lose everything in your house that's not nailed down.

It's More than Magic: How the Internet Works

Since those early Internet days of the late 1960s and 1970s, the network has evolved into today's Internet. Some things still work like they did back then, and some things are different. If you care about your security and privacy, here's a rundown on what you need to know about how the Internet works today. (Pitch alert! If you want to learn everything you'll ever need to know about how the Internet works, check out my book *How the Internet Works*, ISBN 0-7897-1726-3. OK, enough pitches. Now back to your regularly scheduled program.)

The easiest way to understand how the Internet works is to see what happens in a typical Internet session—and see where your security and privacy are at risk when you do it.

What Happens When You Connect to the Internet

Most people connect to the Internet via an Internet service provider (ISP) such as AT&T WorldNet or America Online. (Some people connect via cable modems or from their computers at work from their workplace's local area network. Those are fast connections. Lucky them.)

When you dial into your ISP, usually the first thing that happens is you send a password and username to the ISP, which allows you to log on. So right off the bat, something can go wrong. Someone could find out your username and password and pose as you online. For information about how to stop this kind of thing, turn to Chapter 4, "How to Create Hacker-Proof Passwords."

While you're logging on, your computer is also establishing a connection with the ISP using the Internet's basic protocols that have the mouth-crushing name Transmission Control Protocol/Internet Protocol, usually called TCP/IP for short. (More on TCP/IP later in this chapter. In fact, more on it throughout the book.)

When you've logged on and your TCP/IP connection is established, you're given what's called an IP address. It's an address that only a computer could love and understand—there are no words in it, and it has nothing to do with your physical location. Instead, it's a series of four numbers, separated by periods like this: 147.23.0.124. (Periods are called "dots" in Internet-speak, by the way. Why? I don't have a clue. Makes things sound more important, I think.) This IP address identifies you to the computers and servers that make up the Internet. Without an IP address, you wouldn't be able to do things like browse the Web. Your IP address works with the TCP/IP protocols to do all the kinds of Internet magic that you've grown to know and love.

The Internet Is Based on "Client-Server" Technology

No, it has nothing to do with waiters and fancy restaurants. In client-server technology, the software that runs on your computer is called a *client*, and the computer on the Internet that you contact is called a *server*. Your client and the Internet server work together to do the work of the Internet. So, for example, when you go to a Web site, the client (your Web browser) contacts the server (the computer that runs a Web site). The server (the Web server) then sends your computer a Web page, and your client (your Web browser) displays the page on your computer.

Why should you care about this? Because in this kind of technology, the server can get information from the client—which means that there are ways for an Internet site to get information about your computer and the way you use it on the Internet.

Usually, you're given a different IP address every time you log on to your ISP, although a few ISPs give you the same IP address each time you log on.

You need this IP address to do things like browse the Web. But it can also be used to invade your privacy and compromise your security. Because, essentially, that IP address identifies yourself to computers on the Internet. So, for example, a Web site can track what you do when you visit, because it can identify your IP address and watch what you do on the site. (For more information about this and what you can do to protect yourself, turn to Chapter 12, "What Dangers Are There to Your Privacy and Security on the Web?")

What Happens When You Send and Receive Email

So you've logged on to your ISP. It's time to send and receive mail. You log on to your mail account. You might have a separate username and password for your email account—and again, here's a prime place where you're vulnerable. You don't want anyone stealing your username and password and reading your mail or posing as you and sending out email. (Turn to Chapter 4 to make sure you have a safe password.)

You log on. You read your mail, respond to a few messages, compose a few new messages, and then log off. Believe it or not, there are ways that hackers can conceivably read your mail as it gets sent across the Internet. But there are also ways to keep your mail private. To see how, turn to Chapter 9, "Keeping Your Email Private with Encryption."

What's POP3 and SMTP?

The Internet is full of acronyms, each one more difficult to understand than the last. When setting up your email software, you might come across two of them: POP3 and SMTP. POP3 refers to an Internet mail server (Post Office Protocol) that lets you receive mail. SMTP stands for Simple Mail Transfer Protocol and refers to an Internet mail server that lets you send mail. Often, you have to identify these servers when you set up your email program. They have names like smtp.bigisp.net or pop3.bigsip.net.

The reason your email can be read by hackers has to do with the way that TCP/IP works. And for details about that, read on.

What's This TCP/IP Stuff I Hear About—And Why Should I Care?

As you've probably noticed by now, I keep mentioning TCP/IP. No, it's not that it makes me feel geeky and super-cool to use those acronyms. It's that no matter what you do on the Internet, you're using TCP/IP. So let's take a look at what TCP/IP does, and why it's what makes the Internet so great—and also why it's one of the main reasons the Internet can be such an insecure place.

Earlier in this chapter, we took a trip in the Wayback Machine to visit the groovy, far-out, right-on late 1960s and early 1970s to look at the origins of the Internet. One of the big things that the military and computer scientists cared about back then was making sure that if World War III broke out, computers could still communicate with each other, even if there were a lot of broken connections in the network. They came up with TCP/IP.

TCP and IP go together like love and marriage, like a horse and carriage, like...well, you get the picture. They work really well together. Here's how.

When you send information over the Internet, TCP immediately springs into action. It takes that piece of information and breaks it up into a whole lot of tiny pieces called *packets*. Then it sticks a bunch of information into each packet—things like the IP address of where the information is being sent, your current IP address, the order of the packet, and similar things. Then it takes those packets and sends them on their merry way across the Internet.

Techno Talk

What's a Packet Header?

When TCP breaks something into packets, it puts information into each packet, things such as the IP address where the information is headed. It puts this information into what's called a *packet header*. Routers (which you read about in a second) examine this packet header to figure out where to send each packet.

Now IP takes over. Those packets are sent one after another over the Internet. They go to computers on the Internet called *routers*. Routers do pretty much what they say—they route the packets toward their destination. Using the IP protocol, they examine every single packet that comes their way. They look for the IP address where the information is headed. Then they send that packet to the next closest router to the destination. Each packet usually goes from router to router until it reaches its destination.

Routing things this way makes sure that the packets get to their destination, even if routers along the route crash (or in the case of World War III, in case they're blown to smithereens). Routers constantly check which routers are live and which are dead. So if one router goes down, it simply sends the packet to another router.

Now the packets all start arriving at their destination. TCP takes over again. The receiving computer uses TCP to look inside each packet. Because each packet can take a different route to get to its final destination, they can arrive out of order. But TCP is able to use the information put into each packet to reassemble the information into its original form. All this, by the way, happens lightning-fast.

You're probably thinking that all this sounds pretty neat, but so what? What does it all have to do with privacy and security?

Plenty, it turns out. Here's the problem. Routers aren't the only computers that can look at all those packets whizzing every which way on the Internet. Hackers can look at those packets as well. And they can do more than look at them. They can reassemble them, which means they can look at what information people send to each other. They can get information about your IP address and the receiving IP address. And hackers aren't the only problem. Even Web sites on the up-and-up can get information about you.

This means that you have to assume that unless you or a Web site has taken measures to protect yourselves, whatever information you send over the Internet can be read and used by someone else. In the case of buying online with credit cards, Web sites can use technologies to scramble that information so that hackers can't read it.

The Web Is Not the Entire Internet

Most people use the terms the Web and the Internet interchangeably. But in fact, the Web is only one part of the Internet—one of the newer parts of the Internet at that. When we looked around in our Wayback Machine back in the late 1960s and early 1970s, we found nothing that even resembled the Web. It's a Johnny-Come-Lately that's been around only since the 1990s. There are other parts of the Internet, and they can pose dangers as well. Here's a list of the most common areas and what kind of dangers they might pose:

> ➤ **Email**   It's possible for people to snoop and read your email or break into your email account and use it.

> ➤ **Chat**   Chat lets two or more people type messages to each other in real time, back and forth. There are many different kinds of Internet chat, including the original, called IRC, newer ones such as America Online's Instant Messenger, and a popular chat program called ICQ (pronounced "I seek you"). People can listen in on chats, and they can also get your email address as you chat. You can see an example of a chat session here.

14

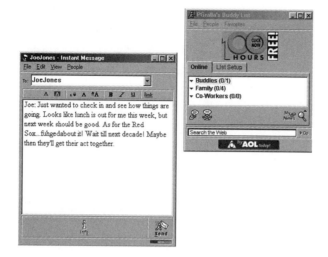

Chat is one of the more popular uses of the Internet—but it isn't secure, either.

➤ **Databases**   There are databases located on the Internet that people could break into. These databases might have private information about you.

➤ **Other Internet resources**   There are all kinds of oddball Internet resources that you've probably never heard of, things like Telnet and rlogin. They each pose their own unique security and privacy problems. You probably don't need to worry about them, though, because you'll probably never use these resources.

All this information is just the tip of the iceberg when it comes to what you need to know about security and privacy on the Internet. For an overview of what kinds of dangers there are to privacy and security when you're online, turn to Chapter 2, "What Dangers Are There to Your Privacy and Security?"

The Least You Need to Know

➤ The Internet has its origins in the 1960s and 1970s, as a way to help the military and computer researchers share information.

➤ When you go online, people and Web sites can see what information you send across the Internet.

➤ The basic protocol that guides the Internet is TCP/IP.

SMILE FOR THE CAMERA!

What Dangers Are There to Your Privacy and Security?

In This Chapter

➤ The ways that Web sites can invade your privacy

➤ Why you need to worry about your email

➤ How credit card information can be stolen when you're on the Internet

➤ The dangers of shopping online

➤ Dangers posed by the Internet to kids and families

In the last chapter, we looked at how the Internet works and why the way it works can pose a threat to your privacy and security. But the dangers there were all theoretical. In this chapter, we begin to see the nitty-gritty—it's an overview of what kinds of dangers there are online. In addition to these dangers, I've also included the chapters you can turn to so you can find out how to combat them. So as you read, don't worry—you have the power to fight back and win.

What Kind of Privacy Dangers Are There?

Let's start off with the scary stuff. Just what kinds of dangers to your privacy are there out there? And how bad is it?

As I said in my introduction to this book, Scott McNealy, head of Sun Microsystems, one of the largest computer manufacturers in the world, was asked about the potential privacy dangers posed by a new Internet technology his company was developing. His terse response was, "You have zero privacy now. Get over it."

Now, I don't think things are quite as bad as Mr. McNealy says they are—you don't have zero privacy. And I certainly don't agree that the only response to a lack of privacy online is that you should "Get over it." Instead, you should fight back, and there's a whole lot you can do, as this book will show you. Still, there are a whole lot of dangers to your privacy out there. Here's the short list. This book shows you how you can protect yourself against all these invasions of your privacy and more:

➤ **Web sites can look at your Internet settings and learn a great deal of information about you.** When you visit a Web site, Web servers can often find out what state you're located in, the operating system you use, the Web browser you use, what site you just visited, possibly what kind of business employs you, and even more information. To see an example of information that can be found out, check out the information Anonymizer.com can gather about you.

When you browse the Web, do you feel like someone is watching you? That's because they can be. The excellent privacy Anonymizer Web site at www.anonymizer.com *shows you some of the information that can be gathered about you when you browse the Web.*

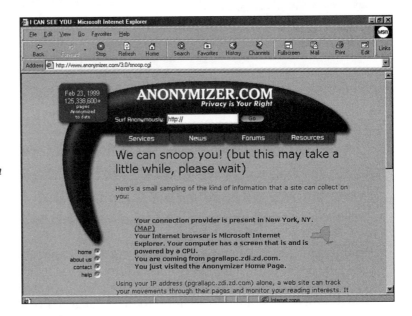

➤ **Web sites can track what you do.** Web sites can do more than just get information about you. They can also track what you do when you visit. So, for example, a Web site can know what pages you look at when you visit, what kind of news and information you like to read, how many minutes you spend at the site, and more. For more information about this and how to combat it, turn to Part 4, "Protecting Your Privacy and Security on the World Wide Web."

➤ **Someone could "steal" your identity.**
So much personal information can be
gained about you from the Internet that
someone can steal your identity—gather
all the information about you and then
pose as you, not only online, but in the
real world. This is called *identity theft*. (Of
course, some days, I must admit, I'd *pay*
someone to take over my identity for me.)
For more information about identity theft
and how to combat it, turn to Part 4.

➤ **Web databases can include private
information about you.** Free, publicly
accessible databases on the Web can contain a good deal of information about you
that you'd prefer not be made public. It's
easy to find out your home address,
phone number, email addresses, and more at many popular Web sites. For how
to fight this, turn to Chapter 5, "Fight Back: How to Remove Your Name from
Web Databases."

Techno Talk

What Are Cookies?

No, I'm not talking about Famous
Amos, Oreos, or ginger snaps.
Cookies are little bits of data that a
Web site can put on your computer
when you visit. That Web site can
then use that cookie as a way to
track everything you do when you
visit.

➤ **Your email can be read.** Hackers have ways of reading your email as it's sent
across the Internet. For more information about this and how to fight it, turn to
Part 3, "Snoopers Everywhere: How to Keep Your Email Private."

➤ **Information about your interests and personal life can be gathered
from public discussion areas.** Old messages never die on the Internet—they
live forever and can be easily looked through to find information about you.
Someone can easily go to a public site such as Deja.com at `www.deja.com`, type
your name, and find out every posting you've made. That means they can find
out your personal interests and read notes that you've sent to others. In essence,
they can create a personal profile of you and your interests. For more information about this and how to protect your privacy, turn to Chapter 17, "Protecting
Your Privacy on Internet Newsgroups and Discussion Areas."

➤ **Someone can steal your passwords.** Think of all the passwords you use
online. There are passwords to log on to the Internet, to get your mail, to get
onto certain Web sites…a whole lot of them, everywhere you go. Some wily
hackers have ways of stealing passwords, which means they can read your email
and do other nasty things. For more information and how to combat this, turn
to Chapter 4, "How to Create Hacker-Proof Passwords."

It's easy to find out some-one's personal interests at a site such as Deja.com at www.deja.com.

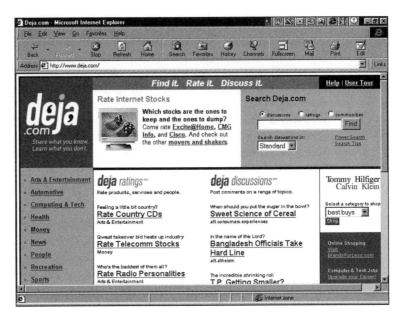

Techno Talk

What Are Usenet Newsgroups?

No, they're not groups of people talking about the news. Usenet newsgroups are public discussion boards where people talk about every topic imaginable, from Japanese cartoons to computers to sports teams to rock stars. To participate, you need a special piece of software called a *newsgroup reader* (which comes with Netscape, Internet Explorer, and Outlook Express), or you can go to a Web site that lets you read newsgroups, such as Deja.com at www.deja.com.

➤ **Marketing groups and companies can compile comprehensive profiles about your buying and Web surfing habits.** Knowing how you spend your money and time is big business, because you can be targeted with ads, junk email, junk mail, and other nasty things that you might not like to see. There are ways to fight back, though. Tips on how to fight back are spread throughout the book, but you'll find advice particularly in Part 4.

Your Credit Card Information Can Be Stolen

Frightening thought: Someone can conceivably steal your credit card information when you send it over the Internet. (Of course, if they stole mine, I'm not sure how much harm could be done, considering it always seems to be maxed out.) Someone can steal credit card information because when information travels over the Internet, there's nothing to stop people from reading it.

Techno Talk

What Is SSL?

No, it's not a new type of supersonic transport. It stands for Secure Sockets Layer, and it's a kind of technology that scrambles information as it gets sent over the Internet. It can be used at shopping sites to scramble your credit card information so that no hackers can read your credit card number—well, they could read it but not make sense of it. Many sites already use it, and eventually, many more will as well.

It's particularly important because great deals can be had when you shop on the Internet—bargains, free goods, and much more. (Pitch alert! For everything you want to know about shopping online, check out my book *The Complete Idiot's Guide to Online Shopping*, ISBN 0-7897-1761-1. Hey, make it easy on yourself. Buy it at an Internet book-buying site like Amazon at www.amazon.com or Barnes & Noble at www.barnesandnoble.com.)

There are ways to battle credit card fraud. You can make sure that you buy only at secure sites—sites that use encryption to scramble credit card information so that no hackers or other snoopers can read it as it's sent across the Internet. (The two book sites I just mentioned are examples.) There are ways to check out a site before buying there. For all the information you'll ever want about how to make sure you're not victimized by someone stealing your credit card online, turn to Chapter 23, "How to Protect Your Credit Card and Buy at a Secure Site."

The Dangers of Shopping Online

When you shop online, there are more dangers than your credit card being stolen. I'm talking about things even worse than buying a lime polyester leisure suit—the kind with the really big wing collars, that used to be known affectionately as the "Full Cleveland." (Note to people in Cleveland: Please don't send me hate mail. I didn't invent the term. I'm just repeating it.) Now I know it's hard to believe anything can be worse than a Full Cleveland in lime. But there are worse things, strange to say. Here's what you should be watching out for, in addition to credit-card theft and bad taste in clothing:

➤ **Can the site be trusted with your credit card?** Before you give your credit card over to a site, you want to know that the site will deliver the goods to you and won't abscond with your credit card. You should know how to check out a site before buying there. Turn to Chapter 23 for more information on how to check out a site.

➤ **Will the site sell or trade information about you and your buying habits with other companies?** When you buy something online, the company you bought from knows a whole lot of information about you. They know what you like to buy. They might know your clothing size or shoe size, your taste in music and books, your address, phone number, email address, age, and a whole lot of other personal information. Will that site sell this information about you? Before you buy at a site, you should check out their privacy rules. Turn to Chapter 23 for more information on how to check out a site to make sure it doesn't do slimy things like this. Pictured here is the publicly posted privacy policy of eToys, an excellent toy-buying site that adheres to good privacy rules.

➤ **Will you be subject to an Internet buying scam?** Scam artists have discovered the Internet big-time, and they've turned out in large numbers. Want to make a million dollars at home in your spare time? How'd you like all your credit-card debt to simply disappear overnight? And if those sound good, how about buying the Brooklyn Bridge, dirt cheap? Every scam imaginable has been tried on the Internet. It's easy to avoid them if you know what to look for. For advice on how to avoid online scams, head to Chapter 22, "Show Me the Money! How Do You Buy Online—And What Dangers Are There?"

➤ **If you're buying at an auction site or classified ad site, can you trust the person you're buying from?** Auction sites have become just about the hottest sites on the Internet for buying all kinds of things—everything from coins to computers to dolls and more. At many of them, you don't buy from the site itself. Instead, you buy from an individual. But how can you be sure the person won't take the money and run or sell you bad goods? There are all kinds of ways to make sure you don't get ripped off at auctions and classified ad sites. For details, head to Chapter 24, "How to Stay Safe When Buying at Auctions."

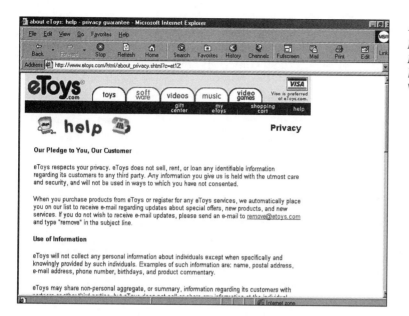

Here's an example of a publicly posted privacy policy (say that four times fast)—the eToys site at www.etoys.com.

Beware of Buying Sports Memorabilia Online

Sports memorabilia is a big business and more and more of it is bought and sold over the Internet, especially at Internet auction sites. A word of warning: Never buy sports memorabilia online. It's become a big scam, and there's no way to check out authenticity ahead of time. How bad is it? Try this case on for size: Someone was offering baseballs that former baseball great Roberto Clemente supposedly had signed. The only problem was Clemente died five years before the balls were manufactured. Either Roberto figured out a way to come back from the dead, or there was a scam afoot—and last time I checked the *National Enquirer,* there had been no Roberto Clemente sightings.

Pick a Number...Any Number—It Identifies You

From the moment you turn your computer on in the morning to the moment you turn it off at night, it can identify you to all comers. It does this by creating a wide variety of numeric IDs—most of which you probably don't know about—and often lets other people see them. Here's a rundown of many of them:

➤ **IP address**   To get onto the Internet, you need a specific Internet address, called an IP address. It's four numbers, separated by dots, like this: 12.133.2.144. Generally, every time you connect to the Internet, you're given a different IP address—although if you're on some company networks, and if you use some Internet service providers, you have a permanent address. When you're online, that number is freely available to the world.

➤ **Windows 95 and Windows 98 number**   Hidden deep in your system, if you use Windows 95 or Windows 98, there's a unique registration number that is only your own. This number is used to create unique numbers that identify you and that are embedded in documents you create, such as word processing files and spreadsheets. When this information was publicly revealed, Microsoft announced it would disable the technology—but only in future ver sions of Windows 98 and beyond.

➤ **Ethernet network card address**   If you're on a corporate network, or if you use a cable modem, you have an Ethernet network card in your computer. You need this card to connect to the network. In turn, the network connects you to the Internet. Every Ethernet card has a unique identifying number called a MAC address that is used to identify your computer. The number is also used in concert with Windows 95 and Windows 98 numbers to create numbers that identify you in documents you create, such as your word processing files and spreadsheets.

➤ **Pentium III chip**   Do you have a computer based on the Pentium III chip? Surprise! There's a unique serial number hardcoded into it that can identify you to the world when you're connected to the Internet. Intel, the manufacturer of the chip, claims that you can block access to the number if you want. Hackers and privacy experts say it's wrong.

➤ **Computer game numbers**   Do you play computer games against others over the Internet? If so, your computer can send out a number identifying

Delete Hidden Numbers in Your Word Processing Files and Spreadsheets

If you don't like the idea of your documents, such as word processing files and spreadsheets, carrying an identifying ID, there's something you can do about it—use two free utilities from Microsoft. One will delete the IDs from files you've already created, and the other will make sure that no future files you create will carry the ID. To get them, head to Microsoft's main site at www.microsoft.com, and go to the OfficeUpdate area. Then look for the security section. You'll find information there about the utilities and how to use them.

you. In some computer games, you need to connect to a large computer on the Internet called a *server* to find opponents to play against. To make sure that you're the real deal and have a registered copy of the software, a number can be sent to the server, which checks it to make sure that you've legally bought the software.

Viruses and Other Ugly Beasts

What Does Download Mean?

When you transfer a file from somewhere on the Internet to your computer, you're downloading the file. It's being sent from a computer on the Internet straight to your computer.

Imagine this: You download a file to your computer and two days later your hard disk crashes. Or you open a file that you were sent via email and you find out that half the files on your computer were deleted. Sound impossible? It isn't. It can happen to you. It's happened to other people. It's happened to me. I've been hit with a virus, for example, and I know a whole lot of other people who have, also.

If you've downloaded something and bad things start happening, a virus has attacked your computer. A virus is a malicious computer program that damages files on your computer. There are all kinds of them, and often they're disguised as friendly programs.

Viruses aren't the only malicious programs out there. There are things called Trojan Horses, for example. And sometimes, you don't even know you're downloading something that can harm your computer. This can happen with things called ActiveX controls or Java applets. (More on those later in this book.)

There are many things you can do to make sure that you're not hit by a virus, other than making sure you always go out with your galoshes on (see, your mother was right about that, wasn't she?). To find out how to protect yourself, head to Part 8, "Protecting Yourself Against Viruses, Trojan Horses, and Other Nasty Creatures."

Online Dangers for Kids

Kids are particularly susceptible to dangers online. By nature, they're curious and are still discovering things about the world. At times, they're rebellious. And they love— absolutely *love*—to go online, find new things, chat with others, and generally spend a whole lot of time in cyberspace. I know all this from experience. I have two kids, and both of them are big-time users of the Internet, so much so that the only way to get any peace around my house was to get them their own computers—and me one of my own.

The Internet is a great place for kids. But you want to make sure that they're safe when they go online as well. To do that, turn to Part 6, "Protecting Your Children and Family Online." Here's a brief rundown on the kinds of things you should know about:

➤ **Your child could view inappropriate material online.** It's a sad fact of the Internet that there's a lot of inappropriate material online, from pornography to violence to hate groups. There's a lot you can do to stop that, though, as you'll see in Chapter 20, "How to Keep Your Kids Safe on the Internet."

Use Site-Blocking Software to Keep Your Kids from Visiting Inappropriate Sites

Software is available that can prevent your children from viewing inappropriate material online. It's commonly called site-blocking software, but it can stop them from doing more than just visiting inappropriate Web sites. It can also block their access to inappropriate discussion areas and other material as well. More on this in Chapter 20.

➤ **Your child could be harassed by someone online.** Someone—another child or an adult—could harass your child by sending them threatening email chat messages or messages that makes them feel uncomfortable. Again, there's a lot you can do to stop that, as you'll see in Chapter 20.

➤ **Your child could develop an inappropriate relationship with someone online—and try to extend it to the real world.** People aren't who they say they are online. That 12-year-old girl who your daughter thought she just befriended could instead be a 45-year-old man posing as a young girl. Again, though, there's a lot you can do to stop this, as you'll see in Part 6.

➤ **Your child's privacy could be invaded, and information given to marketers and others.** You look at your children and see innocence. Businesses look at them and see dollar bills. Children wield an enormous amount of buying power in today's economy—billions and billions of dollars' worth. So they've been targeted as little consumers with access to big wallets—namely, your wallet. Web sites often lure children in with games and freebies, but when your kids are there, the sites sneakily get them to provide personal information about themselves—information that is then used to target them and market to them. Things have gotten so bad that even the federal government has gotten into the act and is threatening legal action unless the Internet sites clean up their acts. Don't count on it, though. You'll have to take action as a parent. It's easy to do, as you'll see in Part 6.

The Least You Need to Know

➤ When you surf to Web sites, those Web sites can gather a great deal of information about you, including what pages you visit and where you're located.

➤ Before giving out your credit card information, make sure you're visiting a secure site that scrambles that information as it travels online.

➤ One of the most common dangers online is the theft of passwords.

➤ Files that you download from the Internet could contain viruses or other malicious kinds of programs.

➤ You should provide your children with guidance when they go on the Internet to keep them safe.

Part 2

Putting Up Your First Line of CyberDefense

To be safe and to protect your privacy online, you've got to be strong. Very strong. Stronger than the starting line of the Green Bay Packers. So strong that even the most determined hacker can't bust through your defenses.

But how can you be strong if, when it comes to hacking and cracking Internet technology, you're really just a 98-pound weakling? Easy. Follow the advice in this part. You'll learn how anyone—even someone just learning to use the Internet—can put up a powerful CyberDefense. You'll find out how to make sure that your Internet service provider doesn't invade your privacy. You'll see how you can create hacker-proof passwords. You'll find out how to get your name out of Web databases. And you'll find out how you can easily protect yourself against the most common Internet scams.

In fact, after you read this part, you won't feel like a 98-pound cyberweakling anymore. You'll put up a line of defense so powerful that even Green Bay Packers of hackerdom won't be able to break through. And you'll never have to worry about hackers kicking sand in your face again.

Chapter 3

SHHHH...

Making Sure Your Internet Service Provider (ISP) Protects Your Privacy

In This Chapter

➤ What information your Internet service provider knows about you

➤ How to choose an Internet service provider that won't invade your privacy

➤ How to make sure your privacy isn't invaded on America Online

➤ What you need to know about cable modems and WebTV

➤ The nasty little secret about privacy in the workplace

The greatest threat to your privacy online might not be from the Web sites you visit or from hackers intent on finding out every aspect of your personal life. Instead, the worst threat might come from your Internet service provider (ISP). Your ISP can know everything about your Web surfing habits, has access to your email and credit card, and can get a lot more information about you.

In this chapter, I'll look at ways you can make sure that your ISP, including America Online, cable modem companies, and WebTV, don't invade your privacy. And I'll look at what kinds of privacy you have at your workplace and what you can do about it.

What Kinds of Information Do Your ISP and Online Service Know About You?

Do you really need to worry about what your ISP knows about you? After all, what do they really do except allow you to dial in and get onto the Internet, right?

Well, let me put it this way: Do the hens in a hen house need to worry if the fox is the one guarding them? Your ISP, more than any Web site, more than any hacker, more than anyone, has the ability to learn just about everything about you. Consider what they can find out if they'd like to know:

➤ Your name, address, telephone number, and other identifying information

➤ Your credit card number

➤ Personal information you might have given them when you joined

➤ Every Web site you've ever visited

➤ The full contents of all email that's ever been sent to you or you've ever sent to anyone else

Keep Up with All the Latest News About Internet Privacy

If you want to find out all the latest news, information, and links to helpful resources about privacy, check out the Privacy Page at www.privacy.org. It's a great site for learning everything you'll ever want to know about Internet privacy—and if you want to get involved to help protect privacy, it tells you how to do that as well.

➤ Every chat session you've ever participated in

➤ What files you've downloaded

➤ What you've bought over the Internet

➤ Everything you've ever done online when connecting through them

They know information such as your name, phone number, credit card number, address, and other personal information because you filled out that kind of information when you applied to join. They can know everything you've ever done when you're on the Internet because of the nature of the Internet—that is, all your Internet communications go through your ISP, who has access to all of it. I mean everything:

every letter to your old girlfriend, every stupid post you ever made on a bulletin board, every time-wasting Web site you ever visited...the whole schmear, as they say in some sections of New York.

Just because an ISP *can* find out all this information doesn't mean it *will* find out the information. And even if it knows this information, the ISP will *probably not* use it in any way. If the ISP does use it, so what? Read on, and you'll see what to worry about, as if you didn't already have suspicions.

Why Should You Care What Your ISP and Online Service Do with Personal Information?

Personal information about you and what you do with your time is worth big bucks to some people. Especially to sleazy marketers. So imagine that your ISP sells all your demographic information, including everything you've ever bought online (including that "Full Cleveland" lime-colored polyester leisure suit) to other companies. You'll spend the rest of your life fighting off telemarketers, junk mailers, junk emailers, and others trying to sell you everything under the sun. Including a few more Full Cleveland leisure suits. And you just might bite.

There's more. ISPs could provide that information to various police and law enforcement sources, including the IRS. (No problem, you've never fudged a little on your taxes, have you? You have? Oh, that's a different story...) If you think this is impossible, consider this: America Online provided personal information about a gay sailor to the Navy, which used that personal information to kick him out of the service.

But wait, as they say on late-night TV, there's more to come. They could provide personal information to private lawyers in a suit against you, so that whoever is suing could pry into your private life in ways never before possible.

Just thinking about all this stuff scares me. But don't worry. There are things you can do to make sure this kind of information isn't gathered or used against you. Next, we'll look at how you can make sure your ISP protects your privacy. Later in the chapter, we'll look at what you can do to make sure online services respect your privacy.

Making Sure Your ISP Protects Your Privacy

There are things you can do to make sure your ISP protects your privacy. The primary thing is to find out the privacy policy, and if you don't like it, find another ISP.

First, if you already have an ISP, or are looking for a new ISP, check its Web site and find out what its publicly posted policy is about privacy. You may or may not find something; not all ISPs post this kind of thing. And you'll probably have to poke around pretty deep until you find it. Here you can see an example of the privacy policy concerning email posted by an ISP called The Internet Access Company (TIAC).

Here's an example of a privacy policy concerning email posted by an ISP— The Internet Access Company (TIAC).

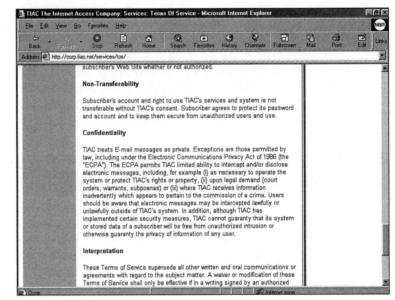

Don't stop with checking out the Web site. Call the ISP and ask for its privacy policies in writing. If it won't give you one, find another ISP. There are many ISPs out there hungry to get your business, so shop around.

The Federal Electronic Computer Privacy Act (ECPA) Provides Some Email Privacy Protection

The ECPA, a federal law passed over a decade ago, provides some protection against your ISP snooping on your email—it bans your ISP from reading or giving your email to anyone it isn't intended for. That's the good news. The bad news is that there are loopholes in it big enough to drive a truck through. For example, if your ISP suspects that someone sending mail is trying to damage the ISP's system or endanger another user on the system, the ISP can read the mail. If your ISP is subpoenaed, it has to turn over the mail. If your ISP gets information that the email might be related to the commission of a crime, it can read the mail. So although the law provides a bit of protection, it doesn't offer a whole lot of it.

When researching the privacy policies of these ISPs, you can figure that you'll be reading a whole lot of legal mumbo-jumbo and hard-to-follow gobbledygook. (After all, what do lawyers get paid for, except to confuse people?) After sifting through the lawyerly verbiage, here's what you should look for when checking your ISP's privacy policy:

➤ **Do they share information about you with other companies, especially direct marketers and other businesses?** Selling lists of people and their personal information is big business. Find out if your ISP sells this kind of information. If it does, look elsewhere.

➤ **Do they maintain logs of your activities online?** Just because an ISP can track your online activity doesn't mean it will. Does the ISP maintain logs of your activities? If so, look elsewhere. Even if it doesn't sell that information, someone from inside the ISP could snoop on you by examining the logs.

➤ **Can you see all the information that the company maintains about you—and can you correct it if it's wrong?** It's your information, so you should be able to get access to it.

➤ **Does the service keep copies of your email after you delete it?** Before email makes its way to you, it sits on an email server at the ISP. Does the ISP keep copies of your email or delete the email after you do? You'd like the ISP to delete the email after you've deleted it—or even after you've fetched it from the server. That way, there's no chance that it can be easily stolen.

What Else You Can Do to Protect Your Privacy with Your ISP

There are a few other ways you can protect your privacy with your ISP. The first thing to do is simply not to give out much private information about yourself. Typically, when you sign up with an ISP, you have to provide information. Expect to provide the usual name, address, phone number, and credit card number. That's fine. There are obvious reasons why it needs that kind of information. But does the ISP really need to know your annual income? Your gender? Your age? Your favorite hobbies? The color of your dog's eyes? Your favorite Beatle? (OK, the world can know it now: Mine was John. Still is, despite his demise.)

Simply refuse to answer any questions beyond the basics. If the ISP won't let you sign up, no problem—tell the ISP to take a hike. There are a whole lot of other ISPs out there who want your money.

Is There Finger Information Available About You at Your ISP?

Finger is an Internet service that allows people to find out personal information about you by simply typing in your email address. Usually, finger information is made available only if you specifically ask it to be made available. However, there's a chance that information is available about you without your knowing it. Check with your ISP and ask that the finger information not be available. To check if finger information is available about you, head to `http://www.cs.indiana.edu:800/finger/gateway` and search for your email address. It not only shows if finger information is available about you—you'll also see the information that is available.

Also, some ISPs let you maintain public profiles about yourself, things such as your email address, personal interests, and the like. If you don't mind the world—including junk mail marketers—knowing about that kind of thing, fine. (Although, do you really want the world to know that your favorite pets are ferrets, and you spend your free time collecting discarded fingernails?) If you don't want that information made public, tell your ISP to pull your online profile. You might not know those profiles are maintained or kept publicly about you, so check with your ISP.

Protecting Your Privacy on America Online

America Online is a marketer's dream. With a vast, captive audience of over 10 million members, it's the largest way that people get onto the Internet in the entire world, by far. No one else even comes close. It's the world's biggest concentrated online audience.

America Online doesn't make most of its money by charging you an access fee. In fact, if that was all the money it got, it would probably go out of business. Instead, America Online makes its money by selling access to its vast audience. That means selling ads, direct marketing by mail, by email, by telephone, and other ways. For you, it means potential invasions of your privacy.

America Online recognizes what a gold mine it has, and it's been quite aggressive about mining that gold—namely your personal information. AOL does things such as sell its subscriber list to direct marketers and other businesses. And it does more than just sell the list—it can also provide information such as your payment history, what computer you use, and other things that you might have thought was your private information.

When America Online advertised in a direct marketing magazine, bragging about the value of its vast list, America Online users revolted (and *were* revolted). As a result of the complaints and bad publicity, America Online agreed to allow people to get themselves off these lists.

That's the good news. The bad news is figuring out how to get yourself off the lists. America Online doesn't make it easy to find out how to do it.

As it turns out, though, it's pretty easy to do. First, use the keyword CHOICES or MARKETING PREFERENCES. When you do that, you are brought to a screen that lets you choose to be taken off a variety of direct marketing lists, such as receiving email, receiving postal mail, getting telephone calls, and the like. Click the list you want to be taken off of, click **Continue**, and finally, click the button that takes you off the list. You can see the process of getting yourself taken off mailing lists illustrated here.

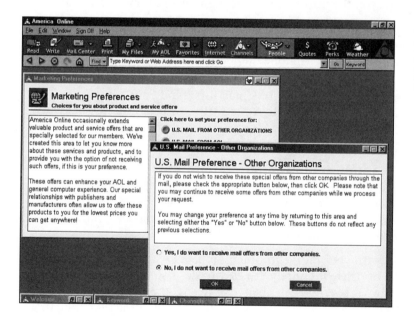

If you're an America Online member, here's how to make sure that you aren't put on marketing lists.

Turn Off Annoying AOL Pop-up Ads

Log on to America Online, and at every click of the mouse, it seems, you get a new ad popping up in your face. Don't just sit there—fight back! You can turn those ads off. Use the keyword CHOICES, click **Pop-Up**, and you'll turn off the ads. I've done it, and it makes using the service a much more pleasant experience.

By the way, there's also information in the Marketing Preferences area on how you can get taken off junk mail lists and telemarketing lists—not just those created by America Online, but by many other places as well. Click **Additional Information** for details. If for some reason the information isn't there, here's how to get your name off lists:

➤ **Get off telemarketers' call lists.** To get off telemarketers' lists, send your name, address, area code, and telephone number to: Telephone Preference Service, Direct Marketing Association, P.O. Box 9014, Farmingdale, NY 11735-9014.

➤ **Get off junk mail lists.** To get off junk mail lists, send your name and address to: Mail Preference Service, Direct Marketing Association, P.O. Box 9008, Farmingdale, NY 11735-9008.

Change or Delete Your Profile on America Online

America Online gives you the option of creating a personal profile—a form that anyone can see, that includes information such as your name, age, gender, marital status, personal interests, and similar information. If you've been on America Online a while, you might have forgotten you filled one out.

If you're uncomfortable with your profile information being widely available, you can change the information or delete it entirely. It's easy to do. Use the keyword PROFILE, and click the **My Profile** button. You can change or delete it. By the way, if you delete your profile, you'll probably get less spam email, because profiles are used by spammers as a way to gather email lists.

Boob Tube Access: How About Cable Modems and WebTV?

Maybe you're a TV kind of guy or gal, and instead of dialing into the Internet, you get on a different way—either via a cable modem or using WebTV. I use a cable modem, myself, and I must say it's a neat way to get online. But both cable modems and WebTV also offer some special privacy issues. Here's what you need to know—and what you can do about it.

Why Are Cable Modems a Problem?

Cable modems let you get onto the Internet at very high speeds. They let you get online using the same cable that comes into your home for cable TV—and you can browse the Internet and watch cable TV at the same time.

A Cable Modem Isn't Really a Modem

When is a modem not a modem? When it's a cable modem. When you get onto the Internet via a cable modem, you're not really using modem technology. Instead, you install something called a *network card* into your computer, and a special device is attached to the network card to let you browse the Internet using the same cable that comes into your house for cable TV.

There are potential privacy dangers with cable modems. Cable modems are different than regular modems—when you have a cable modem and you turn your computer on, it automatically connects to the Internet without you having to do anything, and you stay connected for as long as your computer is on. This means that you can be connected for a dozen or more uninterrupted hours a day. When this happens, your IP address stays the same for the entire day. (See Chapter 1, "Understanding the Internet and Online Security," for information about what an IP address is.) When you have an IP address on for that many hours in a row, there is the potential for a hacker to find it and do some damage. To play it safe, unplug the wire from the cable modem to your network card when you're not using the Internet. It's easy to do. Just unplug the wire right from the cable modem itself, or from where it plugs into your computer. One or the other will be easy to reach. You can also call your cable modem service and ask if they have any special security features you can turn on to stop hackers from getting at your computer.

There's another potential problem. When you're using a cable modem, you're really part of a computer network, and the people in your neighborhood or town are part of that computer network. If your cable modem service is configured a certain way, and if your Windows 95 or Windows 98 computer has certain settings turned on, then anyone in your town or neighborhood can see every single file on your computer—and can copy them to their own computer.

Luckily, there's a way to combat this problem. People can only look inside your computer if you have something called *file sharing* turned on. It's easy to see if you do—and easy to turn it off. To turn off file sharing, open Windows Explorer. Scroll down until you see an icon called Network Neighborhood. Right-click **Network Neighborhood** and choose **Properties**. Next, click **File and Printer Sharing**. You'll see the dialog box shown here. Make sure that both boxes are unchecked. If they're unchecked, no one can look at the files on your computer.

If both these boxes are unchecked, you are safe when using your cable modem.

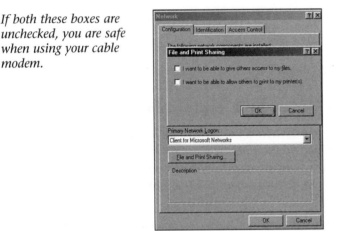

Why WebTV Can Invade Your Privacy

WebTV lets your surf the Web right from your TV. No doubt, you figure that you can watch the Web and your TV, but the Web and your TV can't watch you.

Not quite right. Without fanfare, WebTV has started using a system-polling feature that uploads information about every subscriber's TV-viewing and Web-surfing habits every night. It reports what people watch on TV, what Web sites they visit, and what they click on when they're there. How comprehensive is it? Tom Rheinlander, an analyst at Forrester Research in Cambridge, Massachusetts, told reporter Karen J. Bannan of *Inter@ctive Week Online*, "I don't think people understand the extent of this. It's recording everything they do. This is like having a video camera on them 24 hours a day."

The information is aggregated and given to advertisers, so that they can deliver customized ads. Potentially, information about your personal viewing and surfing habits can be given to advertisers, who can then target you with ads.

What can you do? First of all, complain. Also, WebTV says that it allows customers to turn on or off this kind of polling, so call up and demand that it be turned off if you worry about your privacy.

What Kind of Privacy Do You Have at Work?

If you use the Internet from work—for example, on a corporate computer network—everything you do can be tracked. Easily. And there's not a thing you can do about it, either technically or legally. The courts have ruled that your employer can gather any information it wants about you. You should assume that you have zero privacy at work when it comes to using the Internet.

That means everything. The email you send and receive? Assume that your boss can read every word of it. In fact, people have been fired based on private email they've sent at work. The Web sites you visit? It's a breeze for your employer to know exactly what sites you visit. Any chats you participate in? That too—every word you type can be read.

Again, legally, there's nothing you can do about this, because your employer has the legal right to everything you do on the Internet when you're at work. You should ask your employer what the policy is about tracking what you do on the Internet at work. But let me be honest: Don't trust what they say because no matter what people at the top say, technical people lower down the chain can snoop on what you're doing. In fact, I know of a company in which a fairly low-level technical employee not only snooped on what Web sites an employee was visiting, but also shared that information with the employee's co-workers. Making things worse was that the sites were pornographic in nature.

So what can you do? Assume that every email message you send or receive can be read by your boss and other people at your company. Don't visit personal Web sites at work, and especially don't visit any sex-related sites or participate in any chats that aren't work-related (this is good advice, anyway). Other than that, there's nothing you can do.

The Least You Need to Know

➤ Your ISP can track everything you do when you're on the Internet, including reading your email.

➤ The federal Electronic Computer Privacy Act protects what can and can't be done with your email, but contains big loopholes.

➤ Before choosing an ISP, get its privacy standards in writing—and if you're not happy with the standards, choose another ISP.

➤ Get yourself off America Online direct marketing and email lists by using the keyword CHOICES.

➤ Delete or alter your public profile on America Online or your ISP if you don't want personal information made public.

➤ Cable modems and WebTV pose threats to your privacy.

➤ Your employer can legally snoop on anything you do at work on the Internet, including sending and receiving email and visiting Web sites.

How to Create Hacker-Proof Passwords

In This Chapter

➤ Why you need to worry about your passwords

➤ How hackers can steal passwords

➤ How to manage your passwords to make sure they aren't stolen

➤ Tips for creating hacker-proof passwords

➤ Programs that create hacker-proof passwords for you

One of the biggest threats to your privacy and security is something you have the greatest control over: your passwords. One of the most common ways your privacy can be invaded is by someone getting hold of your password and then wreaking havoc with it.

With a little bit of knowledge, you can create hacker-proof passwords, and you can manage your passwords so that they aren't stolen. Here's what you need to know about managing and creating your passwords so that you don't get burned.

Why You Should Worry About Passwords

On the Internet, you *are* your password. From things as basic as logging on to the Internet through your Internet service provider (ISP) to more complicated things such as checking your email, entering a private area of a Web site, or buying books online, all you are to Web sites and your ISP is a password.

The single most important thing you can do to protect your privacy and security online is to make sure that no one ever steals your password. Here are just a few of the things that could be done if your password is stolen:

➤ Someone could check all your email and pose as you, sending out threatening and phony emails and public messages to others.

➤ Someone could get access to any private areas of Web sites where you've registered.

➤ Someone could "steal" your identity and pose as you, in the real world as well as online.

➤ Someone could use your credit card to buy thousands of dollars of goods online.

➤ Someone could use your account to launch hacker attacks all over the world—and people would believe that you are to blame.

What's a PIN?

Sometimes when you're online you'll find a reference to something called a PIN (no, it's not something that a boy used to put on a girl's clothing in the 1950s to show they were going steady). PIN stands for Personal Information Number, which is a term often used interchangeably with the term password. If you use an automated teller machine (ATM), your password is probably a PIN.

Whoever steals your password could do all these things before breakfast! There's a lot more harm they could do as well. In short, a whole lot of bad things could happen if someone steals your password. If you learn nothing else from this book, learn how to protect your passwords, and believe me, buying the book will have been well worth it. (Of course, the fact that by buying this book, you're helping put my kids through college doesn't hurt, either.)

How Hackers Steal Passwords—It's Not How You Think

If you know how hackers steal passwords, it can help you know better how to protect yours. So how exactly do they steal them? No doubt, you imagine many late-night jaunts of computer-programming magic, fueled by gallons of caffeine-charged Jolt Cola and greasy pepperoni pizzas. (Either that or using a slim portable terminal while whizzing around on rollerblades, as in a certain terrible movie, namely *Hackers*.)

Well, it may be true that hackers prefer pepperoni pizzas to any other kind of food (after all, it contains the four basic food groups: oil, oregano, nitrates, and garlic). But most hackers don't steal passwords by superhuman feats of programming. They use much more mundane tools.

One of the simplest tools is often called social engineering, which simply means that they ask. More people than you can imagine freely give their passwords out. A common tactic is a hacker sends you a message on America Online, claiming that he's working for the service. He asks for your password and username, so that he can fix or check your account. Believe it or not, people respond by giving out their passwords. In some cases, hackers call people up, posing as computer security experts, and ask for passwords.

Hackers can look through someone's desk or garbage can at work, for example, and find a username and password written on a sticky note or other slip of paper. You'd be amazed at how many people write down their passwords this way. In a variation, a hacker could look through your computer while you're away from it and find a list of passwords that you keep on a program.

A very common method is by simply guessing. You'd be surprised at how many people's password is...you guessed it, "password." Or their initials. Or their wife's name. Hackers can use their computers to automate the guessing of passwords. There are programs that keep entering password after password after password—thousands of them—until it finds one that logs on to a system.

The final way hackers can get your password is by sniffing them. It's not that hackers have an especially large proboscis (nose) or sensitive olfactory nerves. (I loved writing that sentence—how often do you get to use the words proboscis and olfactory—in the same sentence, yet?) Sniffing refers to a way in which hackers examine data moving across the Internet. They can look for passwords, and then use them.

The good news is that it's not that hard to foil hackers who try to get your passwords. There are two main ways to do that: be careful how you use your passwords and create hacker-proof passwords that hackers can never crack. Here's how to do both.

How to Handle Passwords So That Hackers Can't Steal Them

It's fairly easy to keep your passwords out of hackers' hands if you just treat your passwords properly. (Feed them well and give them love and care.) Here's what to do:

➤ ***Never* give out your password when someone asks for it.** If someone asks you for your password—either in an email message, by instant message, or by telephone—don't give it out. Employees of ISPs, America Online, and Web sites never ask you for your password.

➤ **Don't share your password with other people.** Friends and family members might want to use your password to log on to the Internet or America Online. Sure, they're your friends, and yes, they're your family. But are you sure that your 13-year-old son won't inadvertently hand out your password to someone else? Here's one instance where sharing is *not* a good thing to do.

Change Your Password After Logging on to Your Email System from Another Computer

Increasingly, there are ways that you can check your email when you're away from your own computer. Cybercafes, for example, let you log on to your email system to check your email. Or you might be at a meeting and use someone else's computer. Or, there is a growing number of public Internet terminals where people can do things such as check their email, either free or for a fee. If you check your email from a computer other than your own, change your password after you log on. It's possible that somewhere along the way, a sniffer has been used to find out your password.

➤ **Change your password weekly or monthly.** There's a small possibility that someone has managed to sniff out your password on the Internet or found out your password in some other way. If you constantly change your password, the thief only has use of your password for a brief amount of time and cannot do a large amount of damage. This is especially important because passwords are easy to "sniff."

➤ **Never write your password on a slip of paper.** It's too easy to leave it lying around where someone can find it. Considering that you don't have the kind of James Bond technology where paper bursts into flame after you've used it, never write down your password.

➤ **Use Windows 95 or Windows 98 screen saver passwords to protect your PC against password stealers.** One way that people can find out your password is to use your computer when you're away from it, looking for passwords, or using your various Internet accounts. It's easy to thwart this: Use the password protection built into Windows 95 and 98 screen savers. To do so, right-click on your desktop, choose Properties, and click the Screen Saver tab. You'll see the dialog box shown here. Choose a screen saver to use, and check the **Password Protected** box. Click the **Change** button, and type in your password. Now, whenever you're away from your desk for a certain amount of time, a screen saver runs that can only be turned off by using a password. You can also password-protect your entire computer, so that no one can turn it off and restart it to get around your screen saver password. Turn to Chapter 28, "Keeping Your PC Safe from Prying Eyes," for details.

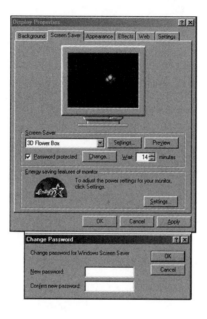

Safety first: Here's how to password-protect your PC with a screen saver.

➤ **Don't save or open attachments to your email unless you know the sender.** Sometimes you receive an email with a file attached, and the sender asks you to open the file. Unless you know the sender, don't do it. The attachment can be a kind of program called a Trojan Horse that can snoop through your hard disk for passwords and then send them back to a hacker over the Internet. For more information about viruses and Trojan Horses, turn to Part 8, "Protecting Yourself Against Viruses, Trojan Horses, and Other Nasty Creatures."

➤ **Don't enable automatic logons to your ISP and America Online.** When you dial in to your ISP, your connection screen gives you the option of automatically saving your password between logons so that you don't have to retype the password each time you log on. The logon screen is pictured here. Don't check the Save Password box; if you do, anyone can log on as you, because your password will be automatically sent to your ISP. The same holds true for America Online—don't enable the option that allows your password to be automatically sent to the service.

To keep your password secure, make sure you don't tell Windows to save it between logons.

➤ **Use different passwords for different Web sites and your ISP.** If you spend any time at all on the Internet, you have many passwords—passwords to log on, to check your mail, to visit certain Web sites, and more. Use different passwords for each site. That way, if someone steals your password, she only has access to a single site, not your entire life.

Check This Out

If You Use Internet Explorer, Don't Let It Save Your Web Passwords

Internet Explorer has a time-saving feature that's also a security risk. When you visit a Web site that requires a username and a password, it automatically saves the username and password if you want. If you're worried about security, never have it save your passwords. Otherwise, anyone with access to your computer can log on to the Web sites as if they were you.

How to Create Passwords That Even Hackers Can't Crack

Handling your passwords properly goes a long way toward making sure your passwords are never stolen. But no matter how you handle them, you're still vulnerable to a hacker who has a program that automatically tries thousands of passwords to see if one is yours. To combat that, you need to create passwords that even hackers can't crack. You can either manually make up passwords that are hard to crack, or you can use a program called a random password generator that creates passwords for you. Here's how to do both.

Rules for Manually Creating Hacker-Proof Passwords

When choosing a password, there's a lot you can to do make sure it can't be cracked. Follow this advice:

➤ **Never use the name of your spouse, children, pets, or anything else associated with you.** If someone knows anything about your life, these will be the first passwords they try. Also, do not use your address, social security number, license plate, initials, or similar information. Remember the principle of "security through obscurity."

➤ **Use at least eight characters in your password.** The longer the password, the harder it is to guess.

➤ **Mix letters and numbers**. When you mix these two, it's that much harder to guess a password than if you use only letters or only numbers.

➤ **If you can use upper- and lowercase, use them both.** Sometimes passwords are case sensitive, which means that the only way to type them correctly is if the proper case is used. If you can create a case sensitive password, make sure to mix upper- and lowercase letters.

Using a Random Password Generator

Another way to create a hacker-proof password is to use a program that creates a random password for you—one that is very hard to crack. These all work in different ways, but in general, they create a completely random password, a collection of random letters, numbers, and characters that is just about impossible to guess.

There are a number of these available on the Internet, such as Random Password Generator (original name, that!), Password Creator, Password Generator, and many others. You can get these programs at many sites on the Internet that let you download files, such as the ZDNet Software Library at www.hotfiles.com.

Using a Web-Based Random Password Generator

One great thing about the Web: Anything you can name is available there, and it's free. There are a number of sites you can visit that automatically generate random passwords for you.

In the site pictured here, PassGen: A Password Generator Java Applet, you type on your keyboard, and based on what you type, the amount of time you press each key, and similar information, a random password is generated. Get to this site by going to http://www.world.std.com/~reinhold/passgen.html.

Visit the PassGen: A Password Generator Java Applet page on the Web, and you can create hard-to-crack passwords.

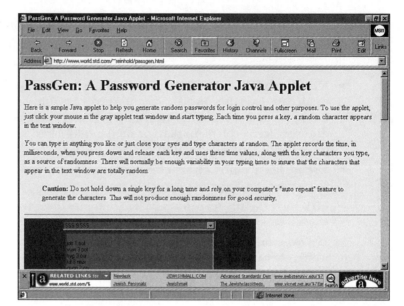

The Least You Need to Know

➤ Never give out your password to anyone who asks for it in email or by telephone. They're most likely hackers looking to steal it.

➤ Never write down your passwords on a piece of paper.

➤ Change your passwords weekly or monthly.

➤ Make sure your passwords are at least eight characters long and contain a mix of letters and numbers.

➤ Don't use your spouse's, children's, or pets' names as passwords.

➤ Random password generation programs can help create hacker-proof passwords.

Chapter 5

Fighting Back: How to Remove Your Name from Web Databases

In This Chapter

➤ What kind of information is available about you on Web databases

➤ The dangers of having information about you made public

➤ How to remove your name from Web White Page directories

➤ How to remove information about you from for-pay Web databases

The whole world is watching! That call from the 1960s should be updated for the new millennium. These days, the call would be about the enormous amount of information about you that's available for the world to see on many databases on the World Wide Web. Almost any kind of information about you that you can imagine—and probably information you've never imagined—is available on the Web for free or for a fee.

In this chapter, I'll take a look at all the kinds of information that are available about you—and more important, I'll show you how you can get your name out of Web databases so that you can retain your privacy.

You Mean, They Can Find *That* About Me on the Web?

If you use the Internet (and often, even if you don't), your life is an open book. Web databases are filled to the brim with information about you. Your name, address, phone number, and email address are often only a click or two away from anyone with a mouse and an interest in prying into your life. Your place of employment might be listed as well.

Things are even worse than that. If someone is willing to fork over some money, they can find out information that you no doubt thought was not available about you publicly anywhere. For a fee, people can visit a variety of for-pay Web sites and find out your Social Security number, driver's license, driving record, credit history, and bankruptcy reports. This kind of information can also be gotten from sources other than the Internet—but the Internet makes it easier than ever to get it, and puts it within anyone's reach, not just private eyes and other professional privacy-invaders.

What's a Reverse Phone Lookup?

If someone knows a phone number, there is a way for him to find out the name of the person at the number and the person's address—from that, it's a snap to find out an email address. Some Web sites allow reverse phone lookups, although most of them won't. Some that used to offer it no longer do because there is a potential danger in offering this service. Someone could call a phone number repeatedly and if he continually finds no one home, could surmise that the people who live there are on vacation. Because he can do a reverse phone lookup, he knows the address, which could be ripe for a burglary.

It's hard to believe, I know. But here's just a small sampling of the information that someone can find out about you for a fee at the A-1 Trace U.S.A. Web site—just one of a number of similar sites on the Internet. You can see a portion of the A-1 Web site in the illustration. I've listed here just a few of the pieces of information the site claims it can find out about people—and the fees to get those reports. There's a whole lot more information about you that sites like this will sell:

➤ Your driver's license number. Cost: $39

➤ Your driving record. Cost: $39

➤ Your Social Security number and postal address. Cost: $29

➤ The property you own and your real estate holdings, including the parcel number of your land, your address, the value of your holding, and the total property value. Cost: $39

➤ Your credit card statement, including all your transactions, daily balances, and whom the charges were made to in any given month. Cost: $189

➤ All your bank accounts, including account balances. Cost: $239

➤ The stocks, bonds, and mutual funds that you own. Cost: $309

Anyone with a credit card and an interest in snooping can find out just about anything about you at sites like A-1 Trace U.S.A.

Does Your Company Provide "Finger" Information About You?

Finger is an Internet service that allows people to find out information about others by typing in a simple command. The only way it will work is if information about you is provided by someone—either by yourself or someone else. Some places of work automatically provide finger information, possibly without telling their employees about it. Find out if your company provides finger information about you, and if they do, you could ask them to delete that information if you don't want it made public.

Pretty scary, isn't it? But it's not just investigative sites like these that contain information about you that you might think is private. There are many, many Web sites—including popular search sites—that let people search for information about you, such as your address, phone number, and email address. Later in this chapter, I'll look at all the major sites that provide personal information about you—and how you can get them to stop carrying it.

Why You Should Worry About What's in Web Databases

So there's all kinds of information that anyone can find out about you on the Web, either for free or for a few bucks. So what, you might think. After all, you don't have a prison record (although if you did, someone could easily find that out, as well), and you have nothing to hide. Big deal. Let anyone find out anything they want.

Well, in fact, there's a whole lot you *should* worry about. Here are some of the dangers caused by all this information being made public about you in Web databases:

➤ **Identity theft**   If someone finds out your name, address, phone number, Social Security number, bank account information, and similar data, they can in essence steal your identity—and more than that, of course, they can steal your money. With this kind of personal information, someone could take out a credit card in your name, charge thousands of dollars, and have the bills sent to you. They could order new checks from your bank and write out checks from your account. They could get government benefits due to you, such as your Social Security checks. They can pose as you and scam other people, giving your contact information.

What You Can Do If You've Been a Victim of Identity Theft

If you're worried that you've been the victim of identity theft, take action immediately. Notify credit bureaus, your credit card companies, banks, the Social Security Administration, the post office, and any other agencies right away and tell them you think you've been victimized. They'll tell you what you can do—including changing your Social Security number.

➤ **Stalkers** It's a scary world out there. Wackos and weirdos abound. Pick up a newspaper almost every day and you find a story about stalkers, sometimes with tragic results. Women in particular need to worry about this possibility. If someone has an abundance of personal information about you, it makes it easier for them to stalk you, by learning your home address and phone number, where you work, what vacation homes you might own, and other personal information.

➤ **Con artists** If con artists know a great deal of personal information about you, it'll be much easier for them to gain your personal confidence. They can call up, posing as a bank employee, because they'll have your bank account information. It also makes it easier for them to target specific scams at you. Feeling overburdened with credit card debt? If a con man knows that, it's easier for him to launch a scam specifically aimed at your circumstances.

➤ **Junk mail** Direct marketers live on demographic information—targeting junk mail and telemarketing calls at people in specific demographic niches. If they get information about you, you're ripe for unwanted phone calls, junk mail, and junk email.

➤ **Use by employers or potential employers** Maybe you don't want any potential employers to know the state of your personal finances—armed with that information, they could try to hire you for as little salary as possible, for example.

➤ **It's just plain creepy** There's no other way to put it. We all like to think that we're unique individuals, free from privacy intrusions and snooping. The idea that anyone can get extremely personal information about you can be just plain creepy—and you shouldn't have to be subject to that kind of snooping if you don't want to be.

Beware of Dumpster Divers

The Web isn't the only way that people can steal your identity and find out personal information about you. There's another way as well—they can sift through your trash, looking for identifying information about you—for example, bank account slips, ATM slips, anything with your Social Security number, and similar information. People who do this are called dumpster divers. To be safe from them, shred any paper that has any identifying information about you that you'd rather not have the world know about.

What a lineup, huh? Don't worry. There are ways you can fight back, as you'll see in the next section of the book.

Keeping It Private: How to Get Your Name Out of Web Databases

You know all the bad news, by now: Your life is there for the taking. Anyone with a mouse, an Internet connection, a credit card number, and bad intentions can find just about anything about you that they want. But there's some good news as well. You can fight back and get your name out of Web databases.

In general, there are two kinds of Web sites that make available information about you. There are the free sites that let people look up information such as name, address, phone number, and email address. These sites tend to have only more public information about you—often called White Page sites. There are also the for-pay sites, such as the A-1 Trace U.S.A. Web site. These sites sell the more private information, such as your Social Security number. In general, it's easier to get your name out of the free sites than the for-pay sites. Here's how deal with each kind of site.

How to Get Your Name Out of Internet White Pages

Internet White Page directories are free, public Web sites that let people search for other people, looking for addresses, email addresses, and phone numbers. There are many, many of them out there, and more come online all the time. Unfortunately, there's no central place where you can get your name off all the White Page lists. You're going to have to go to each individual site and request that your name is taken out of that specific White Page directory. They don't always agree to do it—but many do. (By the way, if you want people such as long-lost friends or relatives to be able to find you, you'll want to keep your name in these databases instead of taking your name out.)

Get Your Name Out of Multiple Databases and Mailing Lists for $2.50

Here's a twist: A Web site that works to get your name off databases, mailing lists, street directories, junk mail lists, and more. Head to the Mr. Postman Web site at www.mrpostman.com, and for $2.50, it sends forms to multiple databases and businesses to get your name off their lists.

Table 5.1 shows a list of the major White Page directories on the Internet and instructions on how to get yourself out of their listings. You have to contact them individually to get your name off. In some cases, the exact directions for getting your name off might have changed from when this book was published. If you don't find the exact pages listed here for getting your name off, don't worry—there is a way to get your name off. Just go to the main page on the site and look for the area that describes how to get your name off the listing. At worst, send a general email to the site, requesting that you be taken off the list.

Here you can see how you can request that your name be removed from the popular Bigfoot (www.bigfoot.com) White Pages.

You can easily get your name out of Bigfoot's White Pages by filling out this form.

Table 5.1 Getting Your Name Out of White Page Directories

Directory	Web Address	How to Remove Your Name
BigFoot	www.bigfoot.com	Search for a name, and from the resulting page, click on the link that lets you remove your name from the directory.
Yahoo! People Search	www.people.yahoo.com	Go to http://people.yahoo.com/py/psEmailSupp.py and fill out the form.
WhoWhere	www.whowhere.com	Go to http://www.whowhere.lycos.com/WriteUs and fill out the form.

continues

Table 5.1   Continued

Directory	Web Address	How to Remove Your Name
Internet @ddress Finder	www.iaf.com	Click Remove from the main page and type in your email address.
Switchboard	www.switchboard.com	Send your listing as it appears on Switchboard to webmaster@ switchboard.com and put "Delete" in the subject field. You can also write to Switchboard, P.O. Box 1296, Westboro, MA 01581.
Infospace.com	www.infospace.com	Do a White Pages or email search and find your listing. Then click on the update/remove link and fill out the form for removing your name.
World Pages	www.worldpages.com	Go to http://www.worldpages.com /docs/feedback.whtml and fill out the form.

What Can I Do About White Page Directories Not Listed Here?

There are many White Page directories on the Internet, and not all of them can be listed here. When you come across a directory, search for your name and see if they have information listed about you. If they do and you want it removed, go to the site's Help, FAQ, or privacy area and look for information about how to remove your listing. If you don't find information, you'll have to send email. Just about every site has an email contact list. Send your request to several people on the list—and make sure to also send the request to the most important executive listed.

Getting Your Name Out of For-Pay Sites

Most of the for-pay sites on the Internet don't compile the information they sell themselves. Instead, they get the information from a wide variety of other places, such as state Departments of Motor Vehicles, registries of deeds, and credit bureaus. So, very few of the for-pay sites provide a way of removing yourself from their data-bases. In fact, there's an economic incentive for them *not* to remove you—the more information they have, the more information they can sell.

In many cases, there's nothing you can do about getting them to stop providing information about you—especially because many of their sources of information are public records. However, there's still a fair amount you can do. Here's how:

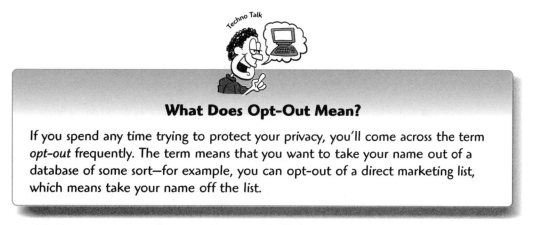

What Does Opt-Out Mean?

If you spend any time trying to protect your privacy, you'll come across the term *opt-out* frequently. The term means that you want to take your name out of a database of some sort—for example, you can opt-out of a direct marketing list, which means take your name off the list.

One of the world's largest—possibly *the* largest—supplier of databases and information about people is Lexis-Nexis. You can find it on the Web at www.lexis-nexis.com. I won't even begin to list here all the information the company sells, because to do so might take up a whole book unto itself. (*The Complete Idiot's Guide to Lexis-Nexis*...hmmm...there's a thought.)

One of Lexis-Nexis's services is a people-finder type of search, called P-Track. The service is designed for attorneys trying to track down people involved in lawsuits and for law-enforcement personnel. It includes people's names and addresses and, at times, other information, such as telephone number and date of birth. You can get your name out of the P-Track database easily. Send an email to remove@prod.lexis-nexis.com, asking that your name be removed, or mail the request to Lexis-Nexis Name Removal, P.O. Box 933, Dayton, OH 45401. You can also fax the request to (800) 732-7672. For the most up-to-date information about removing yourself from the list, call (888) 965-3947.

The Departments of Motor Vehicles have been big violators of people's privacy. In the past, they've disclosed, to anyone with a checkbook, things such as your driving history and your license number. In many states, your license number is your Social Security number, so in essence, they've given out Social Security numbers. Information from Departments of Motor Vehicles (DMV) has been for sale on Web sites, among other places.

You do have a little bit of consumer protection. There is a way to try and salvage a little of your privacy. The federal Drivers Protection Act gives you some control over how DMV information can be used. DMV information can be given to law-enforcement personnel, insurance companies, and the like. But, if you want to make sure that the information can't be used by anyone else, such as direct marketers, you can ban them from using it. For information how, go to a page put together by the Federal Trade Commission at `http://www.ftc.gov/privacy/protect.htm`, pictured here. The page has other helpful information on it, such as how to opt-out of credit card solicitations.

Find Out What Information Lexis-Nexis Has About You

The Lexis-Nexis database giant has a variety of people-finder databases. Wouldn't it be nice to know what information, exactly, they have about you in their people-finder databases? In fact, you can find out for a small fee. Send your name and address and an $8 check or money order to Lexis-Nexis Consumer Access Program, P.O. Box 933, Dayton, OH 45401. You get information that they have in their people-finder databases. Keep in mind, though, that this is just a small portion of the databases the Lexis-Nexis sells to people. You won't be able to find out what information Lexis-Nexis's other databases have about you in this way, however.

For information on how to make sure your state Department of Motor Vehicles doesn't sell information about you, head to this page, run by the Federal Trade Commission.

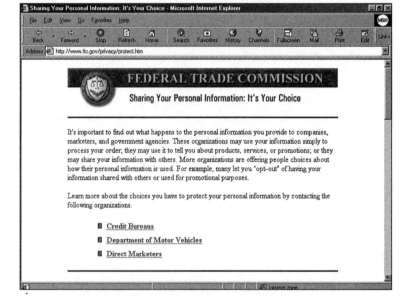

At the same site, you can also find information on how you can get the major credit bureaus Equifax, Experian, and Transunion Corporation to stop sharing information about you with direct marketers. You can contact the individual companies to get them from sharing the information. If you want a quicker way, call 888-5OPTOUT (888-567-8688), and you can be removed from the lists of all three.

What's an Infomediary?

There are so many sites and databases on the Web that can invade your privacy in so many different ways that a new kind of business has sprung up—what some people call *infomediaries*. An infomediary is a site or a piece of software that protects your privacy as you use the Web. It lets you determine what information should be made public about you. Some infomediary sites include www.lumeria.com and www.privaseek.com.

One of the biggest Web-based databases you've probably never heard of is Intelliquest, a market research firm. Whenever you buy something online from one of Intelliquest's clients, you'll find a checked box somewhere as you buy, asking you if you'd like to get information about similar products in the future. If you leave that box checked—and Intelliquest says that from 70 to 80 percent of people do—information about what you've bought is put into a huge database of 200 million people in 100 million households. That information is provided to a variety of marketers and clients who use it to try to sell you products, products, and more products. To keep off the list, make sure to uncheck that box. For more information about filling out forms on the Internet, turn to Chapter 14, "Beware of Registration Forms on the Web."

The Least You Need to Know

➤ Almost any kind of information about you is available on the Web, either free or for a fee.

➤ To remove information about you from White Page directories, check the list in this chapter or visit the site and send email asking to take you out of the directory.

➤ If you think you've been a victim of identity theft, notify credit bureaus, banks, the Social Security Administration, and the post office and tell them.

➤ Visit the Federal Trade Commission site at www.ftc.gov/privacy /protect.htm for information on how to make sure your Department of Motor Vehicles doesn't release illegal information about you.

➤ To make sure the major credit bureaus don't make information available about you to direct marketers, call 888-5OPTOUT (888-567-8688).

Chapter 6

How to Protect Yourself Against the Most Common Internet Scams

In This Chapter

➤ How to recognize Internet scams

➤ Ways you can protect yourself against the most common Internet scams and fraud

➤ What action you can take if you've been the subject of a scam

➤ Best sites on the Internet for getting information about online scams

Con men, scammers, bunco artists, flimflammers, hustlers, smoothies, Ponzi schemers, weisenheimers, and sharpies of all kinds—you'll find them all, and worse, online. They've flocked to the Internet because it's so easy and cheap to do scams there—and because it's so hard to track down the people who've burned you. There's a now-famous *New Yorker* cartoon in which a dog sits in front of a computer and says "On the Internet, nobody knows you're a dog." In the same way, on the Internet, it can be hard to know that someone is a rip-off artist.

Scams are possible on the Internet because it's so easy for someone to pose as a legitimate business. Spend a few bucks building a nice-looking Web site or sending out mass emails, and all of a sudden you're not a chiseler looking to steal someone's life savings—instead you're a legit businessman trying to help some poor schmoe get rich.

Don't worry. It's easy to make sure you don't get conned. And if you have been the victim of a scam, there's a lot you can do about it. In this chapter, I'll clue you in on how you can avoid Internet scams and what you can do if, for some reason, you've been burned. I'll also show you where to go online to find out the latest information about cons, scams, and other nasty schemes.

How to Recognize Online Scams

It's actually pretty easy to spot online scams. Follow this simple, time-honored rule for avoiding any con game: If something sounds too good to be true, then it *is* too good to be true. Instead, it's a flimflam.

Make $100,000 at home in your spare time! Get rid of your credit debt forever—and spend no money! Buy your dream home—with no money down! Sure, and why don't I just give you direct access to my bank account and credit card so you can take out withdrawals whenever you like? And sure, I'll buy that nice bridge you have for sale. What's it called again—the Brooklyn Bridge, you say?

What Is Spam?

No, I'm not referring to the fatty luncheon meat with the cult following. Instead, spam is unwanted email that's sent to you without asking for it. Usually spam asks you to buy something or sign up for an offer. Don't respond to the offer—the odds are, it's a scam. And don't send an email asking that they not send you the offer again, because that only lets them know your email address is a valid one, and they'll keep sending you mail. For more information about how to deal with spam, turn to Chapter 10, "What Is Spam and How Can You Protect Yourself from It?"

It's not just hype like this that you need to watch out for. If you're sent an email with an impossible-to-believe deal or you happen upon a Web site without an address or phone number on it, be wary. In general, any time a Web site, email, or anything else you come across on the Internet doesn't feel right to you, listen to your instincts— they're almost always right.

The Most Common Internet Scams

What kinds of things do you need to watch out for on the Internet? There are all kinds of scams. But here are the most common ones to look out for—and how you can make sure that you'll never get burned:

➤ **Watch out for rip-off artists at Web auctions.** Web auctions are a great way to buy online. But if you're not careful, you can get burned. You can pay for goods that never get delivered, or you can be told that you're buying a rare collectible only to find out that it's a counterfeit. To protect yourself, don't pay the person who you're buying the goods from directly—instead, pay what's called an escrow service. The service holds the money for your goods until the goods are delivered and only releases the money after it's been received by you in good order. Also, never buy collectibles such as rare Beanie Babies or sports collectibles online. Fraud at auction sites has become the most common kind of Internet scam, according to the Internet Fraud Watch at www.fraud.org. For complete information about how to protect yourself when buying at auctions, turn to Chapter 24, "How to Stay Safe When Buying at Auctions."

Know What Kind of Auction Site You're Buying From

There are two types of auction sites: those from which you buy from other individuals, such as at eBay at www.ebay.com, and those from which you buy directly from the site itself. Before buying, know which kind of site you're buying from. If you're buying from individuals, use an escrow service such as TradeSafe at www.tradesafe.com, I-Escrow at www.iescrow.com, and Trade-direct at www.trade-direct.com when buying. If you're buying from the site itself, find out the site's return policies and warranties for the goods that they sell. For more information about protecting yourself when buying at auctions, turn to Chapter 24.

➤ **Beware of business opportunity schemes.** Sell spotted salamanders and make a fortune! Sounds improbable, doesn't it? Stranger schemes have made con artists money. Here's how these schemes usually work: To make a fortune, you first have to buy marketing materials or merchandise (2,000 spotted salamanders, anyone?). And you keep buying and buying and buying...and the only person making the fortune is the person who sold you a bill of goods—or is that a gross of salamanders? In any event, never respond to a business opportunity scheme on the Internet. The only opportunity they provide are for scamsters looking to turn a quick profit.

➤ **Don't respond to credit repair offers.** Got yourself into a bit of financial trouble and now have bad credit? You may well be targeted by an online shyster promising you he can "repair" your credit rating. Beware—there's no way it can be done. Respond to these offers and you'll only get ripped off.

➤ **Stay away from pyramid schemes and multilevel marketing (MLM) schemes.** These are some of the oldest scams on the books. They're also called Ponzi schemes after one of the most infamous perpetrators. In them, you're promised a big-time profit if you pay an initial fee and recruit others to join the plan. Oh, and by the way, you also have to buy marketing materials and pay more fees...and you never end up making money, you only keep paying it. This is one of the more common scams on the Internet. The Federal Trade Commission brought a case against a company called the Fortuna Alliance that allegedly ran such a scheme and then transferred all their loot to a bank in Antigua. Buying this pyramid is like agreeing to buy the Brooklyn Bridge.

➤ **Be wary when signing up for free trials.** Let's face it: You can't get something for nothing. Free trials can end up costing you a bundle. In free trials, you have to first send in your credit card number. You are told that you can back out of the trial before your card is billed. But that free trial might be run by a scammer trying to get his hands on your credit card. Only agree to free trials with large, well-known, reputable Web merchants.

➤ **Don't buy from a site that has no mailing address or phone number.** Anyone can create a slick Web page that looks as if it's on the up-and-up. Behind that page could be a bunco artist looking to get his hands on your credit card. Only buy from a site that has a valid mailing address and phone number—and never buy from a site that lists only a post office box. For more information about shopping on the Web, turn to Part 7, "Let's Go CyberShopping: How to Buy Online Safely."

➤ **Don't buy stocks based solely on advice you come across on discussion boards, chat areas, or via unsolicited email.** Sure, discussion areas are great places to get inside tips about stocks. They're also the shyster's best friend. People looking to bid up a stock so they can sell it quick and get out for a profit often go into discussion areas, use assumed names, and tell grand lies about the stock to artificially inflate its price. Worthless stocks have been run up this way by con artists, and people have been burned. Scammers send unsolicited email promising that fortunes can be made by buying a stock that proves to be fraudulent. The Security and Exchange Commission has been cracking down on stock scams, but they remain one of the most popular scams on the Internet.

Find the Mailing Address and Phone Number for Any Web Site

Not all Web sites include their contact information. But before buying at a Web site—or especially if you've been burned at a Web site—you'll want that information. It's easy to find it out, even if the information isn't listed on the Web site. Point your browser to www.internic.net. Click on the button or link to **Whois**. Type in the name of the site, but leave out the "www". For example, type ebay.com to find information about the www.ebay.com auction site. You then get the site's mailing address, phone number, and often, the names of people who run the site.

➤ **Check your credit card bills for suspicious-looking charges from phony Internet service providers.** In one of the newest Internet scams, a chiseler starts charging your credit card every month for a fee such as $19.95, so it looks like your normal fee from your Internet service provider (ISP). The hope is that you won't notice the fee, because it looks like a normal ISP. Look at your credit card account carefully every month.

➤ **Don't respond to spam.** Spam is unsolicited email sent to your inbox, touting too-good-to-be-true offers such as investment schemes. Users of America Online in particular are targeted for spam. Don't be gullible. Never respond to spam—if you do, you could face worse consequences than mere indigestion.

➤ **Stay away from work-at-home offers.** Make $100,000 a year working at home in your spare time? Sounds good. But it's not going to happen in this life. Stay away from Internet work-at-home offers. You'll be conned into buying a book or series of books or expensive mailing materials and goods. The only person making a number with six zeroes at the end of it is the scammer.

Never Give Out Your Social Security Number

There's no legitimate reason why you should provide your Social Security number to anyone online. Armed with your Social Security number, a con artist can do a world of damage, including assuming your identity. Never give it out.

➤ **Don't call 809 numbers.** You might get an offer some time via the Internet, asking you to call a number with an 809 area code. Beware: It's an area code used for numbers outside of the U.S. and is a favorite of shysters looking to avoid U.S. fraud laws. Dial the number, and you could be put on hold for a long period of time or talk to an operator who claims he doesn't speak English. The whole time, the meter is running—and you can be charged $25 or more a minute.

➤ **Check out online charities before donating money.** Sad but true: Con artists have used the Web to set up sites where you can donate money to what you think is a charity. Instead, you're being bilked out of money. Before donating money to any online charity, get contact information including name, address, and phone number—and make sure it isn't a post office box. Then, check the state where the charity is located to see if the charity is registered and for real.

➤ **Always use a credit card when you buy online.** When you pay with a credit card, the most you are liable for, if you've been scammed, is $50. The truth is, most credit card companies waive even that fee, so only pay with your credit card. If a site says it doesn't accept credit cards and instead wants your bank account number, stay away. Armed with that number, they can fleece you for a whole lot of cash.

What to Do If You've Been Scammed

OK, so maybe you didn't follow my advice about how to avoid online scams and you've been scammed. (I bet you never listened when your mother told you to eat your vegetables, either.) There's a lot you can do to fight it. You might get your money back, and if not, you could get your credit card company to cover most, if not all, of the costs of your scam. You also have recourse to a wide variety of government and private agencies to help you get back your money—and even to prosecute the scam artist who targeted you.

How to Deal with the Company That Burned You

Do you think you've been the victim of a scam? Start off by contacting the company or person you think burned you. Before you do, have all the information about your complaint handy. Here's what you need:

➤ **Product and sales information.** Have ready the product's name, price, serial number, date and time you bought it, and any other identifying information. If you were notified by the company via email about your purchase, have a copy of that. If you filled out a Web form to order and printed out that form, have a copy of that as well. (It's a good idea to print these order forms and email messages and store them in case you need records.)

➤ **A description of your complaint.** Write out exactly why you think you've been wronged.

> ➤ **A cancelled check or credit card bill.** If your check has already been cashed or your credit card billed, have that information ready.

Now, call up the company, ask to be put through to the person handling consumer complaints, and detail your complaint. Take down the name of the person you talk to and take notes about the call, including the date and time of the call and everything that was discussed. Follow up the call with an email and a letter, preferably via registered or certified mail.

Writing a letter preserves your rights under consumer laws. Include information about the sale, detailed in the previous list. Clearly detail your complaint. Include the number of your cancelled check or details about when your credit card was billed. Include information about who you called at the company and what took place in your discussion. And include information about how you can be contacted.

Give them 10 to 14 days to act and tell them you're going to take legal action unless they resolve the complaint to your satisfaction. Make sure they know you're sending copies of your letter to your state consumer agency and your state attorney general. (See below for information on which groups to complain to.)

Do all this, and you'll probably get your complaint resolved. If not, you have a written record of the complaint, which you can then send to your credit card company and government and private consumer agencies.

Getting Help from Your Credit Card Company

Pay with a credit card, and you are covered for all but $50 at most, if you are the victim of a scam. Credit card companies investigate complaints, and if they find you're in the right, you only have to pay the first $50 at most. Many waive that $50 fee, and you end up paying zero, as in zilch.

As soon as you suspect you've been conned, call your credit card company and give them the dirty details over the phone. Follow up with a letter, detailing your complaint. Include the site that scammed you, its mailing address and phone number, the day and time of the purchase, the product you purchased (or thought you were purchasing), and other pertinent information. Describe how you tried to resolve the complaint and include letters or email that you've sent or received.

Complaining to Private Consumer Agencies

If you've been the victim of a scam, or suspect you have, there are people on your side—private consumer agencies. Here's where to go to complain and get help:

> ➤ **Better Business Bureaus**   These are private agencies funded by businesses to promote good business practices and are located locally in each state. They work with businesses to try and get you your money back and keep a record of complaints filed against businesses. They keep your complaint on permanent

file so that other people can be warned about the shyster who burned you. Complain to the Better Business Bureau where the company is located. For a list of all Better Business Bureaus in the country, go to the Better Business Bureau Web site at www.bbb.com, pictured here. You can also file a complaint with the Better Business Bureau's special Web protection site at www.bbbonline.com.

Here's where to go to find a Better Business Bureau near you.

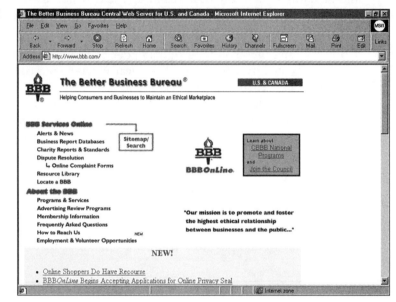

➤ **The National Fraud Information Center** This is another good place to make a complaint. It sends your complaint to the proper state, federal, and local law enforcement agencies. Your complaint also goes into the National Fraud Database maintained by the Federal Trade Commission and the National Association of Attorneys General. You can fill out a complaint form online. Head to www.fraud.org and fill out the form. If you prefer the telephone, call (800) 876-7060.

➤ **The Netcheck Commerce Bureau** This is a private agency that specializes in tracking down online scams and frauds. Head to www.netcheck.com and fill out a complaint form online. The company you're complaining about has 20 days to respond to Netcheck. If they don't resolve it to Netcheck's liking, Netcheck can then forward your complaint to the proper federal organization handling complaints.

➤ **Trade associations** These are good places to make complaints. Just about any kind of business you can imagine has a trade association it can belong to that, among other things, resolves consumer complaints. (The National Soap and Detergent Association? Yup there is one. The National Turkey Federation? There's that, too—and a lot more where those came from.) For a complete list of trade associations, go to the Federal Trade Commission's Web site at www.ftc.gov and find the "Consumer's Resource Handbook." It's a complete guide for consumers that includes a comprehensive listing of trade associations.

Complaining to Government Agencies

A variety of government agencies handle consumer complaints. In some cases, you can file complaints online; in others, you have to do it the old-fashioned way—by writing a letter. Internet fraud has also finally made it onto the radar of the federal government—the Justice Department has begun working with all federal agencies to come up with Internet fraud-busting plans. In any event, here are the agencies to complain to when you've been scammed:

➤ **Your state Attorney General's Office, or your state's Department of Consumer Affairs** These are good places to start. Don't know their addresses? No problem. Head to the Consumer World site at www.consumerworld.org, as shown here. You'll find what is probably the most comprehensive list in the world of government consumer agencies and Attorneys General offices. When complaining, make sure to contact not just the agencies in your state, but also in the state where the Web site does business.

The most comprehensive list anywhere of government consumer agencies can be found at the Consumer World site at www.consumerworld.org.

➤ **The Federal Trade Commission** The FTC is the main federal agency that prosecutes Internet scams. Fill out a complaint at its Web site at www.ftc.com. The complaint goes to the National Association of Attorneys General as well as to the FTC.

➤ **The Security and Exchange Commission**   The SEC at www.sec.gov prosecutes scams involving stocks and securities. It's been extremely aggressive in prosecuting Internet stock scams and fraud and have brought charges against scores of people. You can fill out a complaint on its Web site or email your complaint to enforcement@sec.gov.

Head to This Site for Everything You Want to Know About Internet Stock Fraud

The SEC has put together the most comprehensive page anywhere for information about stock fraud, and it has excellent guidelines to follow when investing over the Internet. Go to the SEC's Investor Assistance and Complaints page at http://www.sec.gov/invkhome.htm. In addition to lots of articles, tips, and resources, you can make out a complaint online.

Tell It to the Judge: How to Use Small Claims Court

Small claims courts are local courts in which you need no lawyer to represent you—make your case to the judge and he decides right then and there whether to award you the amount of money you've been scammed. There's only two drawbacks. The first is that you can only go to small claims court in the locality where the Internet business operates. That means you can only take someone to small claims court if they live in your area. The other drawback is that you can't go to small claims court for a huge amount of money—often it's only for cases of under $1,500 or so. It varies according to locality, so check yours.

Best Sites to Get the Inside Skinny on Consumer Advice and Scams

Do you want to know where to go online if you want to find out about Internet scams and get solid consumer advice? Check out these sites, the best you'll find on the Internet.

Better Business Bureau

`http://www.bbb.com`

Make a complaint about a site, find a Better Business Bureau near you, check out a business to see if complaints have been lodged against it, get advice about doing business on the Internet—all that and more is possible here.

Better Business Bureau Online

`http://www.bbbonline.com`

Help find out if an online site is a reliable and trustworthy one. You can see if sites have complaints lodged against them and lodge your own complaints as well. It also has a seal that Web sites can display if they're members of the Better Business Bureau Online. Click on the link and you can see whether complaints have been lodged against the company.

Consumer World

`http://www.consumerworld.org`

This is probably the most comprehensive site online for finding out information about everything to do with consumers. Especially useful are the links to private and government agencies involved in prosecuting Internet scams or that offer advice on how to avoid scams.

CPA Web Trust

`http://www.cpawebtrust.com`

This group of wild and crazy accountants has created a sort of Web seal of approval. They check out Web sites, and if that site adheres to security and privacy standards, the site can display the CPA Web Trust seal.

Federal Trade Commission

`http://www.ftc.gov`

Here's the site of the main agency that investigates Internet fraud. You can find information about scams and fraud, advice on how to avoid them, and more.

National Fraud Information Center

http://www.fraud.org

Learn about the latest Internet scams, get advice on avoiding con artists, and make out complaints if you think you've been burned.

ScamWatch

http://www.scamwatch.com

Don't be put off by this site's somewhat disorganized look—it's a great place to find out about the latest scams on the Internet. Last time I checked in, it had comprehensive reports on everything from Furbie fraud (people claiming they had the much-desired toys Furbies to sell when they didn't) to a bizarre scam involving someone who claimed to be the legal adviser to the former president of Zaire, Mobutu Sese Seko, trying to get people to open a bank account in the Ivory Coast. There's also great advice on how to avoid scams and links to other anti-scam sites.

Security and Exchange Commission

http://www.sec.gov

Stock scams have become one of the most common frauds on the Internet. This site clues you in on all the latest scams (one warning is shown below), offers great advice on how to avoid them, and lets you make complaints if you think you've been victimized.

Catch up on the latest Internet stock scams at the SEC site at www.sec.gov.

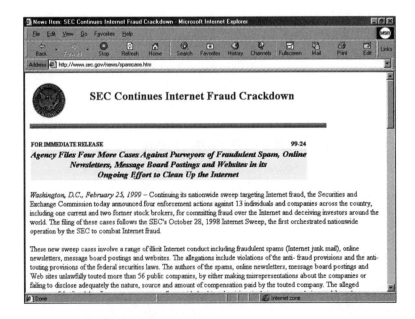

U.S. Consumer Gateway

http://www.consumer.gov

Here's the best place to go to find out all the information federal agencies have about anything to do with consumers—including Internet scams. It links you to great articles, advice, and advisories.

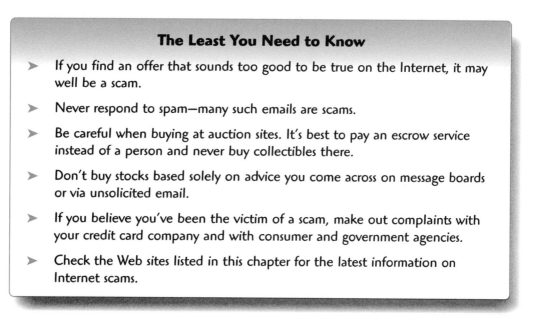

The Least You Need to Know

➤ If you find an offer that sounds too good to be true on the Internet, it may well be a scam.

➤ Never respond to spam—many such emails are scams.

➤ Be careful when buying at auction sites. It's best to pay an escrow service instead of a person and never buy collectibles there.

➤ Don't buy stocks based solely on advice you come across on message boards or via unsolicited email.

➤ If you believe you've been the victim of a scam, make out complaints with your credit card company and with consumer and government agencies.

➤ Check the Web sites listed in this chapter for the latest information on Internet scams.

Part 3

Snoopers Everywhere: How to Keep Your Email Private

Remember that email you sent last month about your company's private plans for expansion into Bali? A snooper could have read it. Or that email your sweetheart sent you last week, pledging undying love? Someone may have intercepted it en route and be cackling about it right now.

And think of all the junk mail you get in your email inbox—what people refer to as "spam." Get-rich-quick offers, scams, solicitations to visit pornographic Web sites—all that and more litter your email box.

Well, Chucky, there's good news on the way. You can protect your privacy and you can fight back against spammers. This part of the book will show you how. You'll learn how email works and why hackers can snoop on it. You'll find out about dangers in email, such as email viruses. And you'll see how you can vanquish them all—how you can make sure your email isn't snooped on and spammers stop sending you mail—and you'll even learn how you can send "anonymous email" so that you can send email and participate in Internet news-groups without people knowing your true identity.

Chapter 7

How Does Email Work, Anyway?

In This Chapter

➤ What happens when you compose an email message

➤ How email is sent across the Internet

➤ What you need to know about email headers

➤ Why you should care about how email works

Email seems to work like magic. You sit at your computer, type a message to someone, click the Send button, and faster than you can say "Jack Robinson," it's sent across the continent. Of course, the only kind of magic at work here is Internet magic.

As you'll find out in the rest of the chapters in this section, there are many ways your privacy and security can be endangered by your use of email. Before you learn how to protect yourself, you should understand how email works. So come along on a guided tour of how email zips its way across the continent in the blink of an eye. You'll learn enough so that you can start protecting your email privacy and security—quicker than you can say "Jack Robinson."

The Mail Starts Here...

To better understand how you can protect the privacy of your email, you need to know how email works. Let's start at the beginning—how you create email on your computer and what happens to it after you send it.

When you create an email message, you use an email program such as Outlook, Outlook Express, or Eudora. The illustration shows a message composed in Outlook. As you're creating that piece of email, only you can see it. It hasn't been sent to anyone on the Internet yet. It's sitting on your computer, all by its lonesome. It's like a letter that you're writing, but haven't finished yet.

Creating a message in the Outlook email program.

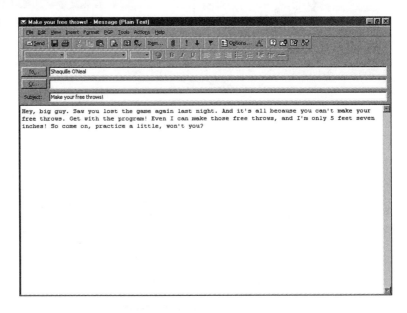

Now imagine you finish writing the email. You want to send the message. What do you do? Click the **Send** button.

What's an MUA?

At some point, you might come across an odd acronym—MUA. (Of course, what acronym *isn't* odd when it comes to the Internet?) MUA stands for Mail User Agent. A Mail User Agent is nothing more than a fancy, ten-dollar word for email software. Microsoft Outlook, Microsoft Outlook Express, and Eudora, for example, are all MUAs.

When you click that Send button, you might think your email is being sent right at that second. If you think that, you're wrong. When you click the Send button, what happens is that your email message is saved on your computer, and your email program makes plans to send the mail. It doesn't yet send it. Before that mail can be sent, you first have to connect to the Internet, and your email program has to send the mail by sending it to a special computer called a *mail server*. Until both those things happen, the mail stays on your computer. Often, it is temporarily put into an Outbox or some similar folder while it's waiting to be sent. After it's sent, it's moved into a Sent folder, or something similar.

When you create that email message, there's more going on behind the scenes than you realize. For the mail to be delivered, a bunch of information needs to be put into it. When you write a letter, you need to put address information on the envelope. In the same way, when you send an email message, extra information needs to be added—and because this is the Internet we're talking about, your mail program adds more than just addressing information.

To handle this extra kind of information, an email message is divided into two parts: the *header* and the *body*. The body is the message that you compose. The header contains the information that's needed to deliver the email message to the proper address. There's not a whole lot you need to know about the body of the message—after all, you composed it! But the header...ah, now, that's where things get tricky. And understanding the header is key to knowing how your email can be snooped on and how you can combat spam. So come with me for a moment, and let's take a closer look at the email header.

Let's Head into the Header

The most basic information in an email header is stuff you put there yourself. You type in the email address of the person to whom you're sending the mail. You put in the subject of the message. If you're sending copies to others, you put in their email addresses. You see all this information as you compose the message.

There's other information the program puts into the header, though. Usually, you don't see this information. When you compose an email message, your email program automatically adds information to the header. It adds the date and time that the message was composed. It also adds two other pieces of information. It creates a message ID, which is a super-long number, followed by your email address. And, most email programs put in a piece of information identifying the program that created the email.

There's a Way to View All the Header Information in Any Piece of Email

Usually, you only view a small portion of the header information in a piece of email—important information such as addresses, the subject line, and the date and time. But email programs also let you see the full header of an email message. As you'll see in Chapter 10, "What Is Spam and How Can You Protect Yourself from It?" seeing these headers can help protect you from spam. To view the full message header in your email program, read carefully through the documentation—very carefully, because that information is often buried deep.

So, for example, if your email address was joe@joejoe.net, and the email program you used to create an email was the Windows version of Eudora Pro, version 3.0, your email program would add that information to the header. Generally, you don't see that information and neither does the person receiving the mail. If you want to, you can see it, but you have to configure your email program in a special way to peek in.

Now, you probably wonder, why spend all this time talking about headers? Because they're key to your email privacy and to stopping Internet spam. Hackers and snoopers can read that header information as your mail message travels across the Internet. And in examining the header information of emails you receive, you can help stop spam.

...And the Mail Goes to There...

Let's get back to the message you've composed. You finished writing it, you told your email software to send it, and your email software put in a few extra pieces of information into its header. Now what?

You connect to the Internet. When you do, your email program notices that you're online (smart program, isn't it?) and sends your message. It does so by contacting an email server run by your Internet service provider. An email server is a computer that handles delivering mail. If you're connected to the Internet at work, your company most likely has its own email server.

What's an MTA?

No, it doesn't stand for the Mass Transit Authority, although it does refer to something that moves things from one place to another. MTA stands for Mail Transport Agent. It's a piece of software that receives an email message from your email software and then delivers that message over the Internet.

Your email software and the email server it contacts do a little dance of sorts—or more precisely, they have a sort of conversation, the kind of conversation that only computers can have, one that you or I can't understand, and wouldn't want to. The result is that the email server adds some more information to the header of the message—under a Received heading. It puts in all kinds of identifying information about itself, such as its own Internet address, the kind and version software it's running, the time and date the message was received, yet *another* message ID, and yes, even more.

After it does that, it sends your message on its merry way. In some cases, it relays your email message to another email server, and that server—yes, you guessed it—that server puts in even *more* information. It puts in its own Received heading, with tons of information. That server may even relay your message to yet *another* email server that puts its own Received heading. And so on. And so on. And so on...

The email servers examine the header of the message and see where you're sending the email. They send it out across the Internet to the intended recipient. As it's sent, computers called *routers*, whose job it is to send information from one computer to another on the Internet, examine the message. So your mail doesn't travel in a straight line. Instead, it might be sent from router to router to router, until it reaches its final destination. (Remember from our discussion of the Internet's structure that the Internet is designed to send packets from one router to another along the best route available at that moment.)

There's another twist as well: Your mail may be sent to one or more other mail servers—called *relays*—before it reaches where you've sent it. These servers do what their name says—they relay it to its final destination, or to another relay. (Sheesh! With all this routing and relaying, it's a miracle the mail ever gets there in the first place!)

Techno Talk

For Email to Work, It Has to Follow Certain Protocols

For the Internet to work, computers have to know how to talk to one another. They communicate using what are called protocols. There are several protocols involved in email. The POP (Post Office Protocol) handles the way your email software gets email from an email server. A newer protocol called IMAP (Internet Message Access Protocol) also handles ways that your email software can get email from an email server. IMAP is more powerful than POP and lets you more easily manage your email. The SMTP (Simple Mail Transfer Protocol) is the basic mail protocol that governs how email servers send messages to one another, and how you send your email to servers.

Finally, the mail is sent to the email server of the person to whom you're sending the mail. When it gets there—yes, you guessed it—it adds even *more* information to the email header. It adds the same kind of information that all the other servers added to the header along the way. It adds a final piece of information as well, called the *envelope sender*—a line of text identifying who sent the message and when it was received. The recipient usually sees this last piece of information courtesy of his email program.

As you might guess, all this header information can get really, really long. In fact, not uncommonly, the header is much larger than the message itself. You can see an example of an email header here.

Holy headers! Here's a typical example of an email header...and it's really long.

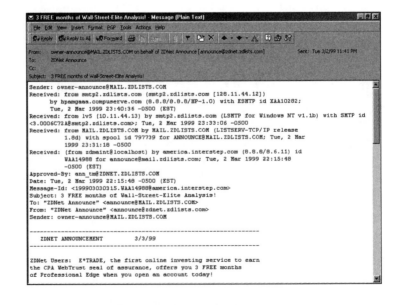

By the way, the whole process of sending and receiving mail sounds as if it could take hours or days. In fact, frequently it happens in a matter of seconds.

Keep in mind that when mail is delivered to someone, it doesn't first go directly to the person's computer. Instead, it sits on the email server. Then, when the person logs on to the server, the server delivers the email message to his computer. Sometimes the email message is then deleted off the server. Sometimes it isn't. It depends on your Internet service provider and your email settings.

Finally, after the email message has been routed from server to server and router to router and relay to relay and all kinds of information has been added to the header along the way, it's delivered to the person to whom you sent the message. All that for saying you can meet for lunch next Tuesday!

The Least You Need to Know

➤ There are two parts of an email message—a header and a body.

➤ The header contains information about who is sending the message, who's receiving it, and what happens to the message as it travels across the Internet.

➤ As email travels across the Internet, it can be snooped on by hackers.

➤ In some cases, your email might be kept by your email server unless you tell the server to delete the message.

TICK
TICK
TICK

Chapter 8

Dangerous Delivery: What Dangers Are There in Email?

In This Chapter

➤ How others can snoop on your email

➤ Why your email can legally be read by your place of employment

➤ What is spam?

➤ What you need to know about email spoofing and mail bombs

➤ How viruses can spread via email

Email—can't live with it, can't live without it. It's one of the most revolutionary ways ever created that let people communicate. It has changed the way we do business, the way we communicate with family and friends, the way we live our lives. It's been a great boon to us all.

But there are some dangers in email. Because the Internet is not a very secure place, your email can be intercepted and read by others. You can be swamped by unsolicited email, called *spam*, and your computer can get a virus from opening an attachment to an email message. In this chapter, we'll look at all the dangers email poses—and in future chapters, you'll see how you can keep yourself safe.

How Your Email Can Be Read by Others

Every time you send out a piece of email, you should assume that it can be read by someone other than the person you sent it to. That memo you wrote about launching a new business on the Internet, selling spotted salamanders and painted turtles online? (www.buyamphibians.com, anyone?) Assume your competitor can read it. A nasty note about your boss? Yup, it can be snooped on. A too-friendly note to an old high-school flame of yours? Yes, it can be perused.

The reason your email can be read by others has to do with the nature of the Internet itself and of how email works. (For more details on how email works, turn to Chapter 7, "How Does Email Work, Anyway?" For details about how the Internet works, head to Chapter 1, "Understanding the Internet and Online Security.") In addition, anyone who has access to the destination computer—say, your ex-flame's current spouse—could read your email as well.

From the moment you send a piece of email to the moment it is delivered to its recipient, it can be read. It starts as soon as you send the mail, because the first thing that happens is your mail is sent to your Internet service provider's (ISP's) email server. Assume that anyone at your ISP can read your mail. It's easy for them to do. The messages are sitting there on a computer, and people at your ISP can simply open them up and read them. There goes the secret of your www.buyamphibians.com business plan. You'll have to make your first million some other way.

What Is Encryption?

To keep your email private, you can *encrypt* it so that only the intended recipient can read it. Encryption scrambles your email so that anyone looking at it (except the recipient) sees a bunch of random letters, numbers, and other incomprehensible gobbledygook. That way, no one can snoop on your mail as you send it across the Internet. Turn to Chapter 9, "Keeping Your Email Private with Encryption," for more information about this subject.

From the ISP's server, the mail gets sent from router to router to router on the Internet. (*Routers* are special computers that send information on the Internet.) Hackers and snoopers can examine your mail as it travels. They can read the message. And they can read the headers, which have identifying information about you and who you're sending the email to, so not only can they read your mail, they can also know who you are. Then, armed with your email address, it's a snap to find out where you live, your phone number, and other personal information. And of course, they can read your message itself. So if you're sending any information that you'd like to be kept secret—like your amphibian business plan—you could be in big trouble.

What to do? If you're worried about email privacy, turn to Chapter 9 to see what you can do to keep your email private. It tells you what you can do to make sure your `www.buyamphibians.com` business plan—or any other email—can't be snooped on by anyone as it makes its way across the Internet.

Your Boss Owns Your Email

Before you hit the Send button at work, consider this: Your boss owns your email. Any email you send and receive at work can legally be snooped on, saved, and used in any way your employer wants. That means anything—email complaining about your superiors, love letters to your spouse, jokes that you send and receive, that note to your friend in accounting where you called your boss Big Butt. Every bit of every note is the legal property of your company, not you.

At Work, Email Is Forever

You're at work. You send an email. Afterward, you think that perhaps you shouldn't have sent it so you delete it. Think it's gone from your work's email system? Well, it isn't. When you send email at work, it's stored various places in your company, such as on an email server and possibly on backup disks. Even if you delete it, that email lives on in company archives. Companies have different rules about how long they keep the email. You should assume that it's kept forever.

Companies increasingly snoop on their employees' email as part of their normal daily business. Consider this: An American Management Association survey found that in 1998, 20 percent of all companies surveyed snooped on their employees' email. It's only going to get worse. Here are just a few instances of what email snooping has already led to, according to an article in *Newsweek* magazine:

➤ Texas Health Resources, a Southwest hospital chain, uses special software that automatically looks into all the email sent by their 3,000 employees, looking for unseemly words.

➤ Content Technologies Inc., which makes email monitoring software for businesses, quadrupled its sales of monitoring software in a single year.

➤ The Salomon Smith Barney Inc. investment firm fired one of its Wall Street analysts for allegedly sending and receiving pornographic email.

➤ Investigators at AT&T reprimanded a husband and wife who worked together at the company because they exchanged affectionate email. (And yes, soap opera fans out there, the mail they had sent was to each other.)

There's not much you can do about your company snooping on your email, because it's perfectly legal. The best advice is this: Never send an email that you don't want your bosses to see. And never, ever call your boss Big Butt.

Why Spam Can Leave a Bad Taste in Your Mouth

If your email inbox is like mine, it's filled—absolutely to the brim—with unsolicited email, the equivalent of junk postal mail, although from my point of view (and many others') it's worse. Email you never asked for from people you don't know is called spam.

Techno Talk

Why Is It Called Spam?

No one is quite sure why unsolicited email is called spam, but many people believe it gets its name from a skit done by the old Monty Python comic group on their television series. In the skit, someone asks what's on the menu in a diner, only to discover that every item contains spam luncheon meat—in fact, spam takes over the entire menu, crowding everything else out. In the same way, spam crowds out your regular email.

It's not uncommon to receive dozens of pieces of spam in a day, and sometimes even more. America Online users are particularly targeted by spammers and tend to receive more spam than do people at other Internet service providers. There's all kinds of spam, but most are commercial offers, often offering shady products and services— work-at-home offers, pyramid schemes, products that don't do what they promise, health and diet scams (Herbal Viagra seems to be a big one these days), phony investment opportunities and stock offers...the list goes on and on. You'll find all that and more offered thanks to spam. Much spam is also pornographic in nature, trying to get you to visit for-pay pornographic sites on the Web.

What's the Beef with Spam?

Sure, spam is annoying, inconvenient, and occasionally offensive, but that aside, what's the matter with it? One reason spam is so popular with spammers is because it's so cheap to send out. But because you're paying for your connection time one way or the other, you're actually paying to receive it. Only a few cents at a time, but that does add up. Think of it this way—would you accept a collect call from a telemarketer?

Spam is offensive and litters your mailbox with so much unwanted mail, it's hard to get to the real mail that needs reading, because there's so much junk. And it's becoming increasingly difficult to figure out what's spam and what isn't, as spammers get more sophisticated. It used to be that you'd see something like "Great business opportunity!!" in the subject line of an email, and you'd know to ignore the message. No longer. Now spammers write in things like, "Hi," "About our talk," or "Good news,"—anything that makes it sound like the message is from a friend instead of a spammer.

Don't think all you need to do to stop getting spammed is to write back to the spammer, asking that they stop bugging you. This doesn't help. In many cases, they've forged their return address, so that if you answer them, it goes to a phony address. In other cases, if you write back, the spammer knows that your email address is a valid one—and he sends even *more* spam.

What Is Spamoflauge?

Often, spammers don't want you to know it's them sending you spam. They hide their addresses by faking information such as who is sending you the message. When a spammer does this, it's called spamoflauge.

There are many ways to fight spam, including getting spam-fighting software that automatically detects spam and deletes it before you ever see it. One such program, Spam Exterminator, is pictured here.

You can kill spam dead with a spam-killing program like Spam Exterminator.

Rule List - AutoCheck Enabled

File   View   Auto-Check   Manage   Help

New   Delete   Settings   Status   Preview   Lists   Clean Mailbox

Criteria	Value	Delete	Beep	Reply	Report	Confirm	Recycle...	Hits
From e-mail Address / Do...	cyberpromo.com	Yes	Yes	No	No	No	No	0
Subject Contains	$$	Yes	Yes	No	No	Yes	No	1
Header Contains	X-Advertisement	Yes	Yes	No	No	No	No	0
From user that is a number	N/A	Yes	Yes	No	No	Yes	No	13
Subject Contains	XXX	Yes	Yes	No	No	No	No	5
Subject Contains	MONEY FAST	Yes	Yes	No	No	No	No	0
Matches Known Spamm...	N/A	Yes	Yes	No	No	No	No	249
Header Contains	X-Distribution: M...	Yes	Yes	No	No	No	No	0
Header Contains	X-Mailer: Extractor	Yes	Yes	No	No	No	No	0
Header Contains	X-Mailer: Floodg...	Yes	Yes	No	No	No	No	0
Header Contains	X-Distribution: B...	Yes	Yes	No	No	No	No	1
Subject Contains	==	Yes	Yes	No	No	No	No	0
Subject Contains	!!	Yes	Yes	No	No	Yes	No	28
Subject Contains	INCREDIBLE D...	Yes	Yes	No	No	No	No	0
Header Contains	airship-list@lists....	Yes	Yes	No	No	No	No	1...
Header Contains	suck	Yes	Yes	No	No	No	No	71
From e-mail Address / Do...	dummiesdaily.com	Yes	Yes	No	No	No	No	346
From e-mail Address / Do...	tipworld.com	Yes	Yes	No	No	No	No	250
Header Contains	Daily New Mem...	Yes	Yes	No	No	No	No	0
From e-mail Address / Do...	Jesse Berst's An...	Yes	Yes	No	No	No	No	73
Header Contains	MS-News Digest	Yes	Yes	No	No	No	No	138
From e-mail Address / Do...	softdeals@hotm...	Yes	Yes	No	No	No	No	1
From e-mail Address / Do...	plarna@aol.com	Yes	Yes	No	No	No	No	1
From e-mail Address / Do...	reminder@gifton...	Yes	Yes	No	No	No	No	2
From e-mail Address / Do...	jackpotx@ix.net...	Yes	No	No	No	No	Yes	1
From e-mail Address / Do...	its@yourchance...	Yes	No	No	No	No	Yes	1
From e-mail Address / Do...	wxcaizo@urs.net	Yes	No	No	No	No	Yes	0

This list is the main control center for Spam Exterminator. Here your may add or modify existing rules that will dictate how your e-mail is handled. To create a new rule press the 'New' button.   ● Help...

There are many other ways to fight spam. For the complete rundown, head to Chapter 10, "What Is Spam and How Can You Protect Yourself from It?"

Why Email Spoofing Is No Joke

Imagine this: Your boss gets a message, apparently from you, calling him Fat Butt, telling him he's the worst boss you've ever had, and then resigning. Or your spouse gets an email, also apparently from you, saying it's all over between the two of you; you want a divorce. Or a piece of offensive spam is sent to thousands of people with your return address, so it looks as if you've sent it. You, of course, have to put up with the hundreds of angry messages sent in response.

Those are all examples of *email spoofing*. In email spoofing, someone sends an email and forges an address so that it looks as if it's someone else's. Email spoofing is tough to track down. You can always try to closely examine the email headers to see if you can trace where the mail came from. See Chapter 10 for some advice on how to do that. The truth is, it is pretty tough to find the culprit. The best way to combat it is to forward any spoofed mail to your Internet service provider and ask it to track down the source of the mail. The ISP might or might not be able to do it, but it can't hurt to try.

Is There Such a Thing as a Mail Bomb?

Mail bombs. Pretty frightening-sounding words. It conjures up visions of emails arriving in your in-box and then blowing your computer to smithereens—or at least crashing your hard disk. The mail simply arrives, and the damage is done, and there's nothing you can do about it.

Well, breathe a sigh of relief. It's not going to happen. No one can send you an email message that on its own destroys your computer or hard disk. (Although, as we'll see, attached files can be dangerous.)

That's the good news. The bad news is that there *are* such things as mail bombs. They're very, very annoying, but they don't destroy your computer.

A mail bomb is when someone sends you (or someone else) massive amounts of mail, so that you get dozens or even hundreds of messages or more, all at once. In the worst case, this can overwhelm your ISP's email server, causing it to crash. In the best case, you are forced to delete hundreds of pieces of email—a very annoying, time-consuming chore.

There are a few things you can do if you get a mail bomb. First, alert your ISP and send it the email. The ISP can then try to track down the perpetrator.

Next, you can take some action on your own. Send a message to the ISP of the sender of the message, telling it about the mail bomb. Depending on the sophistication of the sender of the mail bomb, that might or might not work. If the mail bomb sender doesn't bother to hide his identity, then the ISP can take action. If the identity is hidden well, you don't really know the sender of the message.

A Real-Life Mail Bomb Story

I can write about mail bombs from experience. Several years ago my daughter, who was 11 years old, was subject to a harassing mail bomb. She received dozens of email messages from a single sender in a short period of time, with a not-very-friendly, although not specifically threatening, message. It was quite frightening to her—so much so, that she didn't want to use email anymore.

The first thing I did was check the address of the sender of the message. It didn't appear to be forged. From the content and wording of the message, including its poor spelling and grammar, I guessed that the message was coming from a pre-teen or young teen, which made it more likely that the address wasn't forged. First, I sent a note to the ISP, telling about the mail bomb. Next, I used America Online's email filters to tell the service to reject any email to my daughter coming from the offending address. It worked like a charm—after I took action, she never received another message from the bomber.

Many email programs also let you reject messages from certain senders, or at least flag them or put them into a common folder where you can easily delete them. Turn to Chapter 10 for details on how to do that. America Online lets you block messages coming from specific email addresses. Chapter 21, "Keeping Kids Safe on America Online," shows you how to do that.

Can You Get a Virus from an Email Message?

Probably more myths surround email and viruses than any other single thing about the Internet. All kinds of crazy messages fly around claiming, among other things, that you can get viruses if someone sends you a simple text message, for example.

Let me put your mind at ease. You can't get a virus by simply reading an email message.

Techno Talk

Is There Such a Thing as the Good Times Virus Spread by Email?

One of the most persistent myths that makes its way around the Internet is the existence of a Good Times virus that deletes all the files on your hard drive if you merely read a specific message with the subject "Good Times." It's not true; it can't happen; the message started as a hoax and has since been sent to many millions of people. The hoax first surfaced in 1994, and email about it continues to circle the globe. You can't get a virus from text-based email unless you run a program or file attached to the email message.

Now let me disturb you. Email *can* spread viruses. But to get a virus from an email, you have to open a document attached to the email or run a program attached to the email. If you don't do either of those things, you're safe. There's a very simple way to make sure you don't get a virus from email: *Never* open a file or run a program sent to you via email from someone you don't know. And to be perfectly safe, you shouldn't even run a program sent to you via email from someone you *do* know. If you do open a program from someone you know, though, you should run a virus-checking program, such as Norton AntiVirus. For information about viruses and preventing them, turn to Part 8, "Protecting Yourself Against Viruses, Trojan Horses, and Other Nasty Creatures."

You can even get a virus from a document, such as a Word document, sent to you via email. For example, the most widespread virus in recent years, named Melissa after a certain "exotic dancer," was spread via a Word document sent via email. The Word document had a virus in a macro inside it. For more information about macro viruses, and how to prevent them, turn to Chapter 26, "How to Keep Your Computer Safe from Viruses."

HTML Email Can Be Dangerous

You can't get a virus from merely reading email, but if you're reading HTML-based email, you can get into trouble. Various nasty things can be done to you when you get an HTML message with technologies such as Java, JavaScript and ActiveX. Some email readers that read HTML allow you to turn those technologies off, to keep yourself safe. For example, if you use Outlook, you can turn them off by choosing **Options** from the **Tools** menu, then clicking on the **Security** tab. Now click on **Zone** settings. From here, you'll be able to turn those technologies off. For more information on the technologies' dangers, and more details of turning them off in the Zone settings, turn to Chapter 27, "Keeping Safe from Java, JavaScript and ActiveX Applets."

The Least You Need to Know

➤ Your email can be read by snoopers as it makes its way across the Internet.

➤ Your employer can legally read your email—and many employers do. Don't send email that you don't want read by your boss and others at work.

➤ One way to avoid spam is to use spam-blocking software.

➤ Never open a file or document that you're sent from someone you don't know via email.

Chapter 9

Keeping Your Email Private with Encryption

In This Chapter

➤ Understanding how encryption can keep your email safe from prying eyes

➤ What steps you take when you encrypt and sign your email

➤ How to use Pretty Good Privacy to encrypt and sign your email

➤ How to use a digital certificate to encrypt and sign your email

As we've seen in other chapters, any time you send email over the Internet, it can be snooped on. If you're sending out sensitive material (your www.buyamphibians.com business plan, for example), it can be read by snoops and hackers.

You can make sure that your email stays private by using *encryption*—a way of scrambling information so that only the intended recipient can read it.

Encryption solves another problem as well. It's fairly easy for someone to do email spoofing—that is, forge a message so that it looks as if it comes from someone else. How can people be sure that the message they get from you really *is* from you? And how can you be sure that the message you get from someone really is from the person who it appears to be from? (All this spy stuff is starting to give me a headache...) The answer, again, is encryption, because encryption can create a digital signature that can't be forged. Get an email with a digital signature, and you can be sure it's from who it says it's from. If you send out an email with your digital signature, the recipient can rest assured that it's from you.

In this chapter, I'll take a look at how you can use encryption to keep your email secure and private.

What Is Encryption, Anyway?

What is encryption? You actually know more about encryption than you realize. It's really just a fancy way of saying you're applying some kind of secret code to something as a way to try to hide it from someone. Spies use this kind of thing all the time. Here's your chance to play at being James Bond—or at least Maxwell Smart.

Let's take a simple example of encryption. See if you can decipher this sentence: "on'tday ouyay ovelay ogsfray?"

If you ever spoke Pig Latin as a kid, you'd know that the original sentence was, "Don't you love frogs?" When speaking Pig Latin, you take the first letter of a word, move it to the back of the word, and add the letters ay to the end of it. That's, in essence, a way of encrypting information—scrambling it so that it doesn't look like the original sentence.

Think of all the times you created secret codes as a kid. (Well, at least *I* was creating them things all the time. Then again, maybe I was a weird kid.) Maybe you came up with a code where you substituted the letter z for a, y for b, and so on. You shared the code with a friend, and the two of you could exchange secret messages with each other. Not that you really *knew* anything so important that it needed to be kept from prying eyes—but still, the whole *idea* of the secret code was what was important.

Now, you don't want to send messages out over the Internet in Pig Latin—at least, not if you want to keep your message private—because there are ways to crack encryption codes, especially when someone has a computer to help. And yes, I'm fairly sure that a hacker with a little bit of time will be able to translate "Asswordpay orfay ouyay: uitfray oopslay" into "Password for you: Fruit Loops."

What Is a Cypher?

When data is encrypted, a code or set of formulas of some kind is used—one so complex that it is extremely difficult for anyone to crack. The code used to encrypt information is called a *cypher*.

But you *do* want to send out your email using encryption if you want to keep it private. Encryption can be used in another way as well. It can be used to create a unique digital signature that you attach to your messages so that whoever gets the message knows that the message came from you and not from someone posing as you.

Here's How Encryption Works—And How to Use It

Before you learn how to encrypt your email, it's a good idea to get an understanding of how encryption works. We're not spies or spooks here, so I'm going to keep it pretty basic, but you'll still learn everything you need.

Encryption is based on the idea of keys. A key on your computer, which is basically a file or program of some sort, is used to encrypt information so that it can't be read.

You encrypt your email with a key. Then, another key is used to decrypt the information—put it back into its original form. When sending email on the Internet, you encrypt your email with a key before sending it. That way, no one on the Internet can read your mail, because it's encrypted and looks like a whole bunch of random letters, numbers, and characters. But the person you're sending the message to has a key that can decrypt the email, and when the message gets to his computer, he uses the key and reads the mail.

Encryption programs create these keys. The encryption programs can be completely separate from your email program, or they can be integrated into the program. It's easier to use encryption programs integrated into your email program, because you can do everything from one program—your email software. If you use an encryption program that's separate from your email program, you have to do a bit more juggling to get everything done. Pretty much any good encryption program will work with your email software, so you're in luck.

Techno Talk

What Is a Digital Certificate?

You don't need to have an encryption program to use encryption with your email. You can also use what's called a *digital certificate*. A digital certificate is, in essence, a key used to encrypt and decrypt your email. But the key isn't created by an encryption program on your computer. Instead, a private company called a Certificate Authority, such as a company called VeriSign at www.verisign.com, creates it. You download the key to your computer and can use that key to encrypt email. Often, these Certificate Authorities charge you for the use of the digital certificate, although the price is fairly low. For example, VeriSign was charging $6.95 per year for use of its certificate. Later in the chapter, I'll take a look at how to use a digital certificate from a company like VeriSign.

In general, there are two encryption technologies that use keys. One is called *private key encryption* and the other, not surprisingly, is called *public key encryption*. Here's what you need to know about each.

What Is Private Key Encryption?

In private key encryption, you use a key to encrypt your email, and the person receiving the email has to use the exact same key to decrypt it. Sounds simple and secure, doesn't it? Well, there's a problem with it. How can you get that key to the person receiving the email? If you send the key via email, you defeat the whole purpose of encryption, because the key could be intercepted en route, and the email could be read. In that case, for sending and receiving email, private key encryption isn't really workable. (I guess you could mail the key on a floppy disk, but that's getting a bit complicated for our purposes.)

What Is Public Key Encryption—And How Do You Use It?

The other kind of encryption—public key encryption—is much more workable on the Internet. Just about any encryption program you run will use public key encryption—and I suggest that public key encryption be the only kind of encryption you use.

In public key encryption, the encryption program creates two keys for you. They're a matched pair and work together to encrypt and decrypt email. One key is called your private key, and the other is your public key. Here you can see the Pretty Good Privacy program (usually called PGP) starting to create a pair of keys. The public and private keys work together to encrypt your email when you send it and decrypt your email when it's received.

Some pretty good keys: Here's the PGP program as it starts to create a set of keys for you—one private and one public.

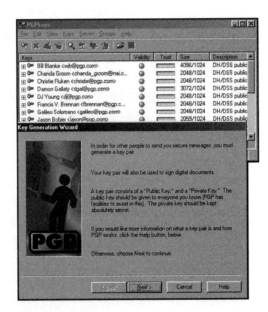

You're the only person in the world who has your private key, so it stays on your computer. But you send your public key out to the world—you want as many people as possible to have a copy of it. To do that, you can put your public key on a public site on the Internet so that other people can download it. Also, you can attach your public key to your email messages, so that anyone who receives your message can have a copy of your public key. You should also get copies of other people's public keys.

Here's the way public and private keys work together. To send someone secure, encrypted email, you need to have his public key on your computer. You use that public key to encrypt mail. After you encrypt it, you send it over the Internet.

After you encrypt the mail with the person's public key, no one can read it except the person you're sending it to. That's because all the public key can do is encrypt email. It can't decrypt it. When it gets sent out over the Internet, it looks like a bunch of gobbledygook to anyone trying to snoop on it.

The encrypted email gets sent to your friend. Here's the cool thing: Your friend can read the email, because his private key can decrypt it. In fact, the only way that mail can be read is with his private key, because he's the only person in the world with his private key.

It works the other way as well. When someone wants to send you secure email, he uses your key to create the encrypted message, sends it over the Internet, and when you get it, you can read it with your private key—no one else can read your mail.

Got that? Good. Let's get away from theory and back to reality now (always a good idea unless you're stuck in a university somewhere, where theory *is* reality). Here are some step-by-step instructions on how you actually use an encryption program:

➤ Get an encryption program, such as Pretty Good Privacy. (Very important first step, that. I'll show you where and how later on in the chapter.)

➤ Next, use it to generate two keys—one private and one public.

➤ Then, make your public key available to as many people as possible by posting it on servers on the Internet and by sending it to friends using email.

➤ Get other people's public keys.

Make Sure to Get Your Public Key into the Hands of Anyone You Exchange Email with—And Get Their Keys as Well

The only way you can exchange secure email with people is if you have copies of their public keys, and they have copies of your public key. Otherwise, encryption doesn't work. So make sure that you get your public key into the hands of as many people as possible—and always ask to be sent copies of their public keys.

➤ When you want to send people secure email, encrypt the messages with their public keys and send the messages to them. They are the only people who can read the mail, using their private keys.

➤ When you get email from someone who has encrypted it with your public key, you are the only person able to read it, using your private key.

Is Pretty Good Privacy Really Pretty Good—And How Do You Use It to Encrypt Email?

There's a fair number of encryption programs available. The truth is, the best one is Pretty Good Privacy (PGP). Don't be fooled by its name: Pretty Good Privacy is more than pretty good. In fact, it's great. It features super-strength encryption and is probably the most common encryption program used on the Internet and so has become a standard of sorts. That means that, by using PGP, you have the widest number of people to exchange email with. Sometimes, encryption programs don't work with one another. But because so many people who use encryption use PGP, you can exchange email with them. Even if people don't use PGP, but use certain encryption technology, you can still send and receive secure email to and from them.

Why Can't PGP Be Exported to Other Countries?

PGP has powerful encryption features. How powerful? So powerful that the U.S. government doesn't allow it to be exported to foreign countries aside from Canada. The government has odd laws governing encryption—it considers encryption to be a military secret of sorts. Because of that, it doesn't allow powerful encryption programs to be exported—and PGP is so powerful, it's one of the programs that can't be exported. Now, anyone in the world can download the program from the Internet merely by visiting the PGP Web site and lying on a form there. And it's pretty easy for anyone from a foreign country to come to the U.S., buy the program, and simply take the disks with them overseas. So, you're probably thinking that it's a pretty useless law, just about worthless. I think the same thing. Does this make any sense? Of course not. But we're talking about the federal government here, an institution not particularly well known for its logic or common sense.

Here's even more good news—there's a version of PGP that you can use for free, if you plan to use it for your personal use and not for business. The program is called PGPFreeware, and it's available from the PGP Web site at www.pgp.com. You can download it to your computer, install it, and use it for free, forever. The truth is, it's pretty much every bit as good as the for-pay version that you can buy on the Web site or in a retail store. True, there are a few bells and whistles missing, but for most purposes, you'll do just as well with the free version of the program.

PGP comes with a manual, and I'm not going to spend time here telling you all the ins and outs of using the program. It works just as encryption programs do as I described earlier in the chapter. Here's a brief rundown, along with tips, on how to use PGP to exchange secure email with people:

➤ When you first run the program, you are asked to generate a set of keys—one private and one public. You are asked how many bits you want to use when creating the key. In general, the larger the number of bits you use to create the key, the more secure your email is. But when you choose a larger number, it also means it takes longer to encrypt the message. My general rule is the larger the better. I suggest using a number no smaller than 2048.

➤ The program is designed to work well with email programs such as Eudora, Microsoft Outlook, and Microsoft Outlook Express. When you install the program, make sure to install the plug-ins that work with your program. That way, it is easier to encrypt and decrypt email.

➤ After you install the program, new icons show up in your email program. When you create mail, you'll find an icon for signing the message and one for encrypting the message. If you only want the person receiving the mail to be sure it's coming from you, click on the icon for signing the message. That way, the recipient will know it's from you when he receives it. If you only click on that icon, though, the mail isn't encrypted—it merely carries your digital signature, and the recipient knows the message is from you. If you want to encrypt the message, click on the icon for encrypting the message.

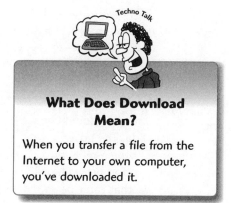

What Does Download Mean?

When you transfer a file from the Internet to your own computer, you've downloaded it.

➤ When you send a message that carries your digital signature, you have to type your PGP password before sending the message. You are prompted to supply your password.

➤ To send the person encrypted email, you need his public key. If you have the public key on your computer, the message is sent automatically. If you don't, you are shown a list of all the public keys you have on your computer, as shown here. Choose a public key from the list, and the person is added to the email message. Then, just send the message, and it is sent, encrypted, and signed, if you chose to digitally sign the message. If you don't have someone's key on your computer, ask him to send you a copy.

Choosing someone's public key from the public keys you have on your computer.

➤ When you receive an encrypted email message, it looks like a whole bunch of random numbers, letters, and characters. You'll see an icon in your email program that automatically decrypts the message and verifies that the sender is who he says he is. Click on it, and it turns those random numbers, letters, and characters into a readable email message—and you are told if the sender is truly who he says he is. Take a look at the nearby figures to see before and after pictures of an encrypted email message. The before picture shows you the message as it's received—encrypted and unreadable. The after shows you the same message after it's been decrypted.

Holy gobbledygook! What in the world is this message saying? It's been encrypted with PGP.

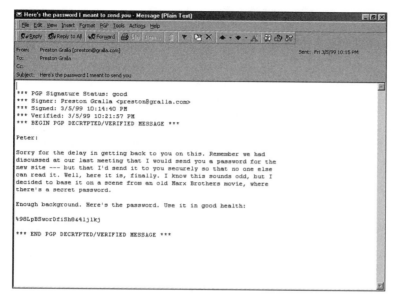

Ah, now I see. PGP comes to the rescue and decrypts the message.

There are a whole lot more ins and outs to PGP. If you want to get down and geeky, there are some truly nifty things you can do with it. But if you're just looking to encrypt and decrypt email, it's pretty straightforward to use. Just remember: You need to have someone's public key if you want to send him encrypted email, and he needs to have your public key if he wants to send you encrypted email.

Help! PGP Doesn't Have a Plug-In for My Email Program. What Can I Do?

Don't despair. You can still use PGP. PGP comes with two programs, PGP Tray and PGP Tools. Each of them allows you to encrypt and decrypt messages, although it takes a little bit longer and a bit of juggling. If there's no PGP plug-in for your program, use one of these tools. Check the documentation for how to use them.

How to Use a Digital Certificate to Encrypt Email

Digital certificates do pretty much the same thing that PGP does. They use private and public keys, they can digitally sign your email, and they can encrypt your email. Digital certificates are often called *digital IDs*.

You get a digital certificate or digital ID from a Certificate Authority. (Sounds impressive and formal, doesn't it?) The most popular one on the Internet is VeriSign at www.verisign.com. Unlike PGP, it isn't free—it costs $6.95 per year for the certificate. After a year is up, you have to pony up the money again, because your certificate won't work any longer.

If you want someone to be able to send secure email to you, you have to send him a copy of your digital certificate—although, in essence, you're really just sending him the public key part of it. And to send secure email to him, you have to get a copy of his digital certificate—although he's really just sending you his public key.

You use your digital certificate to sign and encrypt outgoing email. You also use it to decrypt incoming email. A digital certificate works right within your email program—there's no other way to use it. How you use it depends on your email software, so if you decide to use a digital certificate, check on the authority's Web site for information on how to use it with your email program.

The Least You Need to Know

➤ Encryption programs require that you have two keys—a private key and a public key. You share your public key with the world, but keep your private key to yourself.

➤ Send your public key to as many people as possible and post it on public Web sites. That way, people can send you encrypted email.

➤ Before sending an encrypted message to someone using Pretty Good Privacy or another encryption program, you need his public key. Ask him to send you a public key if you don't already have it.

➤ When you install Pretty Good Privacy, make sure to install the plug-ins specifically designed for your email program.

➤ Digital certificates work much like encryption programs, such as Pretty Good Privacy. But you have to pay an annual fee to use them.

What Is Spam and How Can You Protect Yourself from It?

In This Chapter

➤ What is spam and how is it created?

➤ Techniques to hide your name and email address from spammers

➤ How to use email software and spam-fighting tools to stop spam from ever reaching you

➤ What you can do if you've been spammed

We've all been deluged by the email offers: "Make a million dollars in your spare time!" "New, Guaranteed: Herbal Viagra!" "New Stock—Can't Miss!" "I'm Cindy, Visit Me Online for a Hot Time!"

There's more as well...a lot more. Email boxes all over the world are filled daily with junk mail like these offers, called *spam*, which is the electronic equivalent of junk mail and telemarketers calling you during dinner to get you to get a new credit card or switch your long-distance phone carrier. Any time you're sent an email message from someone you don't know, making you an offer of some kind, or trying to get you to take an action, you've been a victim of spam. Multiply the spam you get in a day by millions and millions of people—and that figure by the cost of transmitting, receiving, and deleting this email—and you have an idea of the scope of the problem.

Spam is one of the most annoying problems you'll face on the Internet. But you're in luck, because there's a lot you can do to stamp out spam and even help lock a spammer in the slammer, as you'll see in this chapter.

What Is Spam and How Is It Created?

So what is spam, exactly? It's email that you never asked to get, sent to you by some-one you don't know. Usually, the identity of the sender of the email has been forged, so it's difficult to know who is sending it. Spam is a popular way to do scams on the Internet, through various get-rich-quick schemes—and it may also offer pornography for sale, or ask you to visit for-pay pornographic Web sites.

Spam Can Be Found on Usenet Newsgroups as Well as in Email

Email isn't the only thing that's bedeviled by spam. So are Usenet newsgroups— worldwide public bulletin boards in which people carry on discussions. Spam is frequently posted on these newsgroups, often to such an extent that it completely overwhelms any legitimate discussion.

Many spam offers are scams, although not all are. (For information on how to recog-nize an Internet scam, see Chapter 6, "How to Protect Yourself Against the Most Common Internet Scams.") Spam has become popular because it's cheap and easy to create, it's often difficult to track down who's created it, and there are gullible people out there who respond to the offers. In other words, there's money to be made and it doesn't cost spammers a lot to try and make it.

Money Matters: The True Cost of Spam

Sure, spam is an annoyance. But in fact, it's worse than a mere annoyance—it costs time and money as well, for nearly everyone but the sender. It clogs up Internet email boxes and mail servers so that mail gets delivered more slowly or not at all. It forces Internet service providers to buy extra bandwidth to be able to deliver all the extra mail. There are other costs and problems as well. Here are the main ones:

➤ Because of the massive volume of spam, you're paying more for your Internet connection than if there were no spam. Estimates of how much email on the Internet is actually spam range from 10 percent to 30 percent or even more. To deliver all that spam, Internet service providers (ISPs) need to buy extra comput-ers and faster connections to the Internet. They have to hire extra staff as well. The Netcom ISP has estimated that about 10 percent of its customers' bills is devoted to handling spam issues, for example. Guess who pays the cost? That's right, you. ISPs pass the cost directly on to their customers.

➤ Spam often disrupts normal Internet traffic. It can clog up the pipes that deliver email and Web sites to you. Things are delivered more slowly to you, or not at all. Spam has also crashed ISPs and corporate networks.

➤ Children are subject to sexually related and pornographic messages. When spammers send out email in bulk, all they have are email addresses—there's no way for them to differentiate adults from children. So sexually oriented spam— estimated by AT&T to make up some 11 percent of all spam—is sent to children.

Calculating How Much Money Is Wasted by Spam

Spam costs money, because it takes up Internet bandwidth and forces Internet service providers to buy more bandwidth than they need. It costs money because every time someone at work has to delete a piece of spam, the person's company has, in essence, paid him to delete that piece of email. Perhaps for a single user, the money doesn't amount to much, but taken over the entire Internet, it adds up to big bucks. A spam-fighting company called Bright Lights has a Spam Calculator on the Web that totes up the total amount of money wasted by spam. Last time I checked, the total money it cost was a staggering $213 million per year. You can even play with the calculator, changing the site's assumptions about how much spam there really is, for example, and see how much money *you* estimate it costs. A neat site and worth checking out. Head to `www.brightlights.com` and click on **Spam Info**.

➤ You have to take time out of your day to delete spam. It takes a few seconds and often more to delete a piece of spam, especially because it's not always easy to know from the subject line what's spam and what isn't. Multiply all the time you spend deleting spam—that's time that you could spend doing other things instead.

➤ Spam leads to scams. Much spam is devoted to scamming people. Because of it, there's more fraud and abuse than if spam were outlawed.

Nasty Business: How Spam Is Created

Before you learn how to fight spam, you need to know how it's created—don't worry, we won't be talking about odd body parts that may go into any luncheon meats.

Let's take an example. Joe Spammer (AKA Joe the Slimeball) decides he's going to try and make a million dollars by sending out spam hyping his extremely illegal business scheme: He wants people to call an 809 number he's set up offshore, and he'll charge them each $5 a minute without them knowing about it. As a come-on to get people to call, he's going to claim in the subject line of the mail, "Free money—call now!!!" And for the body of the email, he'll make up some scam about if people call the number listed, they'll get secret details about how to get free cash from the U.S. Treasury.

So what does Joe do? First, he gets a list of email addresses to send the spam to. There's several ways he can do this. He can take the easy (and more expensive) way and buy the list of addresses from any of the companies that sell bulk email lists. But no, Joe is too cheap to do that—and he has a less-expensive way of doing it anyway. He's going to harvest the names from the Internet using special address-gathering software. This is how many spammers and how many companies that sell bulk email build their spamming lists. Later on in this chapter, I'll show you how you can try and make sure that spammers don't grab your name when compiling their spam lists. So how do spammers harvest their names? Let me count the ways:

➤ They get names from postings to Usenet newsgroups. Newsgroups are worldwide, public Internet bulletin boards. When you post a message to Usenet, your email address is also posted. Software can go into newsgroups and automatically grab the email address from every posting. Later on in this chapter, I show how you can hide your email address so it can't be harvested. And for more information about Usenet newsgroups, turn to Chapter 17, "Protecting Your Privacy on Internet Newsgroups and Discussion Areas."

Keep Your Name Out of Usenet Archives

To a great extent, Usenet newsgroups are forever. The messages are often kept in public archives that people can look at, including the popular Web site www.deja.com. But that means that spammers have an easy central resource for getting email addresses. You can keep your postings out of these archives, though. Just add the following line to your posting's header or to the beginning of your message: x-no-archive:yes.

➤ They get names from public Web White Page directories. There are many White Page directories on the Internet that have people's email addresses on them. Spammers can automatically grab all those addresses. To get your name out of these directories, turn to Chapter 5, "Fighting Back: How to Remove Your Name from Web Databases."

➤ They get names from chat rooms, especially on America Online. Software can automatically watch chat rooms and grab the email addresses of people who come in. Later in this chapter, I clue you in on how to protect your address when in a chat room. And for more information about chat rooms and privacy, turn to Chapter 16, "How to Keep Safe and Protect Your Privacy When Chatting."

➤ They get names from Internet mailing lists. Internet mailing lists are discussions carried on via email. You can subscribe to a mailing list by sending a message to a specific email address. Internet mailing lists are also called listservs, and they're managed by special listserv software. But there is a command that a spammer can issue to the software that in some cases gives to the spammer the email address of everyone on the list. Later in the chapter, I give you information on how to fight this.

➤ They can get names from your ISP's public directory. Some ISPs, including America Online, post a public directory with information about people on the ISP, including their email addresses. You can get your name off of these public directories. I tell you how later in the chapter. For more detailed information, turn to Chapter 3, "Making Sure Your Internet Service Provider (ISP) Protects Your Privacy."

➤ They can get your email address from your Web page, if you've created one. Many people, when they create a Web page, include their email address on it somewhere. Software can automatically check Web pages and gather email addresses listed on them. There are some tricks you can use to keep your address safe from spammers and yet still let people know your email address. I show you how later on in this chapter.

How to Hide Your Name from Spammers

The best way to cut down or eliminate the spam you get is to stop it at the source—don't let spammers get your email address in the first place. Of course, that's a whole lot easier said than done. As you can see from the previous section, your email address might be spread out all over kingdom come on the Internet.

Still, there's a lot you can do to hide your email address from spammers. Here's how to do it.

Hide Your Real Address When Posting to Usenet Newsgroups

Spammers grab lots of email addresses from Usenet newsgroups. It's a fairly simple matter to make sure they don't get yours. There are a number of ways that you can hide your real address when you post to Usenet newsgroups:

➤ **Post anonymously.** Several Web sites and Internet services let you send out email anonymously or post messages anonymously on newsgroups. This means that your name isn't listed along with the posting—and spammers can't grab it. For example, take a look at the Replay anonymous remailer page at `http://www.replay.com/remailer/anon.html`, which lets you post anonymously. There are many others that do it as well. There's only one drawback to this technique—in some newsgroups, people ignore anonymous posters, because sometimes spammers post anonymously as a way to send spam to an entire newsgroup without having their identity revealed. For more information on how to post to newsgroups anonymously, turn to Chapter 11, "Staying Anonymous with Anonymous Remailers," and Chapter 17.

Take that, spammers! Posting to a newsgroup using an anonymous emailer like the one at `http://www.replay.com/ remailer/anon.html` *keeps your email address private.*

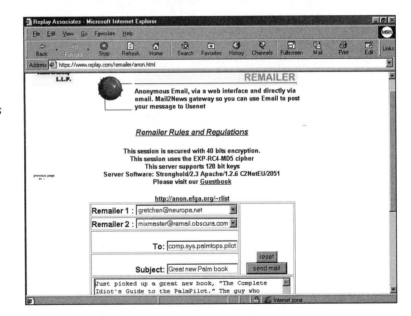

➤ **Use a second email address when posting to newsgroups.** Many sites on the Internet, such as `www.hotmail.com`, `www.bigfoot.com`, and `www.zdnet.com`, give you free email accounts. Get one or more of these free email accounts. Then, when posting to newsgroups, use one of those accounts as your return address—but use it for no other purpose. That way, spam is sent there, but you never have to read it.

➤ **Munge your email address.** Munging refers to a technique you can use so that when you post a newsgroup message using your normal Usenet newsgroup software, your real address doesn't show up—instead, no address or a different address shows up. (Munge? What a word! Leave it to Internet geeks to come up with new uses for language on a daily basis.) Your newsgroup and email software will let you do it. Check the documentation for how. If you use the Outlook Express news reader (it comes with both Microsoft Outlook and Microsoft Outlook Express), here's what to do: Click on the **Tools** menu and choose **Accounts**. Look for your Usenet server in the list that appears and click on it. Click on **Properties**. You'll see the nearby screen appear. In the **E-Mail Address** field, delete your name. Next, put in a phony email address—but make absolutely sure it's phony, something like adam@do-not-send-me-spam-or-else.net. Now, whenever you post to a Usenet newsgroup, your real email address won't appear. The only drawback is that people who want to send you email to follow up on your posting won't be able to because your address won't be listed.

Get lost spammers! Here's how to use the Outlook Express news reader to change the address that is listed when you post to newsgroups.

➤ **Go to www.deja.com to read and post in newsgroups.** When you post to newsgroups at this site, you can use any email address you want—it's easy to munge your address without having to go through setup screens in your news-reader program.

113

There's an Etiquette to Munging

When you munge your email address, there's a generally accepted etiquette about what you should and shouldn't do. An absolute no-no is putting someone else's email address in your postings—whether on purpose or by accident. So check to make sure that any email address you post isn't a real one. And generally, it's considered good form to use a phony address that address-harvesting can't read, but that humans can. For example, if your email address is goodguy@pure.net, you could create a phony email address of goodguy@I-want.nospam.pure.net.

Usenet Is a Way That Spammers Get Highly Targeted Spam Lists

Let's say a spammer is trying to get people to buy antique cars. Sending a spam out to hundreds of thousands of people might not find the spammer many customers, because not many people are interested in antique cars. But Usenet newsgroups allow spammers to gather a highly targeted list of people interested in a specific topic, such as antique cars, Japanese animation, or PalmPilots. That's because the newsgroups are organized by specific interests, and they can gather names only from specific lists. So if you have a special interest, that's all the more reason to protect your email address when posting to Usenet. Later on in the chapter, I show you how.

Go Private: Get Your Name Out of Web White Page Directories

Spammers also harvest names from Web White Page directories, Web sites where you can search for people's email addresses. There are many of these Web sites on the Internet, such as www.bigfoot.com, www.whowhere.com, and www.people.yahoo.com. If you get your name out of those directories, you can cut down on the spam you receive.

Most of these sites let you delete your names out of them, although they don't exactly trumpet that fact. For a list of the major White Page directories on the Web and detailed instructions on how to get your name out of them, turn to Chapter 5.

Go Private, Part II: Remove Your Name from Your ISP's Directory

Another source of email for spammers is your Internet service provider's (including America Online's) public directory. You might not even know that they *have* a public directory, but yes, many of them exist. Or maybe you joined America Online several years ago and created a profile, but now you've forgotten about it. (Age does that to you. I know from experience.)

Check with your ISP—including America Online—and tell it to remove your name from the public directory. Also, ask if it keeps finger information about you. Finger is a feature of some Internet servers that lets people type in an email address and get back information about the person at that address. Tell your ISP you don't want your information available via finger. For more information, turn to Chapter 3.

Protect Your Address in Internet Chats

Yet another way for spammers to get email addresses (boy, they're persistent buggers, aren't they?) is to use software that automatically grabs addresses of people in chat rooms and Internet Relay Chat (IRC) channels. This is a particularly bad problem on America Online.

Not All Spam Is Commercial Offers

Much of the spam sent is commercial offers of some kind—get-quick-rich schemes, come-hither offers to visit for-pay Web sites, goods being sold. But not all spam involves commercial come-ons. There are other kinds of spam, such as email chain letters or political calls to action.

115

The best way to outsmart spammers who harvest your name in chat rooms is to use a separate email address or ID from your real one whenever you chat. That way, spam is routed to that address or ID, and you simply never check that account—that way, you'll never be spammed. To do this, get a free email address as outlined earlier in the chapter and use that when participating in Internet chats. America Online users should create a separate screen name to use whenever they're chatting. The spam is all routed to that screen name, and they can ignore the spam that piles up there.

Protect Your Name in Internet Mailing Lists

Internet mailing lists, often called *listservs*, are great ways to participate in discussions and get information via email. But they can also be a boon for spammers. Several different kinds of software are used to create these discussion lists. Some of them allow anyone to send a "who" message to the software, and the software then dutifully sends back a comprehensive list of email addresses of people who are on the list. This is not a good thing if you want to stop spam. Luckily, there are ways to block the who command. The person running the listserv can simply block all who requests. If the person doesn't do that, you can take matters into your own hands. Two popular programs for handling listservs are listproc and listserv. You can know which software manages yours by the address you had to use when subscribing—it should have either the word listproc or listserv in it. If you aren't sure, send a note to the person managing the list, asking which software the list uses. You can give the software a command to block your email address from being given out when someone issues a who command. Here's how:

➤ If you're on a listproc list, compose an email message to the listproc address where you subscribed, with the line SET *listname* CONCEAL YES in the body of the message. For *listname,* substitute the name of the list where you've subscribed.

➤ If you're on a listserv list, compose an email message to the listserv address where you subscribed, with the line SET *listname* CONCEAL in the body of the message. For *listname,* substitute the name of the list where you've subscribed.

Protect Your Address on Your Web Page

If you create a Web page, most likely you've included your email address in some way. Spammers use programs to automatically harvest names from Web pages, so it means you could end up being spammed. When you put your email address on a Web page, you most likely did it by including a mailto tag in your HTML code. When others click on that link, it automatically launches their email program, with your email address already filled in. The problem is that harvesting programs can get your email by looking for these links.

According to the Multimedia Marketing Group, there's a way around it. Simply put a %20 in front of your email address when you create the link, and you'll foil spammers.

Here's an example of the HTML code you would use if your email address was `goodgirl@nice.net`:

```
<A HREF="mailto%20goodgirl@nice.net">Click here to send me e-mail</A>
```

The mailto link still works with a browser, but the address-harvesting program doesn't recognize there's an email address there and ignores it. For more anti-spam advice from the Multimedia Marketing group, head to `http://www.mmgco.com/nospam`.

Using Your Email Program to Stop Spam in Its Tracks

Maybe you don't want to keep your identity private in Usenet newsgroups. Maybe you want your name published in directories so that old friends and family members can always find you. Maybe you've taken all the steps I outlined previously, but somehow, some way, the spammers are still finding you. What can you do now?

Techno Talk

How Do Email Filters Detect Spam?

How in the world, you might wonder, can an email program or spam-killing software automatically know which mail is spam and which isn't? They do it in a variety of ways. They have a list of known spammers, and whenever an email comes from one of them, it considers it spam. They also search for keywords in the header and sometimes the body of the message—words that are commonly used by spammers. And some of them examine the headers of the messages, looking for certain tell-tale signs that show the sender is a spammer.

Pretty much any email program you use these days has a way of filtering out at least some spam so that you don't have to see it. The program either refuses to accept spam, automatically deletes it, or puts it in a folder so that you can delete the spam yourself. I suggest having your email program put all the spam in a folder, so that you can delete it yourself. These programs aren't perfect, after all, and the last thing you want is to delete a message from your mother (eat your vegetables!) because your email software thought it was spam.

If you use Outlook, it's very easy to turn the spam filter on. Click on the **Organize** button at the top of Outlook and, from the screen that drops down, click on

Junk E-Mail. Then, just turn the spam filters on, and Outlook starts filtering your email. You can tell it to shade the suspect spam a certain color, such as gray or maroon, so that you can tell at a glance that you've been sent spam. Or, you can have it send all suspected spam to a folder, and you can then look at all the spam there. That's how I handle spam. You can see here how to turn on the spam filter in Outlook. Note that there are two kinds of spam filters. One covers garden-variety spam. The other filters out adult content spam.

Spam begone! Here's how to filter spam using Outlook.

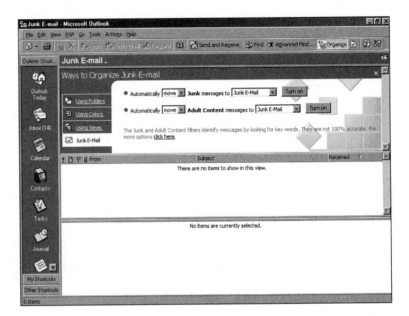

Your spam filter doesn't always know what email is spam and what isn't. Sometimes it misses spam. But you can help your email software detect spam better. When a piece of spam makes it through, you can tell your software that it's spam, and from that point on, all email from that source is marked for what it is—time-wasting, yellow-bellied, nasty spam. The more spam you mark, the smarter your email program becomes. In Outlook, right-click on the offending (and offensive) spam, choose **Junk E-Mail** from the menu that drops down, and click to add it either to the junk mail sender's list or the adult content sender's list. From then on, the software doesn't let the spam through.

118

What If Outlook Considers Certain Email as Spam, But It's Really Legitimate Email?

Sometimes, Outlook (and other email software) mistakenly thinks something is spam when it isn't. You want to let mail from that sender through in the future, without turning off your spam filter. Most email software, including Outlook, has an exception list—email addresses that should never be considered as spam. Here's how to add an address to the exception list in Outlook to always let mail from that address through. From the **Tools** menu, click on **Rules Wizard** and then choose **Exception List**. Then, from the **Rule Description** at the bottom of the screen, click on **Exception List**. Now, add the email address you want to let through. It is no longer considered spam.

Is Bill Gates a Spammer? Outlook Seems to Think So.

Either someone at Microsoft has a sense of humor, or else there's a bug in Microsoft's Outlook email program—or just maybe Outlook is a lot smarter than we think. If you're an Outlook user who subscribes to Microsoft's free Microsoft Office email newsletter, you'll notice something very funny when you get the newsletter—Outlook considers it junk mail! Whenever I get the newsletter, Outlook routes it to my Junk E-Mail folder—and I never told Outlook to put it there. I guess when it comes to junk mail, Outlook really knows what's spam and what isn't.

Using Spam-Fighting Software to Kill Spam Dead

There's another way to make sure that spam doesn't reach you—use spam-fighting software. This software works one of two ways: It can work right inside your email software and detect and kill spam. Or, you can run it before running your email software and it detects and kills spam.

There's a lot of spam-fighting software out there. They generally offer a lot more capabilities than the filters that come with your email software. Good ones are Spam Exterminator, Spam Buster, and SpamKiller, among others. You can try them all out for free by downloading them from many download sites on the Internet, including the ZDNet Software Library at www.hotfiles.com. Pictured here is Spam Exterminator.

Get outta here! Spam Exterminator at work killing spam.

Rule List - AutoCheck Enabled

File   View   Auto-Check   Manage   Help

New   Delete   Settings   Status   Preview   Lists   Clean Mailbox

Criteria	Value	Delete	Beep	Reply	Report	Confirm	Recycle.	Hits
From e-mail Address / Do...	cyberpromo.com	Yes	Yes	No	No	No	No	0
Subject Contains	$$	Yes	Yes	No	No	Yes	No	1
Header Contains	X-Advertisement	Yes	Yes	No	No	No	No	0
From user that is a number	N/A	Yes	Yes	No	No	No	No	13
Subject Contains	XXX	Yes	Yes	No	No	Yes	No	5
Subject Contains	MONEY FAST	Yes	Yes	No	No	No	No	0
Matches Known Spamm...	N/A	Yes	Yes	No	No	No	No	249
Header Contains	X-Distribution: M...	Yes	Yes	No	No	No	No	0
Header Contains	X-Mailer: Extractor	Yes	Yes	No	No	No	No	0
Header Contains	X-Mailer: Floodg...	Yes	Yes	No	No	No	No	0
Header Contains	X-Distribution: B...	Yes	Yes	No	No	No	No	1
Subject Contains	==	Yes	Yes	No	No	Yes	No	0
Subject Contains	!!	Yes	Yes	No	No	Yes	No	28
Subject Contains	INCREDIBLE D...	Yes	Yes	No	No	Yes	No	0
Header Contains	airship-list@lists...	Yes	Yes	No	No	No	No	1...
Header Contains	suck	Yes	Yes	No	No	No	No	71
From e-mail Address / Do...	dummiesdaily.com	Yes	Yes	No	No	No	No	346
From e-mail Address / Do...	tipworld.com	Yes	Yes	No	No	No	No	250
Header Contains	Daily New Mem...	Yes	Yes	No	No	No	No	0
From e-mail Address / Do...	Jesse Berst's An...	Yes	Yes	No	No	No	No	73
Header Contains	MS-News Digest	Yes	Yes	No	No	No	No	138
From e-mail Address / Do...	softdeals@hotm...	Yes	Yes	No	No	No	No	1
From e-mail Address / Do...	plarna@aol.com	Yes	Yes	No	No	No	No	1
From e-mail Address / Do...	reminder@gifton...	Yes	Yes	No	No	No	No	2
From e-mail Address / Do...	jackpobr@ix.net...	Yes	No	No	No	No	Yes	1
From e-mail Address / Do...	its@yourchance...	Yes	No	No	No	No	Yes	1
From e-mail Address / Do...	wpc-aizn@us.net	Yes	No	No	No	No	Yes	0

This list is the main control center for Spam Exterminator. Here your may add or modify existing rules that will dictate how your e-mail is handled. To create a new rule press the 'New' button.   ● Help...

How Can You Filter Out Spam If You Use America Online?

As users of America Online can tell you, they receive tons of junk mail. But you can create filters to try and stem the tide of spam. Use the keywords **Mail Controls**. Then, click on **Set Up Mail Controls**. Follow the directions for putting in the addresses that send you spam. From now on, that mail is blocked and won't reach you.

Fight Back! What to Do If You've Been Spammed

One way or another, you're going to be spammed. You might cut down on spam, but you'll never kill it entirely. Still, if you've been spammed, there are steps you can take to make sure it doesn't happen again or to track down the spam senders and curtail their actions or even put them out of business.

First Find Out Who the Spammer Is

In Chapter 7, "How Does Email Work, Anyway?" I gave details of how email works and spent a bit of time looking at headers of email messages. If you want to find out who a spammer is, you have to look in the email header. So turn back to that chapter for a rundown on the ins and outs and the ups and downs of email and its headers.

By the way, before we go on, a warning here: A smart spammer can trick you. The really good ones can forge a message so completely, you'll probably never be able to track down who created it.

Use a Second Email Address to Protect Yourself Against Spam

When you register at Web sites or fill out forms online, you're often asked to provide your email address. When you do that, you may well be putting yourself on a spam list. But filling in a phony email address might not work—some sites check to make sure the email address you put in is a valid one. Many Web sites, such as www.bigfoot.com, www.hotmail.com, and www.zdnet.com, offer free email boxes. Get a second (or a third) email box at one of these sites and always put in that address when filling out forms. That way, your spam is always sent to that one address.

Spammers can usually forge almost every part of a header, so it's hard to trust any part of a header. But often the most reliable part of the header is the Received header. This part of the header details when various Internet servers received the piece of mail and then forwarded it on to the next server. Often, there are several Received headers, and several of them may be forged. Still, they're worth looking at. Look for the originator of the mail—in other words, the Received header with the earliest date and time. That might well be the location of the true sender. Then again, it might not, but at least you have a place to begin. Also look for the Message ID header. Often, that has the name of the ISP where the spam started, so at least you know where the ISP is sending his mail from. You can then complain to that ISP.

Take These Steps When You've Been Spammed

So you've looked at the header, and you may or may not know the true spammer. In any event, there are actions you can take, even if you don't know the true identity of the spammer. Here's what to do:

➤ **Complain to your ISP.** Your ISP hates spam as much as you do—it forces ISPs to spend more money on mail servers and other costly Internet stuff. Many ISPs have an email address where you can send spam. Forward all your spam to that address—and include the true address of the spammer if you've been able to find it out from the message header. On America Online, forward the spam to the screen name TOSSpam. In all cases, forward the original email, don't copy and paste the spam into a new message. When you forward the spam, all the headers are left intact, so your ISP can do some detective work.

➤ **Complain to the advertiser.** Sometimes spam mentions the name and phone number of an advertiser sponsoring the spam. Call up the number, complain, and tell them you're going to tell everyone you know never to do business with them unless they stop spamming. A legitimate business might listen to you. Scammers won't.

Never Respond to Spam

When you get spam, you'll be tempted to respond to it by sending off an angry note. Or there may be a return email address in the note, saying if you want to get taken off the spam list, send an email message to that return address. *Never* respond to spam. Spammers rarely take you off their lists. By responding, you're only letting them know that your email address is a valid one—and they'll send you even *more* spam.

Visit SpamCop to Stamp Out Spam

There's a simple way you can help stamp out spam: File a compaint with SpamCop at www.spamcop.net. Go to the site and paste in the offending message, including the header. SpamCop will then sift through the headers and try to uncover where the spam originated. It'll then send a note to the Internet service provider (ISP) from where the spam was sent, complaining about the spam, in the hopes that the ISP will stop the spammer from sending mail through them.

➤ **Complain to the ISP where you think the mail came from.** You might be able to find out where the mail originated by examining its header. If you think you know where it came from, forward the mail to that ISP. The ISP doesn't want spammers on the system and might kick them off.

➤ **Complain to your state attorney general.** In some states, such as California, Virginia, and Washington, spam is more than a nuisance—it's illegal. Although the laws vary from state to state, increasingly, states are passing anti-spam laws. The state attorney general is responsible for enforcing them. These laws can have some pretty stiff penalties. In Washington, for example, spammers can be fined $2,000 for every individual piece of spam they send. Considering that most spammers send out millions of pieces of spam, we're talking some big-time money.

➤ **Get more information at these Web sites.** Web sites can help you complain about spam and learn more about how to track down the true senders of spam. Head to the Fight Spam on the Internet site at http://spam.abuse.net/. And the How To Complain About Spam, or Put a Spammer in the Slammer site at http://dlis.gseis.ucla.edu/people/pagre/spam.html is especially worthwhile for figuring out where to complain.

The Least You Need to Know

➤ When posting messages to Usenet newsgroups, alter your email address or use an anonymous emailer to post so that spammers can't get your address from the newsgroup.

➤ Take your name out of Web White Page directories to cut down on the amount of spam you receive.

➤ Remove your address from your ISP's public directory so that spammers can't get your email address from there.

➤ Get a second, free email address at a site such as www.hotmail.com, and when filling out Web forms, put that address as yours. That way, spam is sent to that address, not your main one.

➤ Complain to your attorney general if you've received spam—several states now have anti-spam laws.

➤ Never respond to spam—it only proves to the spammer that your email address is a valid one, and you may get even *more* spam.

Chapter 11

Staying Anonymous with Anonymous Remailers

In This Chapter

➤ Why you might want to use an anonymous remailer

➤ How anonymous remailers work

➤ How to use Web-based anonymous remailers

➤ How to use your email program along with anonymous remailers

➤ Best anonymous remailer sites and services on the Internet

To turn the old *Cheers* theme song on its head: Sometimes you just want to go where nobody knows your name. There might be times when you want to send email to someone or to post a message to a Usenet newsgroup in which you don't want your name known. Maybe you want to blow the whistle on wrongdoing at your company and are worried about the consequences to you if it was known you were the whistle-blower. Maybe you're worried that if you divulge certain information about yourself, you could be ostracized in your community. Maybe you don't want your name ending up in spam lists. For whatever reason, there are times when you would like to send information, but don't want your name known.

Anonymous remailers let you do that. You can send email or participate in newsgroups, and your name and address aren't attached to your postings. This chapter shows you how to do it.

What Is an Anonymous Remailer, Anyway?

An anonymous remailer lets you send an email message or post a message on a Usenet newsgroup without anyone knowing your email address. When someone gets the message or sees the posting, he can't tell that it's you who sent it. Mostly, you don't have to pay any money to use an anonymous remailer, although some for-pay services have sprung up.

As you'll see later in this chapter, there are different kinds of anonymous remailers. Some are Web sites where you fill out a form to send anonymous mail. Others are Internet servers where you send email—with these, you use your own email program to send the anonymous mail—but the server does a bit of magic to make sure that your identity isn't known when the message is delivered.

What's an Email Header?

A piece of email is divided into two parts, the *body* and the *header*. The body is the message itself. The header contains other kinds of stuff, much of which can identify you, such as your email address, the ISP, and other techie stuff that can be used to figure out who you are. For more information on this phenomenon, see Chapter 7, "How Does Email Work, Anyway?"

Generally, here's how most types of anonymous remailers work. When you send your message, the anonymous remailer strips off your email address and other header information that can be used to identify you. After stripping off this header information and putting in new header information, it sends your message on its merry way. Anyone reading the message can't see who originally sent it.

For extra security, some anonymous remailers use what's called chaining. That means the remailer sends your message to yet another anonymous emailer, who in turn strips off the header that your initial anonymous emailer puts on, and puts a new header on. This chain can go on and on. The chaining technique provides greater assurance that your identity can't be found out.

You can also use anonymous remailers to post messages to Usenet newsgroups. Some let you post directly. Others require that you jump through a hoop or two and have your email sent to a gateway that takes the anonymous mail and posts it to the newsgroup. (The Internet can be pretty complicated sometimes, can't it?) But either way, you can use anonymous remailers to post messages on newsgroups.

I'm a Pretty Honest Person. Why Would I Use an Anonymous Remailer?

You're an honest person. You don't beat your dog, spout obscenities in public, or wear white socks with black shoes (at least not in full public view—what you do behind closed doors is your own business). And you're an upright citizen—you always speak your mind and stand behind your words. So why use an anonymous remailer? What have you got to hide? Isn't there something cowardly about sending messages to people or posting notes on discussion boards in which your identity is hidden?

No, there's nothing cowardly about it. There are times when you might want to be able to make your views publicly known or get a message to someone, but you don't want your email address and identity known.

At times, almost anyone could want to use an anonymous remailer. Here are some of the main reasons you might want to use one:

➤ **You want to keep your name off spam lists.** As you saw in Chapter 10, "What Is Spam and How Can You Protect Yourself from It?" Spammers often go to Usenet newsgroups to gather people's email addresses so they can spam them. If you use an anonymous remailer to post messages, your name isn't on your message, and so you can't be spammed.

➤ **You're a whistle-blower and don't want your name known.** Perhaps you've uncovered illegal activity or some other kind of nefarious business at your company or somewhere else, but you don't want your name known. Send using an anonymous remailer and the bad guys get the whistle blown on them without you getting harmed.

➤ **You don't want your beliefs or lifestyle to be known by your employer or the community in which you live.** Maybe your political beliefs or sexual orientation are such that you'd be ostracized in your local community if they were known—but you want to be able to express yourself on the Internet. And perhaps you don't want those beliefs or that orientation known by your employer, either. You can use anonymous remailers to enter discussions and still retain your anonymity.

You Can Be Liable for the Opinions You Express Anonymously

Be aware that when you use many kinds of anonymous remailers, there are ways your identity can be tracked down by law enforcement personnel or others. If you post defamatory anonymous mail, you could suffer the consequences. Recently, the Wade Cook Financial Corp. sued 10 people who posted anonymously for allegedly making defamatory comments about the company on Yahoo! message boards.

➤ **You have a medical or mental condition that you would like to discuss with others and get advice about, but don't want your employers, co-workers, or people in your community to know about it.** There are many conditions, such as mental illness, alcoholism, and AIDS, that people like to keep to themselves. Perhaps you have a problem that you'd like to speak with others about for support, but you don't want your employer, co-workers, or people in your community to know about it. Emailers can solve the problem for you.

➤ **You just plain like your privacy.** The truth is, you don't need a reason to want to post messages anonymously. Perhaps you just feel more comfortable expressing yourself when your identity isn't known. It's your right to do so.

How to Use Anonymous Remailers

This being the Internet, there are different kinds of remailers and—surprise!—they work in different ways. Some are Web-based, some require you to simply send an email message, and some require you to practically jump through hoops to use them—you have to do things like encrypt your message and do other fancy things before sending the message. In general, the more complicated the remailer, the more secure it is and the harder it is for anyone to trace your address. If you're super-paranoid, you have to do a bit more work because you'll want to use super-secret remailers.

What Is a Pseudonymous Emailer?

There's a kind of anonymous emailer that lets you receive messages as well as send them, without your identity being known. It's called a pseudonymous emailer. (Ah, the Internet. Always coming up with new ways to abuse the language.) In a pseudonymous emailer, when you send an email, a false email address is put in place of your own—in other words, your pseudonym. That way, people can send you responses, but they won't really know who they're responding to. If you send pseudonymous email and someone responds to you, first it goes back to the pseudonymous remailer. The remailer uses Internet magic to figure out that the message should be sent to you. It then sends the message to you. You've sent and received email without anyone knowing your true email address.

Be aware, though, that in this kind of remailer, your identity can be discovered. The pseudonymous remailer has to keep your true email address, and it matches it to your pseudo address, so the remailer knows your address. Theoretically, the remailer could turn that information over to someone else. In fact, that's already happened to probably the most popular pseudonymous emailer of all time, a site called anon.penet.fi, hosted in Finland. In 1995, the Church of Scientology wanted to find out who had posted secret church documents on the Internet. They had been posted using the anon.penet.fi remailer. The church asked the Finnish government to get the site to turn over the true name of the person who had posted the documents. The government, in turn, asked that the true address be handed over. The address was revealed, and the church discovered who had posted the documents. The owner of the site eventually shut it down, because he started to get more threats to turn over the names of people who had used the service.

Web-based Anonymous Remailers

Web-based remailers are the simplest to use. Just go to a Web site, fill in a form, and you're done. No muss, no fuss. Pictured nearby is the Web-based anonymous remailer at www.anonymizer.com.

It's easy and safe to send anonymous email using the www.anonymizer.com *remailer.*

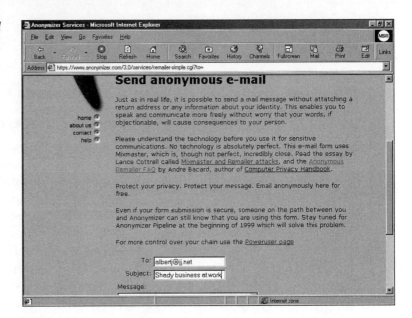

Sometimes Web-based anonymous remailers don't provide the level of security other types of anonymous remailers do. That's not always true, though. The truth is, unless you're pretty paranoid, even the simplest level of anonymity should be good enough for you. Some Web anonymous remailers, such as the one shown here run by the Anonymizer, use very high levels of security. Some of the Web-based remailers let you chain remailers, so you can send it from one to the other for greater security. You can even choose which ones to send to from a list. I know, sounds pretty geeky. But to people who live for the Internet, that's a very cool thing.

The main drawback to Web-based remailers is that more are starting to charge a fee for their services. But there are still enough free ones available that you should never have to pay. A list of them is at the end of the chapter.

Sending Anonymous Email Using Your Email Program

The other way to use an anonymous remailer is to use your email program. You compose a message, add a few extra bits of information that the remailer needs, and then send the message. The remailer does the work for you.

Techno Talk

What on Earth Are Cypherpunk and Mixmaster Remailers?

Not all remailers are created equal. Some offer higher degrees of safety than others. The Cypherpunk and Mixmaster remailers both offer a whole lot of security. In a Cypherpunk remailer, also called a Type-1 anonymous remailer, you can encrypt your email message and send that through a chain of other remailers. As you might guess, it's very secure and pretty tough to figure out who sent the message. However, for the truly raving paranoids among us (ooops, not very politically correct, that; let's just call them very security-conscious folks), there is the Mixmaster remailer, also called a Type-2 anonymous remailer. In this type of anonymous remailer, the message is encrypted and then cut up into a whole lot of tiny little pieces that don't look like they're related to one another. These little encrypted pieces are then sent separately from anonymous remailer to anonymous remailer to anonymous remailer. When the very last remailer gets all these little completely garbled bits of data, it puts them all back together and sends it out as a message. The last remailer hasn't a clue where the original message came from.

The only real problem with these kinds of remailers is that they're kind of tough to use. Here's how to do it using the popular anonymous remailer you can find and use for free by sending your message to remailer@replay.com.

First, find out the address of an anonymous remailer you want to use. There's a list at the end of the chapter. In this example, we're using the anonymous remailer with the address remailer@replay.com. In our example, we'll say that we want to send an email to joe@joejoe.com. (By the way, these instructions all work with the Replay anonymous remailer. You should check other anonymous remailers to see how to post with them.)

Now that you have the address of the anonymous remailer, start composing your message in your email program. In the To field, put the address remailer@replay.com. Next, fill in the subject of the message.

That's it for the easy part. Now the work begins. There has to be some way for the remailer to know where to send the message. There are two ways to do this: the hard way and the easy way.

If you're feeling particularly techie or know your way around your email program, you'll probably want to do it the hard way. Here's what to do. With your email program, create a new header that reads like this:

```
Anon-To: <address>
```

In this case, it would read

```
Anon-To: joe@joejoe.com
```

Your email program may or may not allow you to create headers. And you may or may not know how to do it, even if your email program lets you do it. Check the email's documentation for details.

OK. Now for the easy way. Instead of trying to muck around and edit headers, after you've filled in the address and subject lines, put two colons on the first line of the body of your message, then go to the next line of your message and put in the Anon-To address line. Follow that with a blank line, and compose your message. Now it should look like this:

```
::
Anon-To: joe@joejoe.com
```

You can see here how it would look in the Microsoft Outlook email program.

Here's how to send anonymous email using an anonymous remailer.

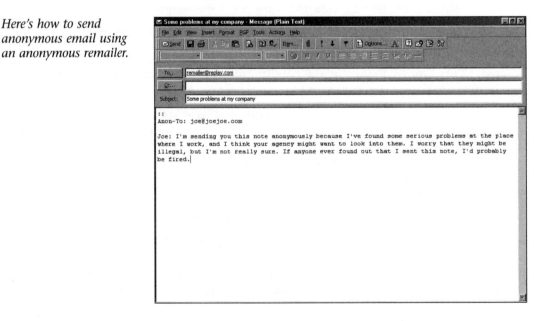

By the way, the anonymous remailer at `remailer@replay.com` can also let you post messages to Usenet newsgroups. It's simple to do. In the Anon-To: line, simply put the name of the newsgroup, like this:

```
Anon-To: alt.rabbitlovers.forever
```

Most anonymous remailers have help information that tell you how to use them. To get information on how to use a specific anonymous remailer, send an email message to the remailer (such as `remailer@replay.com`) with the subject line `remailer-help`.

Where to Find Anonymous Remailers on the Internet

There are a fair number of anonymous remailers on the Internet. Here are some good places to go for information and to post mail anonymously:

➤ **Replay Anonymous Remailer at** `www.replay.com/remailer/anon.html`. Very good Web-based remailer.

➤ `remailer@replay.com`. A remailer run by the Replay people that you access with your email program, as I just described.

The Etiquette of Anonymous Speech

Anonymous remailers allow you speak out anonymously on newsgroups and via email. That's a right you have. But there are some rules you should follow when posting anonymously so you don't abuse that right. You shouldn't use anonymous remailers to spam people, stalk them, or harass them. You shouldn't use it to commit illegal acts. And you shouldn't use it to espouse hate speech of any kind.

➤ **Anonymizer anonymous emailer.** Go to `www.anonymizer.com` and click on the anonymous email link. You get access to a very good Web-based remailer. The site also offers many other privacy-related services, some of which you have to pay for. Remailing is free, however.

➤ **Anonymous remailer list at** `http://www.cs.berkeley.edu/~raph/remailer-list.html`. Big list of anonymous remailers. Also includes some basic information on what commands you can use at the remailers.

➤ **Electronic Frontiers Georgia's Reliable Remailer Lists at** `http://anon.efga.org/Remailers/`. Another big list of anonymous remailers, along with commands for using anonymous remailers and links to related sites and information.

The Least You Need to Know

➤ Anonymous remailers strip off email header information to keep your identity private.

➤ Use anonymous remailers to keep your name off of spamming lists and when you want to send mail or post information that you worry could have consequences for you if your name were known.

➤ Two good Web-based remailers can be found at `www.replay.com/ remailer/anon.html` and `www.anonymizer.com`.

➤ To find out how to use an anonymous remailer along with your email program, send an email to the remailer with the subject line of `remailer-help`.

➤ Never use an anonymous remailer to harass or threaten others, commit illegal acts, or espouse hate speech.

Part 4

Protecting Your Privacy and Security on the World Wide Web

Here's the easiest way to reveal everything about your personal life, including your name, address, kind of computer you use, gender, marital status, annual income, hobbies, the name of your gerbil, and more: Hop onto the World Wide Web. Yes, that's all you need to do to reveal all that. The Web is the greatest information resource ever created—but it's also one of the most effective ways ever created to endanger your privacy and security.

This part will show you how you can combat the many dangers posed by the Web. You'll see how your Web surfing habits can be traced, how personal information can be extracted from you, the dangers of Web registration forms, and how "cookies" (no, not Oreos) can invade your privacy. Better yet, it'll teach you how to keep yourself safe and secure when browsing the Web, so you don't need to worry about any of those dangers.

In fact, it'll teach you so well how to keep safe and secure that you'll even be able to keep the name of your gerbil to yourself. (And considering that you named it "Honeybunch," it's a good idea to keep it to yourself.)

Chapter 12

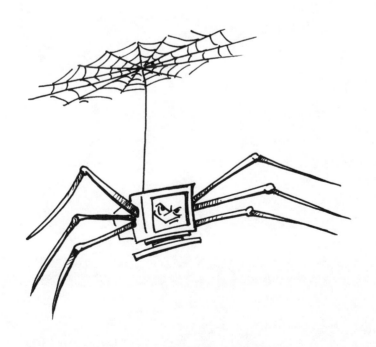

What Dangers Are There to Your Privacy and Security on the Web?

In this Chapter

➤ How someone can snoop on your Web surfing habits

➤ What cookies are and how they are used

➤ Why you should worry about filling out registration forms on the Web

➤ What viruses are and how they can hurt your computer

As far as I'm concerned, the creation of the Web is one of the greatest advances civilization has ever made, right up there with the invention of the wheel, the airplane, and iced decaf cappuccino.

But as with many advances, there come problems (such as, "How do you keep a big head of foam when cappuccino is iced?"). Unscrupulous people and organizations can use the Web to invade your privacy, and you can accidentally download a malicious program to your PC via the Web. This chapter gives you the rundown on the main things you should watch out for. Then the rest of the chapters in this part of the book tell you how to keep yourself safe when on the Web.

How Your Web Surfing Habits Can Be Traced

For you, me, and Web surfers everywhere, the Web is a great place because of all the amazing information, resources, news, music, videos, and just plain fun you find online. We blithely (or not so blithely) point and click away, hopping from page to page and site to site, following our instincts and interests. (Want to know more about the mating habits of Arctic terns or where to go to collect old bricks? You'll probably find information about how to do it on the Web.)

For marketers and online sellers, the Web is a great place as well—in fact, it might be the closest they'll ever get to heaven. (And I believe that after they pass away, marketers are most decidedly *not* heading to heaven. Instead, they're heading to a deep, dark place that also happens to be very hot.) Marketers and online sellers can use the Web to track everything you do—and I mean absolutely *everything*—and can then use that information to put together a profile of your likes and dislikes, what you read about online, how often you tend to stay on a site, how long you stay there, and other information. Based on that profile, they can target ads to send your way, put together targeted email lists, and more.

Think of it this way: Every time you click, they can track what you're doing and can know all the topics you read about and more. In fact, just by examining your browser when you enter a site, they can find out information. Here's a list of the kinds of things Web sites can learn about you:

➤ **Your email address.** It's simple for a site to look into your browser settings and find out your email address. For information on how to stop a site from doing this, turn to Chapter 15, "Holy Cow! My Browser Shows All That Information About Me?"

➤ **Your geographic location.** When you enter a Web site, it often can tell—based on things such as your email address, IP address, and other kinds of information—what part of the country you're connecting from.

What's an IP Address?

When you connect to the Internet, one of the first things that happens is you're assigned an IP address—a series of numbers separated by periods (dots, in Internet speak), like this: 22.155.41.171. As far as the Internet is concerned, that number is you, and it's needed by Internet computers to let you do things such as surf the Web. Most often, you get a different IP address every time you connect to the Internet, although with some Internet service providers and many corporate networks, you get a static IP address—in other words, it's the same every time you connect.

➤ **What kind of business you're in.** Amazingly enough, based on your IP address or email address, a Web site might know what kind of business you're in. Information in your email address can give this away—if your address is Jjoejoe@ibm.com, for example, the Web site would know you are in the computer business. The Web site can buy a database that matches email addresses and IP numbers to types of businesses and can find out what kind of business you're in.

➤ **What operating system and browser you use.** Using Windows 95? Windows 98? The Mac? (Ah, an individualist, are you?) Do you use Internet Explorer or Netscape Navigator, and which version? A Web site can find out all these things in a snap.

➤ **What site you just came from and what site you go to when you leave.** When it comes to extracting information out of your visit, Web sites can get pretty sneaky. They can even know what site you were at *before* you visit, whether you click on a link when you leave, and where that link goes.

➤ **How long you spend on the site.** Do you show up, stay a minute, and leave? Or do you hang out for an hour? No matter which, the Web site can attempt to figure that out.

➤ **What pages you read, what kind of information you're interested in, and what products you might want to buy.** Web sites can track your every click as you go through the site. They know what pages you visit, and based on that, can put together a profile of what your interests are—even what products you're interested in buying. Spending a lot of time reading reviews of computer printers? If so, the Web site knows and realizes that you're interested in buying one. Expect an email or ad pitching you a printer.

Here's Where to Go for More Information about Privacy

There are a lot of privacy-related sites on the Internet. One of my favorites is EPIC (Electronic Privacy Information Center) at http://www.epic.org. You'll find a great list of privacy-related resources, the latest news about Internet privacy, and links to privacy services such as anonymous remailers and sites that let you surf the Web anonymously. You can also subscribe to their free email newsletter that gives you the latest scoop on privacy-related news.

➤ **Other stuff, too.** Internet programmers and marketers are pretty clever. I have no doubt that they've cooked up other schemes that haven't been listed here for finding out what you do on their sites. In general, it's best to assume that anything you do on any site can be tracked.

There are ways to make sure that Web sites can't grab this information about you. To learn how, go to Chapter 15.

Why Web Cookies Can Leave a Bad Taste in Your Mouth

When you visit almost any commercial Web site, it tries to put a little piece of information onto your computer—and you probably don't know that it's being done. For no apparent reason in the world, that little piece of information is called a *cookie*. So yes, your computer is filled with cookies, and they're not Girl Scouts or Famous Amos or Mrs. Fields. And some people think they're not very sweet.

Web sites put this information on your computer for a number of reasons. One big one is to make it easier for them to track what you're doing when you're on the site. They have other ways of watching what you do, but using cookies is just one more way to do it. And cookies can do things that some other technologies can't, so they're useful for that as well.

Often, cookies are used to identify you in some way to the Web site. As you move through the site, it may continually "write" to your cookie. (How romantic—writing to your cookie. Is that like writing to your sweetie?) When it writes to your cookie, it's putting in some new information about you or what you've done.

Cookies can be used to gather information about you and so invade your privacy, but believe it or not, cookies can be your friend, too. They can remember logon information for you so that you don't have to keep typing in a password when you visit a Web site—but keep in mind that this can be a security problem, because anyone using your computer can log on as you. Cookies can also give you extra services, such as being able to customize a site so that it looks and works exactly the way you want.

There are ways to kill cookies. You can configure your browser to ask you before accepting cookies or to never accept cookies—sort of an update of what your mother told you about never taking candy from a stranger. Special cookie programs, such as Cookie Pal pictured here, let you automatically accept cookies from certain sites, automatically kill them from others, and ask you when visiting at yet other sites. That way, you can accept cookies at certain sites that offer features you want and that are available only with cookies. But you can kill them at sites where no extra services are offered. For more information about cookies, turn to Chapter 13, "No, They're Not Oreos: What You Can Do About Cookies."

When It Comes to Cookies, You Have to Balance Privacy Against Convenience and Services

A lot of neat features are made available to you by cookies—things like customizing a site or showing you your own shopping basket with everything you want to buy at a buying site. Cookies can be very helpful. But they can also be used to invade your privacy. So when deciding whether to keep or kill cookies, you have to balance your need for privacy against your desire for extra services.

Cookie Pal: An easy way to toss your cookies online.

Cookie Alert!

If you want to get some idea of how often your Web browser accepts cookies, you can usually configure it to warn you before accepting a cookie. Beware, though— you might find yourself clicking on the warning box more often than you're clicking Web links.

141

The Dangers of Web Registration Forms

Any Web site worth its salt these days seems to have a registration form. Want to get a free email account or a free fax number? No problem. Just fill out a form. Want to enter a contest to win a trip to Maui? Just enter some information, right here. Want to get a free email newsletter? Put in your name, address, and more. How about entering a free, for-members-only area of the site? Just the facts about your life, ma'am, just enter the facts about your life.

Filling in registration forms is a fact of life on the Web today. If you want to fully participate in what the Web has to offer, often you have to fill them out.

So what's the big deal? If you don't worry about your privacy, there's no problem. But if you worry that your name, email address, and personal information will be bandied about, shared by marketers, and generally mishandled and mistreated, then you should worry.

Is It Okay to Lie on a Web Registration Form?

Your parents told you not to lie. In school, they taught you not to lie. Even the Ten Commandments warns "Thou Shalt Not Lie." (Or something like that, anyway.) On the other hand, Moses never had to deal with the sometimes-nefarious uses to which personal information gleaned from Web forms can be used. So, the question is—should you or shouldn't you? In my case, the answer is yes. I'll admit it in public for the first time here—I've lied on Web registration forms. I do that because the forms often ask information that's too personal and is only being requested so they can put it in a database and sell it or use it as a direct marketing tool. My general rule is this: If a form asks for information that's really none of their business, like my occupation or my salary, I often lie. So far, I've been a crab census counter, toothpick maker, and a Yenta Yeti.

The reason you should worry is that your name is worth money to Web marketers. In fact, it's as good as gold. Web sites make money on advertising, but the real money comes from people selling things to you. And if they know your name, your address, your email address, your income, your home address, and other personal information, it is easy for them to sell things. You could get deluged with email come-ons, phone calls, and other kinds of annoying offers.

Worse than that is that after a site has your name and personal information, you never know where it will end up, who will use it, and how it will be used. Sites can sell lists of names and personal information to other sites or to direct marketers. Those sites or direct marketers, in turn, can sell them to other parties. Pretty soon, everyone knows your name and your annual income.

As if that weren't bad enough, sometimes the forms you fill out are not secured. This fact means that anyone can tap in to your personal information (such as your home address) as it floats through the Internet. A secured site prevents this snooping, but you still have to wonder how the site will use the information.

Does that mean that if you want to get all the neat services on the Web, you have to give up your privacy? No. There's a lot you can do, such as only filling out certain fields on a form, reading the fine print to make sure you're not agreeing to be spammed for the rest of your life, and checking out a site's privacy policy before filling out a form—and if a site doesn't have a privacy policy, watch out! You can see an example of a privacy policy nearby, as posted on the ZDNet Web site at www.zdnet.com. Turn to Chapter 14, "Beware of Registration Forms on the Web," to learn the best way to handle filling out Web registration forms.

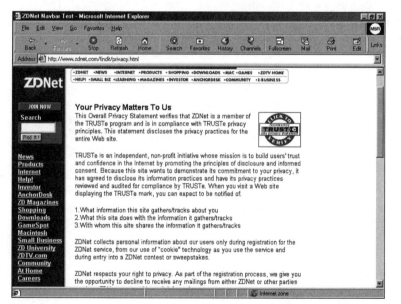

An example of a publicly posted privacy policy (say that five times fast!) on the ZDNet Web site at www.zdnet.com.

Beware of Viruses and Other Malicious Programs

Some of the neatest things the Internet has to offer are programs that you can download for free to your computer and then use. (Download means to transfer something to your computer from the Internet.) Many of these programs you can use for free forever; some you can only try out for a month or so, because they stop working after that; and still others ask that you pay after 30 days, but they still run after that time period.

Many people, like me, live to download. (In fact, I'm in charge of the ZDNet Software Library at www.hotfiles.com, one of the biggest download sites on the Internet.) But there's a potential problem in downloading. Not all download sites check their files to make sure that the files don't have viruses in them. There's a chance that something you download can be infected with a virus, and it can attack your computer.

What Is Shareware?

Spend time on the Internet, and you'll probably come across the term *shareware*. Shareware is software that you can download to your computer and use for a time—often 30 days—for free. After that time, you're supposed to pay for it. The program usually still works after 30 days; shareware works on the honor system. Freebies are, not surprisingly, called *freeware*.

Viruses are programs that invade other programs and then launch themselves and do damage. If you download a program with a virus in it, the program you downloaded might appear to work fine. But after you run the program, unbeknownst to you, the virus gets loose and starts doing its nasty business. There are all kinds of viruses, from ones that do no harm at all and perhaps only display a taunting message on your screen to others that can kill your hard disk and the data on it.

There are many different kinds of viruses that work in different ways. The best way to protect yourself against them is to use a virus scanner—a program that detects viruses, and when it finds them, eradicates them. Pictured here is Norton AntiVirus, the one I use.

Better safe than sorry:
Using Norton AntiVirus
to check a computer for
viruses.

Viruses aren't the only things you download from the Internet that can do bad things to your computer. When you visit Web pages, often there are things sent to you called ActiveX controls (sounds like *The X-Files*, no?) or Java applets (is that some kind of combination of coffee and little baby fruit?). They can do damage as well.

What Is a Trojan Horse?

A common kind of virus is a Trojan Horse—a program or file that masquerades as being something useful, but in fact is a destructive program or a virus. For example, a file could say it was a personal finance program, but in fact behind the scenes was deleting files from your hard disk. In fact, one of the most infamous viruses in recent memory, the Melissa virus, was a kind of Trojan horse. It claimed to be an important email message, but in fact, it looked into the Outlook email program's address book, made copies of itself, and then mailed itself out to people listed in the address book.

By the way, the term Trojan Horse gets its name from the *Iliad*, in which the Greeks gave a huge wooden horse to their arch-enemies the Trojans. The Trojans wheeled the horse into their city, and at night, Greek soldiers crawled out of the hollow horse, and opened the city's gates, allowing the Greek army to plunder, pillage, and generally wreak havoc.

So to keep yourself safe in modern times, remember the Trojan Horse, and keep in mind a new twist on an old saying: Beware geeks bearing gifts.

There are steps you can take to protect yourself against viruses, ActiveX Controls, Java applets, and any other nasty creatures hanging around the Internet. Turn to Part 8, "Protecting Yourself Against Viruses, Trojan Horses, and Other Nasty Creatures," to see how.

The Least You Need to Know

➤ When you go to a Web site, the site can track everything you're doing—and can also find out personal information about you, such as your email address and sometimes even what business you're in.

➤ Cookies are little bits of data put on your computer so a Web site can track you or give you extra features and services.

➤ You can use a special cookie program to kill certain cookies and let others be put on your hard disk.

➤ The information you put into Web registration forms can be used by direct marketers, so check out a site's privacy policy before filling one out.

➤ To be safe when downloading files, use an anti-virus program.

Chapter 13

No, They're Not Oreos: What You Can Do About Cookies

In This Chapter

➤ What web cookies are and why Web sites use them

➤ The sweet and sour of Web cookies

➤ Where your browser stores its cookies

➤ How to delete cookies from your hard disk

➤ How to stop Web sites from putting cookies on your hard disk

Who doesn't like cookies? They're sweet, they come in all flavors and sizes, and every time you buy one from a Girl Scout, you do a good deed.

But when it comes to the Web, cookies leave a bad taste in some people's mouths. Cookies are little bits of information that Web sites put on your computer's hard disk when you visit them. They use those cookies to track what you do on the site and to offer you extra services, such as customized Web pages. They're also used to deliver ads pitched to your interests.

If you don't like the idea of Web sites putting cookies (or anything at all) on your hard disk, there's something you can do about it. This chapter shows you how. And even if cookies don't bother you, read on, because you'll learn everything there is to know about cookies, except for perhaps how to bake mocha chocolate chip ones.

What Are Web Cookies?

Strange but true: When you visit many Web sites, they actually put information on your hard disk that you don't know about. Those bits of information are cookies.

Each cookie a site leaves on your hard disk is a very small text file. If you looked at most of those files, they would make about as much sense to you as an ancient Sanskrit manuscript. (Although if you were a Sanskrit scholar, or an Internet geek, it might make a lot of sense to you.) If you look close enough inside them, you might be able to make some sense of them, but not enough to be useful.

Cookies have become ubiquitous on the Web. Just about any Web site you visit uses them, and many Web sites use more than one. If you were to look at your hard disk to see them all, you'd be amazed at just how many there are. The following figure shows some of the cookies from sites that I've visited. I'm a busy guy on the Web, I know, but this is ridiculous!

More cookies than the Girl Scouts! A list of some of the cookies that sites have put on my hard disk.

Why Are Web Sites Serving Cookies?

Why should a Web site go to the trouble of storing cookies on your computer? A big reason is that it gives the site an easy way to track what you do when you visit the site. It uniquely identifies you, so the Web server can know what you're doing whenever you visit. From visit to visit, it can more easily build up a profile about you. That profile is worth a lot of money to Web sites, because after they have that profile, they can sell advertising targeted at people's specific interests. Spend a lot of time on a site reading about child-care for children under the age of one? Diaper companies love to advertise to you. Do you retrieve stock quotes quite frequently from a site? Online brokerages pay big money to put an ad in front of your face. And Web sites love to get that money.

Only the Web site that places a cookie on your hard disk can read that cookie. So when you go to the *New York Times* site on the Web and it puts a cookie on your hard disk, the Web portal Yahoo! cannot read that cookie, and vice versa. This exclusivity helps ensure your privacy to a certain degree. If sites could read each other's cookies, the amount of information that could be obtained about you would be absolutely mind-boggling; and it would mean that sites could obtain your user name and password at other sites and other information you don't want made public.

The people who designed the technology of the Web made sure that sites couldn't read each other's cookies, as a way to protect your privacy. But some companies have managed to find their way around the technology. I won't go into all the technical mumbo jumbo and rigmarole of how it's done, but the Internet advertising agency DoubleClick.com has built up a network of Internet sites that in essence can read each other's cookie information. All that information is put together, and profiles are built on Web visitors. It's not the kind of information that's dangerous—it is based on the Web pages you visit, so that advertising can be targeted at you—but it makes some people uncomfortable.

Techno Talk

What Ingredients Are There in Cookies?

Cookies are data files placed on your hard disk. Each cookie is made up of two elements—the cookie's name and the value. The value is the actual data in the cookie itself, and each Web site can put all kinds of different data into the value. There is often an expiration date (the date the cookie expires—kind of like a Sell By date on real cookies); the domain (the address of the server that delivered the cookie to you); and things such as usernames and passwords. Often, much of the data is scrambled, so that only the Web server can understand it, not you.

Cookies Can Also Be Sweet

I don't want to give you the impression that cookies are some wicked plot to destroy civilization as we know it. In fact, cookies can provide some of the coolest services and content for you on the Web, as well as big benefits—and you don't even get fat using them. Here's a list of some of the things that cookies can do:

➤ **Log you on automatically to Web sites.** Many sites offer extra services in areas for which you need to log on. It's a pain to type in your username and password each time. Cookies can log you on automatically. Keep in mind, though, that this can be a security risk if anyone else ever uses your computer. When logging on, you are given the option of whether the username and password should be stored on your computer. When you say Yes, the information is stored in your cookie. When you say No, it isn't.

➤ **Let you customize what you see on a Web page.** Maybe you want information about politics and entertainment, but not business and sports. Or when you visit a Web page, you'd like to see your local weather and news and a listing of local movies. Some sites recognize that the Web isn't one-size-fits-all, and so they let you choose the information you want to see whenever you visit. To do that, they need to use cookies. You can see here how you can customize a section of Yahoo! to give you the precise information you want every time you visit. To customize it in this way, you need to use a cookie.

Have it your way. Cookies let you customize the information you see on a Web site. This picture shows how to customize a portion of Yahoo!

➤ **Give you information you want without your having to ask for it.** From your previous Web surfing, a Web site knows that you always check the Celtics box score, the Boston traffic, the Massachusetts lottery number, and the weather in the Bahamas (if your number hits, you'll be able to afford a vacation in someplace balmy). It uses a cookie to show you that without you having to ask.

➤ **Show you advertising you'd be interested in.** Don't smirk, now. Some people actually *like* advertising, because it can tell them about good deals on products they're interested in buying. If your cookie tracks that you've been checking out information on a new Palm VII pocket computer, an ad telling you about a cheap deal for it would be a welcome sight.

➤ **They can do much more.** The minds of men and women are infinite in their capacity for figuring out creative ways to use technology. Have no doubt: New ways of using cookies are being cooked up right now, and I assume they won't be half baked.

Where Are Cookies Stored? (No, They're Not in Your Cupboard)

When a Web server puts a cookie on your computer, it puts it into a specific location on your hard disk. Sounds simple. But, of course, this is the Internet, and nothing is simple. Where that cookie is put depends on whether you use Microsoft Internet Explorer or Netscape Navigator and even what version of those browsers you use. Thank you, technology companies, for making all our lives so much easier.

Microsoft Internet Explorer and Netscape Navigator handle cookies a bit differently from each other. Here's what you need to know about each.

Where Microsoft Internet Explorer Stores Its Cookies

If you're using Microsoft Internet Explorer, look in either the Windows\Cookies or Windows\Profiles\UserName\Cookies directory, where UserName is your name. That's where you find all your cookies...and your cookies...and your cookies. If you spend much time on the Web, that folder will be chocked full of the little goodies.

Believe it or not, you can tell a good deal about a cookie just by looking in a directory that holds them. In Internet Explorer, each cookie is a separate text file and ends with the extension .txt. The cookie starts with your abbreviated name, next is the @ sign, followed by the name of the Web site that put the cookie on your hard disk, and it ends with the extension .txt.

For example, if your abbreviated name is joejoe, and you visit the Web site www.homeruns.com, it puts a cookie on your hard disk with the name of joejoe@homeruns.txt. That means you can know which Web sites have put cookies on your hard disk just by looking in the Cookies folder.

You can also see the date and time it was put there or modified. Look at the date and time for the file in the directory. That's the latest time the Web site touched the cookie.

Sometimes you can find out more about the cookie. For example, you might be able to see whether it's used to put in your name and password and other information. Of course, usually, you find garbled and incomprehensible characters, but it can't hurt to take a look.

To look inside a cookie, double-click it. You'll see something that looks like this.

What's inside this cookie? As usual, a bunch of garbled text and letters.

What's An Extension?

The files on your computer have a period (dot, in computer-speak) near the end of them, followed by three letters, such as DOC or TXT, like this: article.doc or readme.txt. Those last three letters tell the computer (and you) what kind of file it is. For example, a .txt file is a text file, and a .doc file is a Microsoft Word document.

By the way, Windows sometimes hides the extension from you; in that case, you can still tell a text file by its icon.

Sometimes you see English words in there that might give you a clue as to what the cookie is doing, and you might even see your username and password.

Where Netscape Navigator Stores Its Cookies

Netscape handles cookies differently from Internet Explorer. Instead of creating separate text files for each, it stores all your cookies in a single text file called...yes, what else, cookies.txt. (How surprisingly logical. They'll never let *that* happen again.) Look for the file in the folder, C:\Program Files\Netscape\Users\Username, where Username is, of course, your username.

Techno Talk

Some Cookies Can Reveal Your Web Passwords to Snoopers

If you look through your cookie files, you might be surprised to notice that some cookies list your usernames and passwords for Web sites. Usually cookies encrypt those usernames and passwords on your cookies, but not all do. If it's not encrypted on your cookie, that means anyone with access to your computer can open your cookie files and steal your passwords. If you're worried that someone other than you has access to your computer, delete those cookies that show your user name and password. See the section later in this chapter "Fighting Back: How to Make Cookies Crumble," for information on how to kill cookies.

The picture nearby shows a typical cookies.txt file. You can see the name of the Web site that put the cookie on your hard disk, and the usual incomprehensible information, along with the occasional English word. You don't see the date and time the cookie was put there, though.

```
cookies.txt - Notepad
File  Edit  Search  Help
# Netscape HTTP Cookie File
# http://www.netscape.com/newsref/std/cookie_spec.html
# This is a generated file! Do not edit.

e12.zdnet.com:8080      FALSE   /clear  FALSE   946684783   cgversion       2
.msnbc.com      TRUE    /       FALSE   937396814   MC1
GUID=53d6f2f34c8f11d19c9d08002bb003f0
.excite.com     TRUE    /       FALSE   946641528   registered      no
.amazon.com     TRUE    /       FALSE   2082787122  ubid-main       1928-6749868-3066801
members.zdnet.com       FALSE   /       FALSE   946699127   ZDNET_LOGIN     prgralla:1gpg
.zdnet.com      TRUE    /       FALSE   946616320   browser 1880295E365C231D
.amazon.com     TRUE    /       FALSE   929822397   group_discount_cookie   F
www.netscape.com        FALSE   /       FALSE   942197277   NGUserID
cfc84949-23461-898412554-1
.homeruns.com   TRUE    /       FALSE   2051222532  SITESERVER
ID=1c4ba00608dc8c06961e0f516c47b19e
.netscape.com   TRUE    /       FALSE   1293839979  UIDC    24.128.41.45:0909070680:815898
.netscape.com   TRUE    /       FALSE   946684740   NSPOP   |ncr1b|ncr1c
home.netscape.com       FALSE   /       FALSE   942189140   NGUserID
d18fc718-20466-909070732-2
.zdnet.com      TRUE    /       FALSE   946616319   cgversion       3
shop.barnesandnoble.com TRUE    /       FALSE   1133413070      SHOPPERMANAGER%2FBNSHOP
4W9CR8HFJNSH2KU700LHRNKKFSNGR86N
.netscape.com   TRUE    /       FALSE   978307221   NS_REG
SHA1=%838%BF%CA%3C%26%A3%80%12%29%8F%0B%80%17%24%2DM%21U%2D[-]UR%5FEMAIL=pgralla%40tiac%2Enet[-]U
R%5FREG%5FID=DFGMKGIIRJSSPTS
.nscp-partners.com      TRUE    /       FALSE   978307172   NS_REG
SHA1=%c0%83%87%d6%12%d9w%f5%e8%05%a74%f6%b8%40U%de%5d%7es[-]UR%5FEMAIL=pgralla%40tiac%2Enet[-]UR%
5FREG%5FID=DFGMKGIIRJSSPTS
www.zdii.com    FALSE   /       FALSE   994230476   ELOGIC%5FZDII%5FPP      zd+fasmx+fpurx
.nytimes.com    TRUE    /       FALSE   946684770   RMID    9b2863ab367a79d0
expedia.msn.com FALSE   /       FALSE   1325419138  tpid    1
www.ne.mediaone.net     FALSE   /       FALSE   946598400   m1LPdefault     True
www.necnews.com FALSE   /       FALSE   945489484   NETSCAPE_LIVEWIRE.pref_vidtype  _rv_t1
```

Here's how to look at cookies in the cookies.txt file of Netscape Navigator.

Fighting Back: How to Make Cookies Crumble

You don't have to allow Web sites to put cookies on your hard disk—after all, whose computer is it, anyway? And you can also clean cookies off your hard disk. In fact, there's a good deal you can do to ensure your privacy and make cookies crumble. Without a whole lot of work, you can

➤ Check out a Web site's cookie policy

➤ Delete cookies from your hard disk

➤ Stop new cookies from being put on your hard disk

➤ Allow some cookies to be put on your hard disk and stop others from being put on

Now I'll show you how to do all that and more.

Checking Out a Web Site's Cookie Policy

If you're worried about cookies and how they're used by Web sites, there's something easy you can do—check out a site's policy. Unfortunately, not many sites post those policies, but some do. Look for the area of the site titled "Privacy Policies" or "FAQ" or "Help" or something similar. Some sites spell out in great detail exactly what they use cookies for. In fact, if you find a site willing to publish this information so freely, it often means they're not using cookies to invade your privacy, because that's not something they're likely to share with the world. You can see Yahoo!'s cookie policy, available in its Privacy Policy area, in the illustration.

Open to the world—
Yahoo!'s cookie policy

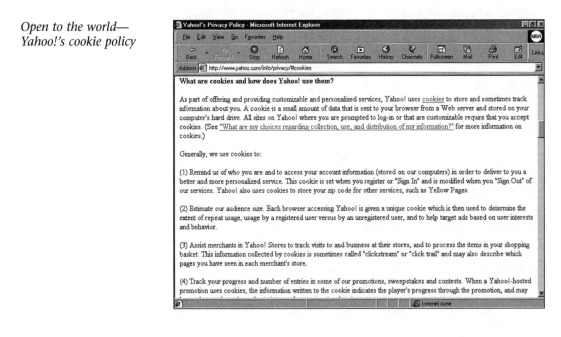

If you don't find a cookie policy at a site, go to the Contact area and send an email requesting it. Often you don't get a note back, but sometimes you do.

How to Delete Cookies from Your Hard Disk

It's quite easy to delete cookies from your hard disk. You can do it yourself, but often a much better way is to use a cookie-killer program, a program that lets you delete and manage cookies. If you're worried at all about cookies, I strongly recommend that you get one of these programs. There are many of them out there. My favorite is Cookie Pal—the most comprehensive solution I've found to killing and managing cookies. You can get it at many download sites on the Internet, such as the ZDNet Software Library at www.hotfiles.com. You can also find it at www.kburra.com. You can try the program for free before deciding whether to buy it, so it's a can't-lose deal.

If you're not using a cookie-killer program, you can still delete cookies from your hard disk. In Microsoft Internet Explorer, go to the Windows\Cookies or Windows\Profiles\UserName\Cookies directory, where your cookies are stored. Then, to delete a cookie, simply delete it as you would any other file. That's it. It's over. The cookie is history. Delete as many or as few as you'd like.

Techno Talk

Why Are My Deleted Cookies Showing Up in My \Windows\Temporary Internet Files Directory?

If you've deleted Internet Explorer cookies, you might be surprised to see them in the directory that temporarily stores Internet files. Well, believe it or not, you see the cookies in that directory, but they don't really exist! Because of the peculiar way Internet Explorer handles cookies, the names of those cookies show up, even though they've been deleted. Don't worry, the cookies are really gone. Web sites cannot use them, because they don't exist, even if it looks as if they do. Ah, computing!

In Netscape Navigator, you cannot delete cookies one by one. Instead, you have to either delete every Netscape cookie or none at all. To delete all the cookies, go to \Program Files\Netscape\Users\Username and delete the cookies.txt file. There. All gone. To leave them, don't do a thing.

By the way, a word of warning here: Don't try to edit your cookies.txt file. Bad things could happen. Netscape didn't design the file to allow it to be edited.

Programs such as Cookie Pal let you delete individual cookies, whether you use Netscape Navigator or Microsoft Internet Explorer. Pictured here is Cookie Pal in action.

Fighting the good fight: Cookie Pal deleting a Netscape Navigator cookie.

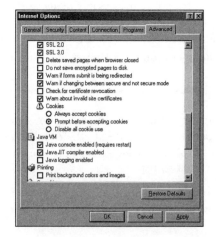

How to Stop Cookies from Being Put on Your Hard Disk

If you don't like the taste of cookies, you can do something even better than deleting them—you can stop them from being put on your computer in the first place. To do so, you can use a program like CookiePal, or you can customize Microsoft Internet Explorer and Netscape Navigator to do it.

To do this in Internet Explorer, select the **View** menu and choose **Internet Options**. Then click the **Advanced** tab. Scroll down until you see the Cookies section, pictured here.

Here's how to turn off cookies in Microsoft Internet Explorer.

To stop all cookies from being put on your hard disk, choose **Disable All Cookie Use**. When you do this, every cookie is automatically rejected. I don't suggest going this far—after all, many cookies have their uses. Instead, I recommend choosing the **Prompt Before Accepting Cookies** option. That way, every time a cookie is going to be put on your hard disk, you are first asked, so you have the option of whether to accept it or not.

To do this in Netscape Navigator, select the **Edit** menu, choose **Preferences**, and click **Advanced**. As in Internet Explorer, you can reject all cookies or instead be asked whether to reject individual cookies.

When You Disable Cookies, You Also Give Up Web Services

A word of warning: If you disable all cookies, you also give up special Web services such as customization. And you won't be able to use some Web sites at all.

You Should Really Get a Cookie Killer

The best option is to get a cookie killer like Cookie Pal. Rejecting all cookies means you give up a lot of great Web content and services. Accepting all means your privacy might be invaded. And being asked every time a cookie is about to be put on your computer can be very annoying, indeed.

That's where a program like Cookie Pal comes to the rescue. It allows you to automatically let some sites put cookies on your computer, but automatically rejects others. You tell it which sites to accept and which to reject. It's very easy to use and also lets you easily delete cookies.

It's the solution I use. Sites where I get great extra services by allowing cookies— I tell Cookie Pal to accept those cookies. All others I tell Cookie Pal to reject. Pictured here is Cookie Pal doing its work.

The best of both worlds: CookiePal automatically rejects cookies from some sites and automatically accepts them from others.

The Least You Need to Know

➤ Web cookies can invade your privacy, but they also let you get special Web services and content.

➤ Microsoft Internet Explorer stores cookies in the Windows\Cookies or Windows\Profiles\UserName\Cookies directory. You can delete individual cookies there.

➤ Netscape Navigator stores cookies in the \Program Files\Netscape\Users\ Username directory. You can delete the cookies.txt file there, but you can't edit it.

➤ Both Explorer and Navigator ask whether to accept or reject cookies, automatically, every time a Web site wants to serve one.

➤ The best way to handle cookies is to use a cookie-killer utility such as Cookie Pal.

Chapter 14

Beware of Registration Forms on the Web

In This Chapter

➤ How Web sites use registration forms

➤ Why there are so many questions on registration forms

➤ How to check out a site's privacy and registration policies before filling out a form

➤ How the TRUSTe Web site can protect your privacy when you fill out registration forms

➤ Insider tips and techniques for making sure registration forms don't invade your privacy

What's in a name? Plenty, if it has demographic information attached to it, like your age, gender, annual income, spending habits, way you access the Internet, marital status, number and age of children, and more. That information is worth a whole lot more than its weight in electrons to Web sites, marketers, and advertisers. Because if they know that information about you, they can pitch products at you—products that they think you'll purchase, based on your profile. And the odds are, if they pitch those products at you, and make the right pitch, you're going to buy things. And if you buy things, they make money.

That's why Web registration forms are so ubiquitous. They can be a great invader of your privacy. But as you'll see in this chapter, there's a lot you can do to make sure that, when you fill out forms, your privacy need not be invaded.

Why Are Registration Forms Used?

These days, free services abound on the Internet. Want a free email address? Sure, you can get dozens of them, from many different Web sites, yours for the asking. How about free software that does things like let you play video, watch TV stations, and tune into radio stations and live broadcasts at no cost? Sure you can do that, and you don't have to pay a penny for it. Or the newest twist: A free fax number of your very own so that anyone can send you a fax—and it's delivered to your email box as an attachment? In the can-do world of today's Web, you can get several of those for free as well. There are thousands of sites that offer free customization, stock quotes, customized news, email newsletters, and more.

What's going on here? How can anyone make any money on the Web if they're giving all this stuff away for free?

The answer is that stuff isn't quite free. To get it, you have to register for it. You might think that's a pretty good bargain, and the truth is, it is. In fact, considering all you can get for free on the Web, it might be one of the best bargains you'll ever find anywhere, any time.

You Are Asked to Fill Out a Registration Form When You Pay by Credit Card

You have to fill out registration forms not only when you want to get free services, but also when you want to buy things on the Web. These forms aren't used just to confirm your credit card number—they're also used to get demographic information about you. Your name and demographic information, when linked to a credit card, is worth oodles of money to Web sites and advertisers. That's because they know you're willing to part with your money over the Web, which means you're a live, paying customer. These sites and advertisers desperately want to pitch products at you, and they use the information you've put in your registration form to make the pitch.

Web sites can afford to give all this stuff away for free, because your name and demographic information is so valuable to them. By selling advertising to you based on your demographics, and possibly by selling your name and demographic information to direct-marketing lists, they can recoup their costs and make a profit to boot. So when you fill out a form, the Web site adds your name and demographics to its large list and figures out ways how to make money off of that list.

Depending on how much you value your privacy, this can be a good deal—give up a little information in exchange for a lot of free goodies. On the other hand, if you're not careful how you register, marketers, advertisers, and Web sites can end up learning a whole lot about you—and you'll never know in whose hands that information ends up.

Do They Really Need to Know All That Information About Me?

There are registration forms, and then there are registration forms. Some are like Jack Webb on the old *Dragnet* TV Show: "Just the facts, ma'am." Still others are more like today's confessional talk-show hosts: They want to know every detail about your life, including, no doubt, at what age you were potty trained and when you experienced your first kiss.

I've filled out more than my share of registration forms in my time, and here's a sampling of the kinds of things that forms have asked me for:

➤ Name, address, phone number, fax number, and email address

➤ Age and gender

➤ Exact birthdate

➤ Occupation

➤ Marital status

➤ Number of children and their ages

➤ Annual income

➤ What books you like to read

➤ What music you like to listen to

➤ Mother's maiden name

➤ What computer you use, including its make, model, amount of RAM and hard disk size, and operating system

➤ What kind of hardware and software you expect to buy in the next year

➤ Method by which you access the Internet, and what speed you access it at

➤ Number of hours a month you spend on the Internet

➤ More and more and more; just about any question you can think of, you'll get asked on a registration form

Never Give Out Your Social Security Number

On rare occasions, a site might ask you for your Social Security number when you fill out a registration form. Never, absolutely never, give your Social Security number when filling out a form. There's not a reason in the world a site should need that number. And after someone has that number, he can find out virtually any information about you and can even steal your identity and pose as you—possibly getting his hands on your bank account.

How much of that information does the site need to give you free services? Very, very little. Most of it is used to put together a demographic profile on you. And that profile is used to sell you things; or, the Web site might sell your profile to other marketers or list creators, so *they* can try and sell you things; or they can sell your name to other companies which try and sell you things. Your name and demographic information goes around and around, and there's no way to track it back down. Like a genie, after it's out of the bottle, there's no putting it back.

Your First Line of Defense: Checking Out a Site's Privacy Policy

The first thing you need to do if you don't want your registration information abused or revealed to others is to check out a site's privacy policy *before* registering. After you register it's too late.

Head to the area of the site called something like Privacy Policies, if there is one. No great surprise—often the link to this is in very small type at the bottom of a page. If you can't find a Privacy Policies area, look for something like FAQ, Help, or something similar. Many sites don't post their policies. If you come across a site that doesn't, assume that every piece of information on your registration form will be sold to the world. Some sites, though, such as ZDNet at www.zdnet.com, post their privacy policies, as you can see here.

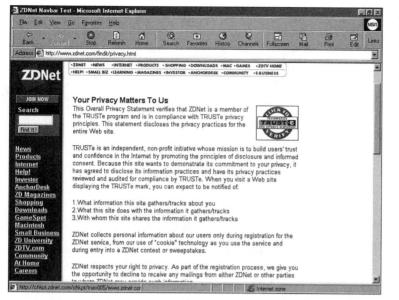

A detailed explanation of a privacy policy and registration forms at the ZDNet Web site at www.zdnet.com.

Let's say you find a site that posts its policy. Just because its policy is posted doesn't mean it's a good one. Here's what to look for in a privacy policy:

➤ **Does it tell you what kind of information it collects from you?** If you know this before you register, you know whether to even bother filling out a registration form.

➤ **What does the site do with the information it gathers?** Does it keep the information to itself, or does it share it with others? If the site shares your information with others, who does it share with? And in general, how is the information used—so you can get extra services, so they can send you advertising, or some other reason?

➤ **Is information about you shared individually or in the aggregate?** Some sites gather information about individuals primarily to put together demographic information about the site as a whole—not to track individuals. They then show that aggregate information to advertisers to prove how valuable their Web site is to customers. This action is not an invasion of privacy, because it never reveals your name and personal information. However, other sites release the personal information—and you should know if they do.

➤ **If they share information, who is it shared with?** Is it shared with advertisers, direct marketers, list-sellers, or their favorite Aunt Sally? (If it's Aunt Sally, don't worry—I have it on good faith that she's an honorable old lady.)

When You Enter Contests or Participate in Polls, You Might Need to Register

They get you coming and going—to enter contests on Web sites, you usually have to fill out a registration form. After all, you can't get something for nothing, can you? And some sites ask you to fill out a registration form before participating in polls.

➤ **Is there a way to correct errors in the registration information you give?** Your personal information, in the long run, should belong to you. If you want to correct it, there should be a way for you to do so.

➤ **Can you opt out of mailings?** Web sites ask for your email address not because they're curious (although, I must admit, most Webmasters I've know are very curious people, indeed), but because they want to send you email asking you to buy things or to visit the site. You want to be able to opt out of getting those mailings if you don't want to get them. You should be allowed to opt out, and you should be shown how to do it.

➤ **Is there contact information?** To whom can you complain if you think your privacy has been violated? There should be a person or email address to send your complaints to.

➤ **Does it carry a TRUSTe trustmark?** TRUSTe, at www.etrust.com, is a company that sets standards for protecting privacy on the Internet and makes sure that any companies that participate in its program adhere to these privacy rules. Check to see if a company has the TRUSTe trustmark on its site, pictured here. In the next section, we look a little more closely at TRUSTe.

If you see this logo, it means the site adheres to the privacy principles of TRUSTe, a privacy-watch site.

Why You Can Trust TRUSTe

When it comes to registration forms, and privacy in general, the TRUSTe site at www.etrust.com is one of your best friends. It's an independent service whose only purpose is to make sure that people's privacy is protected online.

164

TRUSTe creates standards about how personal information that's gathered via registration forms and other methods can be used. If a Web site wants to use the TRUSTe logo on its site, it has to adhere to those standards—and TRUSTe also checks to make sure the standards are adhered to. TRUSTe also resolves any privacy complaints filed against Web sites that display the TRUSTe logo. In general, TRUSTe sets rules so that you control your own private information and so that Web sites don't misuse information you give to them.

You Can Complain to TRUSTe If a Site Displaying Its Logo Invades Your Privacy

Have you been at a site with a TRUSTe logo and suspect the site has invaded your privacy? Don't just sit there and stew—take action! Go to `http://www.etrust.com/users/users_watchdog.html` and fill out a form complaining about the site. TRUSTe will investigate.

Smart Techniques for Protecting Your Privacy When Filling Out Forms

You've checked out a site's privacy policy. It seems OK. Or maybe there's no policy posted, but there's some stuff you want to get on a site, and the only way to get it is to fill out a registration form. You figure it's worth the gamble to fill out a form. What can you do to make sure your privacy isn't invaded?

There's a whole lot you can do. After all, you're the one filling in the information on the forms—the power is in your hands. Follow this advice for filling out forms, and your name—and your demographic information—will be protected.

➤ **Look for the opt-out policy.** Most Web forms tell you, in very innocuous terms, that they're going to send you mass or targeted email, or they're going to let advertisers send you email. That means you've been put into someone's list. Usually, the site lets you opt out—that is, ask that you not be put on the list—and no mail will be sent to you. It's usually a small check box, somewhere at the bottom of the form. Read the form carefully to see whether you need to check or uncheck the box if you don't want to receive mail. It's often hard to tell.

➤ **Only fill out the fields that are required.** Most registration forms have fields that you're required to fill out to register and fields that you aren't required to fill out. Often, people miss the distinction. Those fields you need to fill out often have asterisks or other small marks next to them, or note that they're required. Fill those out and no others.

➤ **Read the fine print.** You might be surprised at what you agree to when you fill out a registration form. Even though most of the fine print is dull and written in legalese, read all of it before signing up. You don't want to find out that you've given away your first-born child (then again, maybe you do...).

Don't Let Your Children Fill Out Forms on the Web Unless You're Present

Children are an immensely lucrative market for advertisers. Not only do they spend and influence the spending of billions of dollars each year, but they're also young and impressionable. If a company can get a child's loyalty today, they'll have it for scores and scores of years. Because of that, many Web sites induce children to fill out forms with personal information on it by offering prizes, games, and the like. Tell your children not to fill out any forms unless you're present. For more information about protecting your children's privacy online, turn to Part 6, "Protecting Your Children and Family Online."

➤ **Get a second, free email address that you use whenever you enter your email address.** Web sites ask for email addresses so that they (and their advertisers) can send you email. If you don't want your main email box littered with junk, get a second, third, or fourth free email address and use that when filling in your information. That way, the junk mail is sent to the other addresses, not your main one. You can get free email addresses at many sites, including www.yahoo.com, www.hotmail.com, www.bigfoot.com, www.zdnet.com, and many others.

➤ **When all else fails, lie.** Let's not beat around the bush here—feel free to lie on Web registration forms. It's a war, after all—they want to invade your privacy and you want to protect it—and all's fair in love and war. If they ask questions that are too personal, they should expect to be lied to. They want to know your profession? Fine; no problem. Tell them you're the Emperor of Ice Cream. Want to know your annual income? Sure, let them go ahead and ask—it's $2.5 billion. How many children do you have? Thirty-seven sounds like a good round number. Look at it this way: They can't invade your privacy if nothing you tell them is true.

The Least You Need to Know

➤ Web sites offer free services as a way to get you to fill out registration forms.

➤ Information from registration forms might be shared with direct marketers and advertisers.

➤ Check the privacy policy of a site before registering, and see if it has the TRUSTe trustmark.

➤ Use the opt out options on registration forms if you don't want to receive a lot of email.

➤ Only fill out the required fields in a registration form; these are often labeled with an asterisk.

➤ Feel free to lie about your profession, income, and other questions that seem too personal.

Chapter 15

--USED TO BE A BEDWETTER. HAS A MOLE ON RIGHT BUTTOCK SHAPED LIKE RHODE ISLAND...

Holy Cow! My Browser Shows All That Information About Me?

In This Chapter

➤ What information Web sites can find out about you from your browser

➤ How to delete information out of your browser's cache

➤ Making sure that no one can see which Web site's you've recently visited

➤ Keeping your email address and Usenet newsgroup information private

➤ How you can surf the Web anonymously

Head onto the Web with your browser, and you're announcing all kinds of personal information about yourself. Your email address. What newsgroups you're interested in. Recent Web sites you've visited...and a whole lot more.

In this chapter, you'll see all the kinds of information that your browser can reveal about you, and you'll see how, with just a little bit of work, you can protect your privacy so that it need not tell the world about you—no matter how much of a blabbermouth it is.

No Escape: What Kinds of Information Does Your Browser Show About You?

Every breath you take

Every move you make...

Every step you take

I'll be watching you

Remember that old song from the Police? Well, it was a love song. (Sort of a creepy one, when you think about it, but a love song, nonetheless.) Take those same words, twist them around a little bit, and they might as well be the anthem for your Web browser. That little helpmate of yours that lets you view Web sites can also reveal an enormous amount of information about you to all the places on the Web you visit. Merely by pointing your browser to a site, you can reveal an enormous amount of information about yourself.

Don't believe me? Head to www.anonymizer.com. Click the text that says the site knows information about you. You see a page that reveals a bunch of information about you, as you can see pictured below. The truth is that what you see on that page only scratches the surface of the kinds of things your browser can reveal about you.

Holy smokes! My browser reveals all that about me? See what it finds out about you at the Anonymizer Web site at www.anonymizer.com.

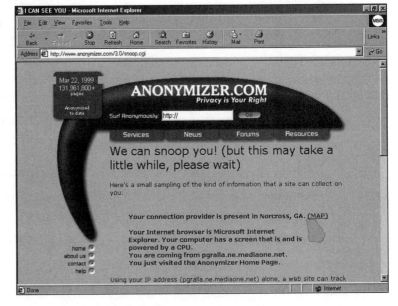

There's a whole lot of other things your browser can reveal about you. Here's the rest. Read it and weep:

➤ **Detailed information about the newsgroups you've visited.** It can reveal the newsgroups you've visited, the headers you've downloaded, and any graphics files you've viewed. (Of course, you haven't visited any adult-oriented newsgroups. But some spammers post naughty pictures to all the newsgroups they can think of, so you might still have some explaining to do to.) And Internet Explorer can even reveal the full text of everything you've read in those newsgroups.

What's a Newsgroup Header?

Newsgroups are Internet bulletin boards in which you can read and post messages about any kind of subject you can imagine. Each message you can read contains a header, which tells you what the subject of the message is, who sent it, and other details. To make it easier to decide which messages you want to read, you can first view newsgroup headers before deciding which messages you want to read.

➤ **Your user ID.** When you install Internet Explorer and Netscape Navigator, you're asked to provide a user ID. Web sites can look inside your browser and find out what it is.

➤ **Your email address.** Yes, your browser reveals that about you as well. Isn't anything secret any more?

➤ **Detailed information about your browsing habits.** What pages do you click to go to on a site? Do you prefer reading about sports or financial information? All that and more can be revealed by the use of cookies that Web sites place on your hard disk. For information about how to handle cookies to protect your privacy, turn to Chapter 13, "No, They're Not Oreos: What You Can Do About Cookies"

➤ **What browser and operating system you use.** No great surprise here: Your browser can tell a Web site whether it's Internet Explorer or Netscape Navigator, what version of Explorer or Navigator it is, and what operating system you use.

➤ **Recent Internet sites that you've visited.** It's easy for a Web site to find out which sites you've visited. Your browser keeps this kind of information in several places. It keeps it in the URL window at the top of the browser; click the drop-down arrow to the right, and you can see the history of sites you've visited. It keeps even more detailed information in a special area of your computer called a *browser cache*. That cache contains not only a record of where you've visited, but graphics, text, and other pieces of the actual Web pages themselves.

What's a Browser Cache?

When you visit a Web page, the information on that page is downloaded to your computer, including all the graphics, the HTML pages, and anything else on that page, so that you can view the page. All the elements of the page are put into a directory on your hard disk called a *cache directory* or *browser cache*. That's why, when you hit your browser's Back button, you can see the page or pages you visited so quickly—it's viewing them from a cache on your computer and doesn't have to go out to the Internet and grab them.

Pretty amazing what your browser can reveal about you, isn't it? But don't worry—you don't need to give away all this information every time you visit a Web page. In the rest of this chapter, I show you that there's a lot you can do to protect your privacy when your browser hits the Web.

What Information Is Kept in Your Browser's Cache—And What You Can Do About It

As I explained before, when you visit Web sites, entire Web pages and all their elements are kept in a special browser cache on your computer in a special directory. Exactly where these files are kept depends on the browser you use and its version number. However, Internet Explorer usually puts them in the c:\Windows\Temporary Internet Files folder and Netscape Navigator puts them in c:\Program Files\Netscape\ Users\username\Cache, where username is your Netscape username. Pictured here is the Netscape cache on my computer.

As you can see in this picture, it's pretty tough for normal human beings like you (assuming, of course, that you're a normal human being—a big assumption, I know) to see what's going on in your cache, for it looks like a bunch of weird-looking names. In fact, there are ways to reconstruct the exact Web pages you've visited from this browser cache. You can even download programs from the Internet that can do that for you.

There's a whole lotta browsing going on. Here's the contents of my Netscape cache directory.

It's actually pretty easy to clean out your browser caches. Both Internet Explorer and Netscape Navigator have ways to let you do that. In Internet Explorer, first choose **Internet Options** from the **Tools** menu. Then, in the section under Temporary Internet Files, click the **Delete Files** button. That cleans out all the files in your Internet Explorer browser cache. The screen where you do that is pictured here.

A good place for house-keeping: Here's how to clean out your Internet Explorer cache.

Internet Explorer also has a neat feature that cleans out your browser's cache for you every time you shut down the program. That means you don't have to do it your-self—your browser does your housecleaning for you. To get there, first choose **Internet Options** from the **Tools** menu. Then click the **Advanced** tab. Scroll down until you see the Security section. Check the box next to **Empty Temporary Internet Files When Browser Is Closed**. Now, every time you close down your browser, your cache is cleaned, with no muss and no fuss.

To clean out your Netscape Navigator cache, choose **Preferences** from the **Edit** menu. Then click the + sign next to Advanced and choose **Cache**. Click **Clear Disk Cache**. That action deletes all the files from your browser cache. You can also click **Clear Memory Cache**. Doing so deletes all the files currently in your computer's memory.

You Can Get Software to Clean Out Your Caches Automatically

It can be kind of a pain to have to remember to constantly clean out your browser cache. Many programs, though, automatically clean your cache for you at intervals you specify. For example, Cache and Cookie Washer (there are separate versions for Internet Explorer and for Netscape Navigator) and Cache Killer Pro do that for you. To get them, and other similar programs that do the same thing, go to any of many popular Internet download sites, such as the ZDNet Software Library at www.hotfiles.com. You can download them and try them out, but if you want to keep using them, you're expected to pay a fee to their author.

How to Kill the Information in Your History List

Your browser has a much better memory than you do. (At least, it has a better memory than *I* do. But then, I can't even remember simple things like where I put my car keys whenever I need to leave the house.) It remembers where you've been on the Web. And it's a blabbermouth—it hands over that information to any Web site that wants it. How indiscriminating!

If you want your browser to keep its mouth shut and not reveal where you've been, you can clean out your history list. It's easy to do. In Internet Explorer, you can find it on the same screen from which you can delete files from your cache. To get there, choose **Internet Options** from the **Tools** menu. In the section under History, click **Clear History**. That deletes all your history files.

In Netscape Navigator, choose **Preferences** from the **Preferences** menu and click **Clear History**. You can also clear the listing of recent files in your location bar by clicking **Clear Location Bar**.

Kill Your History List Altogether

If you don't like continually having to kill your history list, you can kill it altogether. In Internet Explorer, in the History portion of the Internet Options screen, set the days to keep pages in history to zero. In Netscape Navigator, set the pages in history to expire after zero days. In both instances, you can browse without a history list.

How to Hide Your Email Address

When you surf the Web, your browser can reveal your email address to the world. It's not that hard for sites to find it out.

However, if you do a little bit of work, you can hide your email address—or even put in a false email address if you like. You only need to change your browser settings or the settings in your email program.

In Netscape Navigator, it's a straightforward process. If you use Netscape 4.0 or later, choose **Preferences** from the **Edit** menu and then click **Identity**. You see three fields: for your name, your email address, and your organization. Delete the text from any of those that you want to keep secret. (Write down the information somewhere, though, so that you can put it back in if you want.) Your email address and name are now hidden when you visit a Web page.

In Microsoft Internet Explorer, click the **Mail** button and then choose **Read Mail**. Doing so launches your email program. You now have to delete your name and email address from your email program. Every program handles this differently, so check your manual on how to do it. To do so in Outlook, choose **Accounts** from the **Tools** menu, click **Mail**, and click your email account (or accounts). Click **Properties**. You see fields for your name, email address, and organization. Delete the text from any of those that you want to keep secret. (Write down the information somewhere, though, so that you can put it back in if you want.) Your email address and name are now hidden when you visit a Web page.

Keeping Newsgroup Information from Prying Eyes

When you're browsing the Web, sites can look into your browser and see information about how you use Usenet newsgroups. Sites can see your address information and might also be able to see what newsgroups you read and subscribe to.

In Internet Explorer 4, you have to launch the Outlook Express newsgroup reader. To do that, click the **Mail** button and choose **Read News**. Outlook Express's newsgroup reader loads. Right-click your newsgroup server. You see fields there that have your name, your email address, and your organization. Delete the text from any of those that you want to keep secret. (Write down the information somewhere, though, so that you can put it back in if you want.) Your email address and name are now hidden when you visit a Web page.

Don't Use Your Browser to Read Newsgroups for Even More Anonymity

The simplest way to make sure that no site can check what newsgroups and messages you're reading is to not bother with newsgroup software. Instead, you can use the Web itself to read and post to newsgroups. Go to Deja.com at www.deja.com, and you can participate in newsgroups. If you're worried about anonymity, simply don't use your real name or email address. There are other ways to post anonymously to newsgroups. To see how, turn to Chapter 11, "Staying Anonymous with Anonymous Remailers," and Chapter 17, "Protecting Your Privacy on Internet Newsgroups and Discussion Areas."

You can also make sure that Web sites can't tell which messages and headers you've been reading in newsgroups. To do that, click the newsgroup server. You see a listing of all the groups you're subscribed to. Right-click each, choose **Properties**, and click the **Local Files** tab. To get rid of all the information about what you've read in each of the newsgroups, click the **Delete** button. Everything you've read in those newsgroups is deleted.

Of course, still listed are the newsgroups that you subscribe to. To hide those newsgroups, you have to unsubscribe to them. To unsubscribe, right-click the newsgroup and choose **Unsubscribe** from this newsgroup.

In Netscape Navigator 4.0 and later, to hide your email address, follow the directions as outlined in the previous section. To hide other details about newsgroups, choose **Preferences** from the **Edit** menu and click the **Identity** tab. Delete the information in the other fields listed there, click the **Mail Server** category, and delete the information listed there. If your server information doesn't show up, you can get to it by clicking **Mail & Groups** instead of Identity.

In Navigator 3.0, Select **Mail and News Preferences** from the **Options** menu. Click the **Servers** tab and delete information from there. After that, click the **Identity** tab and delete that information.

Using the Veil of Darkness: How to Surf Anonymously Without a Trace

As you can see from the rest of this chapter, if you want to surf the Web and still protect your privacy, it takes a whole lot of work. In fact, you can spend all your time deleting your cache, killing cookies, and hiding your email address...which leaves you no time at all to surf the Web. (Good solution, in a weird way, I guess: If you don't surf the Web, you don't need to worry about protecting your privacy there.)

In fact, there's a much easier way. You can use a Web site designed to let you surf anonymously. It's simple to do. You go to a Web site designed to hide your identity when you browse the Web. Then you type in the name of the Web site you want to visit. When you do that, you go to the site you want to visit—but all traces of your identity are wiped clean. No cookies. No email address. No newsgroup information. No nothing. Nada. The best-known site is the Anonymizer at www.anonymizer.com. I'll show it here again so you don't have to flip back in the book.

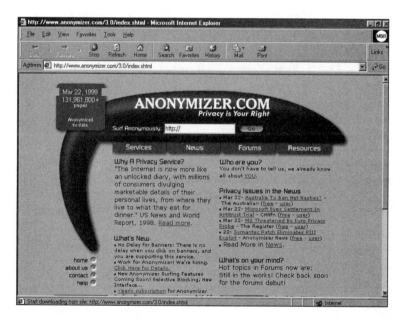

Hide your identity when you browse from the Anonymizer Web site at www.anonymizer.com.

Some of these sites charge a fee for their services. The Anonymizer, for example, lets you use it for free for basic services. When you use the free basic services, your Web surfing can be a little slow, and you see a big, fat banner ad on the tops of your pages. To surf faster, kill the banner and get some other extra privacy services—for this you have to pay a fee.

I could explain how this anonymous surfing works, but it would get pretty technical fast (and pretty dull, too). It has to do with things like proxy servers...I can see your eyes glazing over already. I'll spare you the details. Believe me, though, it works.

Protecting Your Identity Online—Becoming Schizophrenic

How can you be in two places at once if you're not anywhere at all? Easy. Use one of the new identity-hiding and identity-switching programs that make it easy to hide your identity online. These programs do more than merely hide your identity—they actually let you create different identities for yourself when you surf online, complete with different email addresses, different newsgroups information, and more. Kind of like that old movie *The Three Faces of Eve*, except you're in control, not your different personae. And there isn't an evil one...unless, of course, you want to create one.

These are programs that you download to your computer, and they let you create these different personalities with your browser. As I write this, these identity-switching programs aren't quite released yet, but by the time you read this, they might be. The giant networking company Novell at www.novell.com has one called DigitalMe. And a little-known company called Zero Knowledge Systems at www.zks.net has similar software called Freedom.

The Least You Need to Know

➤ Browsers can reveal a surprising amount of private information about you.

➤ Delete information out of your browser's cache directory and kill your history list to keep your browsing habits private.

➤ You can easily delete information from your browser about your email address and the newsgroups you visit so Web sites can't find it.

➤ To make sure Web sites can't find out what newsgroups you visit, go to www.deja.com.

➤ For the most privacy when browsing the Web, go to a site that lets you surf anonymously, such as www.anonymizer.com.

Part 5

Protecting Yourself in Chat Areas and Usenet Newsgroups

Can we talk? I mean a real heart-to-heart chat, just between us two? Good. Lean a little closer. Whisper all your secrets into my ear. I promise, I won't tell anyone else about them...

Gotcha! Chat and participate in discussion groups online, and you'll have no secrets—the world will know about them. Not only that, but you'll be giving out your name to junk email senders, called spammers, so they can flood your inbox with junk mail. And direct marketers will be able to put together a pretty comprehensive profile of your likes and dislikes, and even the name of your gerbil, Honeybunch. (No, not that! Anything but that!)

But there are simple ways you can protect your privacy and security when chatting or participating in discussion groups. This part will show you how. So don't worry, all your secrets are safe when you head online. Even Honeybunch's name.

Chapter 16

How to Keep Safe and Protect Your Privacy When Chatting

In This Chapter

➤ How you chat online

➤ What kinds of dangers are there when you chat?

➤ How to make sure that you're protected when using Internet IRC Chat

For many, the neatest thing about the Internet is the way it allows them to communicate with people all over the world. And the way they like to communicate is to chat—to talk to others via keyboard.

Chat's great. But it also carries dangers. In this chapter, you find out what those dangers are and how to keep yourself safe when chatting.

What Kinds of Ways Are There to Chat on the Internet?

What different types of chat are there on the Internet? Let me count the ways...no, that might take too long.

The word chat, when used on the Internet, is very confusing—and it's applied to a lot of different things. So first, I'll give you the rundown on what chat means—and what it doesn't.

When you chat on the Internet, you don't actually speak to someone else, or hear what they're saying. (Thank you, Internet, for taking even simple-sounding words and making them difficult to understand.) Instead, when you chat online, you type messages on your keyboard, and other people can see what you type. In turn, they type messages on their keyboards, and you see what they type. It's all done live. Most chats are group chats—many people chat simultaneously.

Techno Talk

What Does Real-Time Mean?

You might sometimes hear the phrase *real-time chat*. No, it's not another word for that hackneyed, meaningless phrase *quality time*. It just means that you're chatting live—you see what people type at that moment, and they see what you type at that moment. And because all chat is live, the term real-time doesn't really add any meaning to the term chat.

Chatting is like a giant free-for-all. You can talk to the entire group of chatters (or is that chatterers?), or you can instead carry on a side conversation, one on one. Most chats are focused on a topic, such as pets, car care, romance, or just about any other kind of topic you can name. There are all kinds of different technologies for chatting and all kinds of different kinds of ways you can chat. Here's the rundown on the most popular ones:

➤ **Internet Relay Chat (IRC)**   Here's the granddaddy of all chats. This is the first kind of chatting ever available on the Internet and is still one of the most popular. You need special IRC software to participate in IRC chats. My favorite is mIRC, shown nearby. You can download it from download sites such as the ZDNet Software Library at www.hotfiles.com or www.mirc.com. You can chat using many other kinds of chat software as well. There are some potential security holes in using IRC that could cause you trouble. I outline the problems—and how you can easily plug them—later in this chapter.

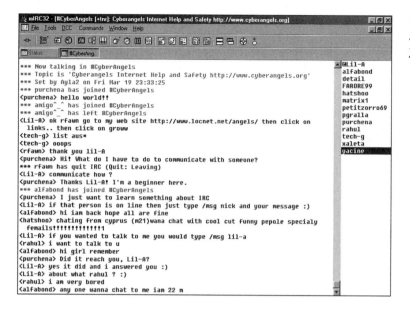

Yak away using software, such as mIRC, that lets you chat using IRC.

➤ **Chats on America Online** To a great extent, America Online was built on chat. It's a yakkers paradise. Pick a subject, and you'll find others who want to chat about it. For those who like to chat with others, the joint is jumping. Of course, for some, AOL is also synonymous with security holes.

➤ **ICQ (pronounced "I Seek You")** This software started out as an underground phenomenon and took the Internet by storm. Millions of people use it to chat with one another. You can only use it to chat with others who use ICQ. Get it at download sites such as the ZDNet Software Library at www.hotfiles.com or at www.icq.com.

ICQ lets you know when your friends are online and sends them instant messages.

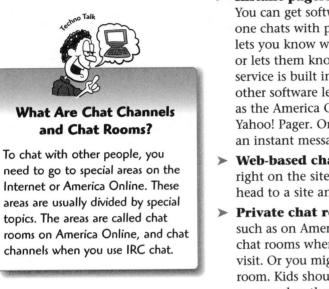

What Are Chat Channels and Chat Rooms?

To chat with other people, you need to go to special areas on the Internet or America Online. These areas are usually divided by special topics. The areas are called chat rooms on America Online, and chat channels when you use IRC chat.

➤ **Instant pagers and instant messengers** You can get software that lets you have one-on-one chats with people on the Internet—and also lets you know when your "buddies" come online, or lets them know when you come online. This service is built in to America Online, but a lot of other software lets you do it on the Internet, such as the America Online Instant Messenger and the Yahoo! Pager. On America Online, it's known as an instant message—IM, for short.

➤ **Web-based chats** Some Web sites let you chat right on the site itself. No software needed—just head to a site and yak away.

➤ **Private chat rooms** In some kinds of chats, such as on America Online, you can create private chat rooms where you and those you invite can visit. Or you might be invited into a private chat room. Kids should never go into a private chat room unless they know the person who created it.

What Dangers There Are in Chatting—And How You Can Stay Safe from Them

There are a number of different dangers you and your family can face while chatting—everything from dealing with a rude or unpleasant person to having your email address taken and put on spam lists to having your children targeted by adults. In this section, I look at advice on how you can avoid dangers when you chat. As I mentioned before, the use of IRC has a different set of dangers associated with it. I cover all that later in the chapter.

Gender Benders and Other Strangers: People Might Not Be Who They Say They Are

There's a famous cartoon in the *New Yorker* magazine in which a dog, poised near a keyboard, says something like, "On the Internet, no one knows you're a dog."

Take that a little bit further. On the Internet, you don't know whether the 12-year-old girl your daughter is chatting with is really a 45-year-old male pedophile. You don't know whether the pleasant, mild-mannered man you're chatting with who says his hobbies are raising orchids and studying chess is really a raving lunatic. The whole point of chatting is to make friends, and so it's hard for you to believe that people can be hiding identities like that. But they can. So be careful what information you give out about yourself to anyone you meet in chats.

Moderated Chats Are Safer than Unmoderated Ones

Most chats are freewheeling: anybody can say anything they want, and they usually do. But some chats are moderated, which means that there's someone who watches what goes on and can kick people out of the chat area if they're getting out of hand. (Hanging from the chandeliers is usually considered okay, though, so you're safe on that account.) It's best if children participate only in moderated chats. And if you're offended by sexually oriented talks or abusive behavior, you should consider looking for moderated chats as well.

Report Abusive Behavior to Moderators or the Online Service

There's something about chats that pushes some people over the edge. The partial anonymity—and the fact that nobody's liable to punch them out for being rude— gives them a license to act abusively, to harass people, and in general to act as all- around jerks.

If you're in a chat area and someone is exhibiting abusive behavior, in particular if they're harassing you, report them to a moderator (if there is one). If it's a chat on America Online, report their behavior to the service. On a service like America Online, people can be kicked off the service for abusive behavior. If the behavior bothers you and there is no moderator or it's not a chat on an online service, leave the chat area.

Use a "Bozo Filter" to Block Messages from Bozos

If someone is being abusive on a chat, but you don't want to leave the chat room, don't let the jerk force you off—there's a way you can stay in the chat room and not face abusive behavior or harassment. Many types of chats let you block messages from certain people so that you never see any of their messages. Think of it as a Bozo filter. If only we could do this in real life! Of course, if we could, no one would ever have to hear another word any politician ever spoke...not a bad thing, when you think about it.

What's a SYSOP?

People who moderate chat areas go by a number of different names. A common one is SYSOP—short for System Operator.

Check the specific kind of chat software you're using to see how you can block the Bozos. (Don't look under Bozo in the documentation, though, because you won't find it listed there.) Pictured here is how you do it using mIRC.

The fastest way to get rid of the Bozos: Block messages from people when you use mIRC.

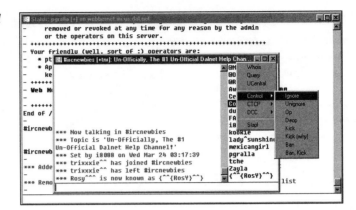

You Can Issue Warnings and Take Away a Harasser's Privileges with America Online's Internet Instant Messenger

America Online's Internet Instant Messenger lets you block people from sending you messages—but it goes well beyond that. You can also issue a warning to someone. When you issue a warning to someone, that person can send and receive fewer messages than he could before the warning. And if he receives enough warnings from people, he isn't allowed to send and receive messages at all. It's the best way of all to block the Bozos.

Never Give Out Your Real Name, Address, Telephone Number, or Other Identifying Information in Chat Rooms

People can often seem so friendly, so good-natured, and just so plain nice in a chat room or via an instant message that you are tempted to give out identifying information about yourself. Well, I have three words for you if you face that temptation: *Don't do it*! Stalkers and harassers can seem charming at first—that's how they can insinuate their way into people's lives. But if you give out identifying information about yourself, you can be stalked. This identifying information can also be used in scams. Remember, on the Internet, no one knows you're a dog—or a stalker or a scam artist.

If You Agree to Meet Someone You've Chatted with Online, Meet in a Public Place

Sometimes relationships born online can blossom into real-life friendships. I can speak from personal experience here: Someone I met in a writer's discussion area later became a good friend of mine after we found out we lived in the same area and met for lunch. But you need to be careful when meeting someone in real life—you don't really know what that person is like. If you agree to meet someone in person, only agree to do it in a public place, such as a coffee shop or a restaurant. *Never* agree to meet at or near your home.

Don't Give Up Your Life for an Online Stranger

The story has become so commonplace that it's become a cliché. Two people meet online. One or both are already married. They develop such a close relationship that one decides he's head over heels in love with the other and gives up his entire life—friends, family, job, and all. In brief order, the relationship turns sour, because real life can never stand up to fantasy. And so a person's life is destroyed...and in some cases, there's physical violence as well.

Never give up your life for an online stranger. It won't work out. Keep fantasy a fantasy and real life real life.

Kids Need Special Guidance When Chatting

Kids love to chat. But they're also more vulnerable than adults to stalkers and harassers. There's a lot you can do to protect your kids when they chat. For advice on how to do that, turn to Chapter 20, "How to Keep Your Kids Safe on the Internet," and Chapter 21, "Keeping Kids Safe on America Online."

Keep Your Email Address from Spammers

People who send out spam often gather email addresses from chat rooms as a way to build up their junk email lists. This is a particular problem on America Online. There are ways to make sure that you aren't subject to spam after entering chat areas. America Online users should create a separate screen name to use whenever you're chatting. That way, the spam is all routed to that screen name, and you can simply ignore the spam that piles up there. You can also create a new screen name every time you chat, and then abandon that screen name. That way, the screen name no longer exists by the time it's spammed. Of course it is harder for friends to keep track of you if you use disposable screen names.

For other kinds of chats, outsmart spammers by using a separate email address or ID from your real one whenever you chat. That way, spam is routed to that address or ID. You simply never check that account, and you are never spammed. To do this, get a free email address and use that when participating in Internet chats. To find out how to get free email addresses, turn to Chapter 10, "What Is Spam and How Can You Protect Yourself from It?"

What Is a Chatterbot?

Yes, you read that right. That's not a chatter*box*, it's a chatter*bot*. Chatterbots are programs that have some artificial intelligence built into them, and they participate in chats on IRC channels. They're pretty stupid and basic at this point—but then again, so are a lot of people who frequent chat rooms. The next time you're chatting to someone, don't be surprised if it's not a person at all and is really a chatterbot.

Don't Let IRC Irk You: The Special Dangers of IRC Chat

When you chat using IRC, you should heed all the advice about chats in general to keep yourself safe. But IRC poses its own special dangers. Because of a security hole in IRC, it's easy for people to send you viruses and Trojan horses and damage your computer or even steal your passwords and take control of your computer. (For information about viruses and Trojan horses, turn to Part 8, "Protecting Yourself Against Viruses, Trojan Horses, and Other Nasty Creatures.")

The cause of the potential trouble is two IRC features. One is the capability to run what are called scripts. The other is a way to communicate known as DCC. Here's what you need to know to keep yourself safe if using each.

Beware When Running IRC Scripts

Chatting on IRC is pretty simple. But the truth is, underneath it all, IRC is extremely complex and has all kinds of hidden capabilities and powers. One of those capabilities is running *scripts*. When you run an IRC script, your computer performs a series of commands that the script tells it to do. Commonly, you get scripts when people send them to you over IRC.

The problem is that unless you know what you're doing—and I mean *really* know what you're doing—you don't know before a script runs what it really does. Sure, a person might *tell* you it does all kinds of neat stuff, but for all you know, the script in fact searches through your computer for all your passwords and silently sends those passwords back to a hacker.

Even if a friend tells you a script is safe, don't believe him. Unless your friend is a true wizard, there's no way for him to know what the script really does. And some legitimate, useful scripts have been created to do damage.

So unless you're a wizard yourself, don't run scripts. They're too dangerous to mess around with.

Beware When Using DCC

When you issue a DCC command in IRC, you're opening up a direct connection between you and another person. This can be helpful because it lets the two of you chat directly with no lag time (normal IRC sometimes has a lag time). And with DCC, you can send and receive files to and from the person with whom you've opened up the connection.

Therein lies the rub. When you open up a DCC connection with someone, you're opening yourself up to all kinds of attacks. Someone can send you files of all kinds—including Trojan horses. And when they do that, they can literally take control of your PC, without you knowing about it.

What Does DCC Stand for?

DCC is an acronym for Direct Client to Client—it's a way to establish a fast one-on-one connection with another person on IRC.

This DCC connection was used by hackers to get an infamous Trojan horse called Back Orifice onto thousands of computers. Back Orifice allows a hacker to take complete control of a computer across the Internet—a hacker can look at every single file on the computer, steal passwords, delete and move files, run programs, and in fact can control a computer just as if he were sitting at a keyboard.

Normally, if someone wants to open a DCC connection with you, you get a request. Then, if he wants to send you a file, you get another request. There's an easy way to make sure you don't run into trouble: When someone wants to open a DCC connection with you, turn it down. And if you've opened a DCC connection with someone and he wants to send you a file, just say no.

Simple, yes? Ah, but this is the Internet we're talking about, so nothing is truly simple. When you're using IRC software, you get to set the DCC options. Check those settings. Because there's a setting in DCC that leaves you open to any passing hacker or cracker out there. If your DCC settings are set to Auto-Get, then you never get a warning when someone tries to send you a file—it is sent to you automatically. After you get that file, you could be in big, big trouble.

Read your chat software documentation and check your DCC settings. Make sure it is *not* set to Auto-Get. For maximum safety, set it to Ignore All. When you do that, no one can ever send you files. You don't even need to get a warning—the file is automatically turned away. Nearby is a picture showing how to do that in mIRC.

Maximum safety: How to change your DCC settings in mIRC.

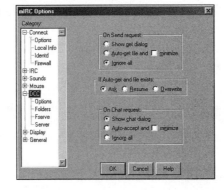

The Least You Need to Know

➤ Realize that people often disguise their identities and personalities when they chat.

➤ Moderated chats are safer to participate in than those that aren't moderated.

➤ Never give out your real name, address, telephone number, or other identifying information in chat rooms.

➤ If you agree to meet someone you've chatted with online, meet in a public place.

➤ Use "Bozo filters" to block messages from people who are abusive or harassers.

➤ When using IRC, don't run scripts sent to you or accept files sent via DCC.

Chapter 17

Protecting Your Privacy on Internet Newsgroups and Discussion Areas

---

In This Chapter

➤ What Usenet newsgroups and other online public discussion areas are

➤ How your privacy can be invaded when you join in public discussions online

➤ How you can protect your privacy when you participate in online public discussions

➤ What to do about abusive or harassing behavior on newsgroups and in discussion areas

➤ How to get your postings out of sites that archive newsgroup postings, such as Deja.com

---

Cyberspace is a vast, freewheeling place where you can talk to others in public discussions about anything under the sun and over the stars…and all places in between.

That's the good news. The bad news is that these freewheeling discussions can be used to invade your privacy. When you participate in discussions, people can put together a profile about your likes and dislikes, can put you onto spam mailing lists, and can abuse your privacy in other ways. In this chapter, you see how you can protect yourself when participating in public discussions on the Internet and online services.

Can We Talk? What Are Usenet Newsgroups?

Quick, without thinking, tell me what you think newsgroups are. Are they a) Roving packs of journalists; b) The usual gang of gasbags and blowhards who bloviate about current events on cable news channels; or c) None of the above?

What Does Bloviate Mean?

In a discussion, some people offer reasonable opinions that coincidentally agree with yours. The other participants bloviate.

If you answered c) None of the above, you'd be right on target. You'd think that something called newsgroups would have something to do with the news—but nooooo. This is the Internet we're talking about, and nothing is what it says it is. As for why they're called Usenet newsgroups…don't ask. Suffice it to say that the name was derived from the term User Network.

Newsgroups are discussion areas on the Internet in which you can talk about anything you want. Do you like talking with others about pranks? Head to `alt.shenanigans`. Are you a fan of the TV show *Buffy the Vampire Slayer*? You're not alone, as you can find out at `alt.tv.buffy-v-slayer`. A space cadet, are you? Meet like-minded others at `sci.astro`.

What's a Flame?

Here's another instance on the Internet where words are not what they seem. A flame is when someone in a newsgroup or another discussion area verbally and vociferously attacks someone else—often for no clear reason. It can also be used as a verb, as in to flame or to be flamed (that is the question…). There are people who love nothing more than to go online and flame people, just for their little bit of fame. (A fame flame?)

To participate in newsgroups, you need a piece of software called a *newsreader*. Both Netscape Navigator and Microsoft Internet Explorer have newsreaders built in to them, and there are many others you can find at download sites such as the ZDNet Software Library at `www.hotfiles.com`. Pictured here is Internet Explorer's newsreader, called Outlook Express.

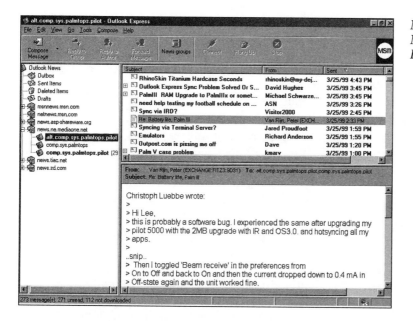

My newsreader of choice: Microsoft's Outlook Express.

You can also participate in newsgroups by going to the Deja.com Web site at www.deja.com. Go there and you don't need any special software—you can do everything right from that page via your Web browser.

Can We Talk Some More? What Other Kinds of Discussion Areas Are There?

Newsgroups aren't the only kinds of discussion areas on the Internet and online services. There are plenty more as well. America Online has very active message boards, as do other online services such as CompuServe. And many Web sites have Web-based discussion areas as well.

Although these discussion areas use different technology than newsgroups, many of the privacy issues they pose are the same, as you can see in the following section.

What Dangers Are There in Newsgroups and Discussion Areas?

What could be wrong with talking to people about *Buffy the Vampire Slayer*, whether Pluto is truly a planet (at last look it still is), or good April Fool's jokes? By itself, maybe nothing. But there are a lot of problems you might come across when participating in public discussions—everything from getting your name on spam lists to being harassed to people being able to put together a profile of your interests with only a few mouse-clicks. Here are issues you should be concerned about:

➤ **You can reveal information about yourself that you don't want an employer or people in your local community to know about.** Maybe you've talked in discussion areas about your personal life, medical condition, or political beliefs—and they're things that you don't want employers, would-be employers, or people in your local community to know about. It's easy for employers or would-be employers to check out your postings.

➤ **Anyone can put together a detailed profile of your interests and personality by doing a search at Deja.com at `www.deja.com`.** Deja.com is a Web site that lets you post and read newsgroup messages. But it also lets people search for every posting you ever made to Usenet newsgroups, and so it is very easy for someone to put together a personality profile about you.

➤ **You can be put on spam lists.** Spam is unsolicited email sent to you from people you don't know about things you don't want. It's very annoying and can clog up your email box. Spammers often go to Usenet newsgroups and harvest names to put into their spam lists.

➤ **You can be harassed by people online—and they can also find out your email address and harass you via email.** Most people on the Internet are normal (well, at least *near* normal), but there are also a lot of weirdos out there who might harass you because they object to something you said about Buffy, or for no discernible reason.

Check This Out

Deja.com Isn't the Only Site That Lets People Search Through Newsgroups

Other sites, not just Deja.com, let people search through all the postings made to newsgroups. For example, the AltaVista search engine at www.altavista.com lets people search through a comprehensive archive of newsgroups postings.

Help to the Rescue: How to Protect Your Privacy in Newsgroups and Discussion Areas

You can see there's a whole lot of reasons why you want to protect your privacy in newsgroups and discussion areas. Don't let that scare you away, though. There's a lot you can do to protect your privacy online. Here's everything you need to know.

Hide Your Email Address in Your Newsreader

When you post a message to newsgroups, your email address is right there, for all the world to see. That's because you put information into your Web browser or newsreader with your email address.

But what you put in, you can also take out. You can also make a phony address. If you take out your email address or put in a phony one, you go a ways toward hiding your identity from spammers and others.

Check your newsreader to see how to hide your email address. For detailed instructions on how to hide it if you're using the Netscape newsreader or Microsoft's Outlook Express newsreader, turn to Chapter 15, "Holy Cow! My Browser Shows All That Information About Me?"

Make Sure Your Posts Aren't Put into Databases

Sites such as Deja.com at www.deja.com take every post ever made in Usenet newsgroups and in essence put them into an easy-to-search database so anyone, anywhere, anytime can search through them. That means your words live forever. Someone can put together a profile of you based on all your postings.

There's a way for you to keep your name out of these kinds of databases. You can add a special header to your posting. Then sites like Deja.com know you don't want your posting put in their databases, and you are left out of them.

Techno Talk

What's a Header?

A newsgroup message or piece of email is made up of two parts: the body, which is the message itself; and the header, which contains identifying information such as your email address, the date and time of posting, and similar information. Newsreaders generally let you edit headers as well as bodies of messages.

Put this line into the header of your message:

```
X-no-archive:yes
```

When you enter that, sites like Deja.com don't put your post into their databases. Check your newsgroup reader's manual to see how to edit the header. See the section later in this chapter for more information about Deja.com and privacy.

Post Newsgroup Messages Using Deja.com

Although Deja.com can be used to invade your privacy, you can also use it to hide your identity when posting messages, as you can see in this picture. Go to the site and post a message. Your real email address doesn't appear in the posting. Instead, the address is the email address that Deja.com gives you; and they block spam to that email address. It's one of the easiest ways to participate in newsgroups without anyone knowing your identity. See the section later in this chapter for more information about Deja.com and privacy.

Use Deja.com to retain your anonymity when posting newsgroup messages.

Use a Separate Screen Name When Posting Messages on America Online

America Online lets you create several screen names. When you post a message on America Online, it automatically identifies you by your screen name. So, create a separate screen name to use whenever you're posting a message. (Perhaps in addition to the separate screen name you use to chat, as I suggest in the previous chapter.) That way, you are identified by that screen name, and if anyone sends you spam or harasses you, it is on a separate screen name. You can also create a new screen name every time you want to post a message and then abandon that screen name. That way, the screen name no longer exists after you get rid of it.

Report Any Harassing Behavior to Your Online Service or Internet Service Provider

If you're being harassed in postings, report the harasser to your online service, such as America Online. If the harassing occurs on a newsgroup, report it to your Internet service provider (ISP).

Use an Anonymous Remailer to Post Your Messages

An anonymous remailer lets you post a message on a Usenet newsgroup without anyone knowing your email address. (As you might guess from the name—smart you!—you can also send email with them anonymously.)

There are many different kinds of anonymous remailers. My favorite is the Anonymizer at `www.anonymizer.com`. For lists of other remailers, head to a list of them at `http://www.cs.berkeley.edu/~raph/remailer-list.html` and to the Electronic Frontiers Georgia's Reliable Remailer Lists at `http://anon.efga.org/Remailers/`.

For more information about how to use anonymous remailers, turn to Chapter 11, "Staying Anonymous with Anonymous Remailers."

Don't Abuse the Ability to Hide Your Identity When Posting Messages

Being able to hide your identity when posting messages can be liberating, but you don't want to abuse the privilege of privacy. When posting anonymously, you shouldn't use hate speech, harass people, try to manipulate stocks by planting false rumors, or send out spam.

Why Your Words Live Forever: Deja.com, Your Permanent Profile, and What You Can Do About It

As I've mentioned several times in this chapter, Deja.com keeps a permanent record of every posting made to newsgroups. It is easy for someone to put together a profile of your likes, dislikes, hobbies, and personality. (Likes rabbits, hates sea monkeys, hobby is collecting toenail clippings, personality is multiple.)

Deja.com also gives you ways to protect your privacy. You can delete any posting you want out of the site, so that when people search through it, they find only the postings you want them to find. (It's okay to let them find postings on your affection for rabbits, not okay to find them on your toenail collection.)

In Deja.com parlance, when you want to delete a posting, you nuke it. So how do you nuke a posting? Simple. Fill out an Article Nuke Form pictured here. Head to `http://www.deja.com/forms/nuke.shtml` to fill it out and nuke at will.

Yes, nukes! Here's how to nuke your postings at Deja.com at `www.deja.com`.

You Can Be Held Legally Liable for Postings You Make Anonymously

Just because you post a message anonymously doesn't mean that you're exempt from the legal consequences of postings. Courts have ruled that if you do something illegal, such as libeling a company, when you post anonymously, you're still liable for your actions.

198

If someone is using Deja.com and posting messages that you feel are abusive or harassing, you can report them to the site, which can take action against the person. To report someone, send the person's email address and information about the posting to abuse@deja.com.

The Least You Need to Know

➤ To protect your privacy when you post messages, hide your email address in your newsreader.

➤ To keep your posts out of sites that archive newsgroup messages, put this line into the header of your message: X-no-archive:yes.

➤ When you post a newsgroup message at Deja.com at www.deja.com, your real email address is hidden.

➤ To hide your true identity when posting to a newsgroup, you can use an anonymous remailer.

➤ Report any abusive posting behavior to your online service or your Internet service provider.

Part 6

Protecting Your Children and Family Online

Many parents are justifiably worried about their children using the Internet. They've heard stories of stalkers, they worry that their children may come across inappropriate material online, and they worry that their kids' privacy may be invaded when they surf the Web.

But the truth is, there are ways to keep your kids safe online. It's not hard at all—and it won't interfere with their enjoyment of the Internet, either. In this part, you'll find out the best tips for teaching your kids so they'll stay safe online, you'll get parenting and technical advice on keeping them safe, and you'll see how to use site-blocking software so that they don't come across inappropriate material online. And since so many children use America Online, I'll also teach you how you can customize that service to keep your children safe and secure as well.

So when it comes to your kids getting online, don't worry, be happy. Because they'll be able to get all the amazing resources of the Internet and they'll be safe and secure as well.

Chapter 18

What Kinds of Dangers Are There for Children Online?

In This Chapter

➤ What you should know about online stalkers

➤ How children can come across inappropriate material online

➤ What site-blocking software is

➤ The ways in which your children's privacy can be violated online

The Internet is a great place for kids—it's a combination of the world's biggest library, playground, amusement park, school, and den for hanging out with their friends.

But it can also pose dangers as well. Your children can be stalked online, can come across inappropriate material, or can have their privacy violated. That doesn't mean they shouldn't spend time online, because they should. But you should know the dangers they can face online—and know what to do about them. In this chapter, we look at the kinds of dangers your children face online, and I give brief advice on how to handle them. Then in the next chapters, I give in-depth advice on how you can keep your kids safe and protect their privacy online.

What Are the Dangers That Children Face on the Internet?

Just about every week, it seems, you hear yet another story about the dangers posed by the Internet to children. Of how easy it is for them to come across pornographic or other kinds of inappropriate material. Of how they can be targeted by stalkers. Of how their privacy can be invaded by marketers of every kind and stripe.

Yes, the stories are often true. But they're also rare occurrences. You shouldn't be frightened away from letting your children use the Internet any more than you should be frightened away from letting them walk in your neighborhood, go to the public library, or even read the Bible. (Talk about inappropriate material—some of the scenes in that book are pretty steamy, when you get down to it!)

Because the truth is, the Internet is a great place for kids to go. They can visit amazing locations, they can learn from the earth's largest virtual library, they can get homework help, they can make friends on many continents, and they can learn a great deal about the world and their place in it. And let's not forget that they're kids—so they can have loads of fun as well.

I know all this from experience—I have two children of my own, Gabriel and Mia. (Hi, kids! Nice seeing your name in print again, isn't it?) They've learned and grown from using the Internet, they've done better in school because of it, and they've certainly had fun on it. (Right now, I'll bet, Gabe is on some alien world on Battle.Net engaged in interplanetary and interspecies warfare in StarCraft. And Mia, no doubt, is chilling and chatting with her online buds on America Online.)

Just as you need to make sure that your children are safe in the real world, you also need to make sure that they're safe when they're online. In general, there are three types of dangers that you need to be concerned about when your kids go online:

➤ **They can be targeted by stalkers or those who might take advantage of them.** Your adolescent daughter might think she's becoming best online friends with a 14-year-old girl, when in fact, it's a 45-year-old man—and he wants to set up a meeting with her.

➤ **They can come across inappropriate material such as pornographic pictures or violence and hate sites.** The Internet is a vast, free-wheeling place, and there are nasty nooks and crannies they might come across.

Yahoo for Yahooligans!

The Internet is a vast place, and often the best way to find information on it is to go to a search site or Web portal such as Yahoo! or Excite. But when kids do searches on those sites, they might find inappropriate material in the searches—and the searches generally are targeted at adults, not kids. The solution to the problem: Have your kids visit a kid-centric search site such as Yahooligans! at www.yahooligans.com. It's safe, the information your kids find across the Internet from there is all designed for kids, and there's a lot of cool kid stuff for them to check out as well. For more kid-friendly sites, head to Chapter 20, "How to Keep Your Kids Safe on the Internet."

➤ **Their privacy can be invaded.** Kids love contests. They love games. They love getting things for free. Big companies and advertisers know this, and they often induce children into giving away information about themselves and their family online, so that your kids', and your, privacy may be invaded.

In the rest of this chapter and the rest of this part of the book, Part 6, "Protecting Your Children and Family Online," I'll show you how to keep your kids safe from all that and more.

Are There Really Stalkers Online?

Perhaps the thing that kids love to do the most online is communicate with others. They love making friends, learning about other people and places, and hanging out with their friends. To a great extent, that's how kids learn who they are—by talking with others. Chat, email, and Internet telephones all make it easy for kids to find friends. And the Internet's international reach lets kids have pen pals from all over the world.

That's great and should be encouraged. But there are dangers to that as well. Your child can be harassed and stalked or victimized by adults looking to take advantage of children's trust and innocence. There are a whole set of rules your kids should follow to make sure that they aren't victimized. Two of the most important are:

➤ They should realize that the people they communicate with might not be who they say they are.

➤ They should never agree to meet any of their online acquaintances unless you're present with them and it's in a public place.

Get to Know Your Kids' Online Buddies

As a parent, you like to know who your kids' friends are. The same should hold true in the online world—try to get to know their online buddies. You often can tell more clearly than your child if those buddies really are your children's age or are pretending to be their age. Drop in on your kids when they chat online, ask them to tell you about who's in the chat room with them, and look at the screen to see what the chat is about.

There are other rules they should follow as well. For more, turn to the rest of the chapters in this section: Chapter 19, "Best Rules for Keeping Kids Safe and Protecting Their Privacy," Chapter 20, "How to Keep Your Kids Safe on the Internet," and Chapter 21, "Keeping Kids Safe on America Online."

How Can Kids View Inappropriate Material Online?

Free speech is messy, especially on the Internet. The same basic right that has protected us from tyranny for over 200 years is also used to post material online that is truly objectionable—sexually oriented material, violent material, and sites devoted to hate.

If a child wants to find that material, he or she will no doubt be able to find it. All they need to do is spend a few minutes at a search site or Web portal, and they can find what they want.

Even if a child doesn't go searching for that material, he or she may find it. Surfing the Web, visiting chat rooms, participating in Usenet newsgroups, even just getting email—all of this can inadvertently expose your children to material that you find objectionable.

There are many things you can do about your kids finding objectionable material online. Here are some of the most important:

➤ **Use common sense parenting.** Your children are bombarded daily with objectionable material on television and the radio, in newspapers and in magazines—just witness the often-salacious reporting on President Clinton and Monica Lewinsky. Just as you discuss objectionable material available on the airwaves and in print, also discuss with them anything they find on the Internet that's objectionable. Encourage them to come to you with questions they may have.

➤ **Use site-blocking software.** You can get software that blocks objectionable sites on the Internet, such as those that are sexual or violent in nature. This is called *site-blocking software*. You can also block the kinds of sites your children visit on America Online. For more information about site-blocking software, turn to Chapter 20.

Site-Blocking Software Can Block Sites You Might Want Your Children to See

Site-blocking software is far from a perfect solution to the problem of your children seeing objectionable material online, and many parents might not want to use it. The software might also block important, useful sites that you would like your children to see, such as sites about breast-cancer prevention or the dangers posed by AIDS.

➤ **Know where your children spend time online.** When your children leave the house, you want to know where they're going. If they go somewhere after school, you want to know where they are as well. The same should hold true for the online world—know where your children spend their time, and it'll help make sure they aren't visiting inappropriate sites. Drop in on your children when they're using the Internet, see where they visit, and talk with them about it.

There are many more tips about what you can do about your children coming across inappropriate sites online. Turn to Chapter 20 for more details.

Find Out Your Library and Schools' Internet Access Policies

Many libraries and schools offer access to the Internet, and your children might be getting onto the Internet there. Find out what those policies are. Do they use site-blocking software? What can you do if you want your children to have full access to the Internet, without site-blocking software? What are the policies for chatting? Do more than just find out—get involved in setting those policies, if they're still being set, by attending and speaking at public meetings.

How Kids' Privacy Can Be Violated

To many companies, your child is a potential gold mine. Children spend billions of dollars a year and they influence the spending of many billions of other dollars in spending. (Don't believe they influence billions in spending? Just try taking your child to the supermarket and passing the candy aisle. Or count the number of times you've bought Beanie Babies or Furbies, and countless other dolls, toys, and games in the past year.)

Not only that, kids are impressionable and, at an early age, begin to notice brands. If a company can get your kids to become loyal customers, that company might have customers for life. Have you noticed how often your kids sing jingles from commercials—or worse yet, extol the virtues of MCI over AT&T? They're a marketer's best dream.

Marketers have found that the Internet is the best way to get personal information on your children—information that will be put into databases and will no doubt follow them around for the rest of their lives.

Ninety Percent of Child-Oriented Web Sites Collect Personal Information about Children

The Federal Trade Commission, looking into the issue of how kids' privacy can be invaded online, did a survey and found that nearly ninety percent of child-oriented sites it visited collected personal information from children. They did this by using contests, games, guest books, and other means. Less than 10 percent of those sites tried to obtain the parents' consent about collecting that information.

Many kid-oriented sites on the Web gather personal information about children and then use that information themselves or sell it to other marketers. And we're not talking just names and email addresses. Web sites have gathered highly personal information from children, such as whether the child had gotten gifts in the form of savings bonds, stocks, mutual funds, cash, or other financial services—and whether the children's parents own mutual funds. That same site publicly posted the full names, ages, and full addresses—including city, state, and ZIP codes—of kids who won a contest.

The best way to protect your children's privacy is to make sure that they never give out any information about themselves or your family that you don't think should be revealed. For more information on how to protect your children's privacy online, turn to Chapter 19.

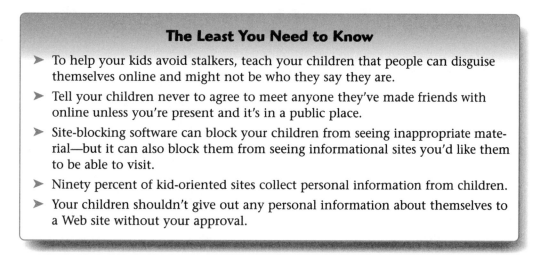

The Least You Need to Know

➤ To help your kids avoid stalkers, teach your children that people can disguise themselves online and might not be who they say they are.

➤ Tell your children never to agree to meet anyone they've made friends with online unless you're present and it's in a public place.

➤ Site-blocking software can block your children from seeing inappropriate material—but it can also block them from seeing informational sites you'd like them to be able to visit.

➤ Ninety percent of kid-oriented sites collect personal information from children.

➤ Your children shouldn't give out any personal information about themselves to a Web site without your approval.

Chapter 19

Best Rules for Keeping Kids Safe and Protecting Their Privacy

In This Chapter

➤ Why good basic parenting helps keep your children safe online

➤ What your kids should know about safety before heading onto the Internet

➤ How you can protect your children's privacy on the Internet

There's a lot that technology can do to help you keep your kids safe and secure when they're online, as you see in the next few chapters. But even more important than technology is to teach your kids how to stay safe and protect their privacy when they're connected. And there's a lot of rules you should know for making sure that your kids' online experience is a happy one.

In this chapter, you take a look at those rules. And you spend time seeing, not only how to keep them safe, but how to protect your kids' privacy when they hop onto the Net.

The Best Line of Defense: Good Parenting

There's all kind of advice, tips, software, and Web sites that can help you keep your kids safe and protect their privacy when they go online. They're all necessary and they're all useful. But the truth is, there's something a whole lot more important than all of that put together—that's to be a good parent. Sounds trite, I know. After all, aren't we all good parents? (You *have* stopped renting your child out as a *sherpa* on Mt. Everest expeditions, haven't you? Well, haven't you?)

Yes, we're undoubtedly all good parents (except for those of you still renting our your kids as *sherpas*). But I've noticed that when it comes to the Internet, parents can get strange. They act as if somehow the Internet is separate from the rest of their lives and their children's lives. They can start to trust their children less, or be less secure that the things they've taught their children about the real world will carry over into the online world.

Overriding everything else in this chapter is to apply the same common-sense rules of parenting to the Internet that you do in the real world. Go back to the basics: Teach your kids right from wrong and what's appropriate for them to do and view online and what isn't. Recognize that the online world is like the real world, and you need to know who their friends are and where they're visiting—but you don't want to be overbearing or intrusive about it. Most of all, you want your children to trust you—enough that they come to you if they need advice, want to know whether visiting certain Web sites is suitable, or are uncomfortable by things that have been said to them in chat rooms or via email.

As many of us have learned the hard way, often the best way to get your kids to trust you is to show that *you* trust *them*. That means, although you want to know what your kids are doing online, you should be careful about not being intrusive, and you shouldn't try certain ways to find out what your kids are doing online without them knowing about it.

Get a Helpful, Free Pamphlet on How to Protect Your Children

An excellent resource for any parent concerned how to keep his children safe online is "Child Safety on the Information Highway," by the National Center for Missing and Exploited Children and the Interactive Services Association (8403 Colesville Road, Suite 865, Silver Spring, MD 20910). Much of the information in this section of the book is inspired by that pamphlet. You can also read the entire pamphlet and get more information at the National Center for Missing and Exploited Children Web site at www.missingkids.org.

I can tell you from personal experience that this works: I've given my kids pretty free rein in what they do online, and it's paid off. They regularly ask me before they download files from the Internet, whether they can register at certain sites, and they come to me when they come across something online that makes them uncomfortable. So just make sure that, however you handle your kids' online use, it brings you together instead of pushes you apart.

Rules for Keeping Kids Safe Online

Good parenting is the basis of how to keep kids safe. Still, there are specific things you need to do regarding the Internet and online services to protect your kids. The best thing is to teach them rules about how to stay safe—in essence, teach them to be what's known in the real world as street smart, but that we call CyberSmart. (Note the quirky capitalization in the middle of the word—that's the easiest way to make any word sound high-tech and Internet-cool.)

The children most at risk online tend to be teenagers. One reason is that you're more likely to leave them unsupervised than younger children. Teenagers go online largely to meet other kids, send and receive email, participate in bulletin boards, and chat...and chat...and chat. Not only do teens tie up your phone line by talking on the telephone; they also tie it up by dialing in to the Internet to chat. In fact, my teenage daughter Mia can often be found talking into the phone while chatting online at the same time—often to the same people! Talk about wanting to stay in touch!

This tendency to talk and chat has always been normal for teens; but online it has the potential for danger, because a person can pose as someone your child's age, but really be an older person targeting your child.

Your kids face three kinds of risks online. He might be exposed to inappropriate material of a sexual or violent nature. Your kid also might give out information to a stranger online or arrange a face-to-face encounter that could risk his safety—witness cases in which pedophiles gained a child's confidence and then arranged a personal meeting and molested the child. Your kid might also be exposed to messages via email, bulletin boards, chats, or instant messages that are harassing, demeaning, or hostile.

Techno Talk

What Does "IM me" Mean?

Watch your kids online in a chat session, and you might frequently see the phrase "IM me." What in the world does that mean? IM stands for Instant Message, which is a way for two people to have a private, one-on-one chat, especially on America Online or using America Online's Instant Messenger on the Internet. When one kid asks another to IM him, it's an invitation to a personal chat. Kids often participate in a public chat room, as well as several Instant Message sessions simultaneously.

There are ways to protect them against all these dangers. Here's how to do it:

➤ **Block their access to certain portions of the Internet.** There are ways that you can block kids' access to certain Web sites and other areas of the Internet and online services that might be unsuitable for them. You can do this using what's called site-blocking software or by using the parental control areas of online services. To see how, turn to Chapter 20, "How to Keep Your Kids Safe on the Internet," and Chapter 21, "Keeping Kids Safe on America Online."

➤ **Spend time with your children online.** Site-blocking software is no substitute for spending time with your kids when they're online. Ask them where they go, watch what they're doing, and suggest places that you think they might want to visit. That doesn't mean you need to always be there when they go online, but if you regularly drop in and ask what they're doing, it goes a long way to ensuring that they don't visit inappropriate places or do inappropriate things.

➤ **Make sure they don't give out personal information.** Data such as home address, school name, or telephone number should never be revealed in public or private message areas such as bulletin boards, chat rooms, or via Instant Messages or email. The person your 11-year-old daughter believes is another 11-year-old girl might well be a 40-year-old man. Also, consider unlisting your child's name in public directories on America Online or the Internet. To learn how do that, turn to Chapter 21 and Chapter 3, "Making Sure Your Internet Service Provider (ISP) Protects Your Privacy."

You Can Block Email from Specific Individuals to Your Kids

If your children complain that a specific person is sending email that makes them uncomfortable, or for some other reason, they don't want to get messages from a person, there's a simple action you can take. You can configure their email software to block the messages from a person or have those messages put automatically into a special Junk folder, so they can easily delete it. On America Online, you can block email from specific individuals. For details on how to do all this, check out Chapter 20 and Chapter 21.

➤ **Don't allow your child to meet someone person-to-person that they've meet online without getting your approval.** If you agree to such a meeting, you should go along, and the meeting should be held in a public spot.

➤ **Tell them not to respond to messages that are suggestive, obscene, threatening, or that make them feel uncomfortable.** If your children come across any messages like that, they should tell you about it. Then contact your online service or service provider, send them the message, and ask for their help. If the message is truly threatening, contact the police.

➤ **Child pornography is illegal.** Laws regarding adult content on the Internet are currently being tested in the courts, but child pornography is illegal on or off the Internet. If you become aware of any use or transmission of child pornography online, contact the National Center for Missing and Exploited Children at (800) 843-5678 and notify your online service.

➤ **Make sure that your children know that people might not be who they say they are.** They should always keep in mind that it's easy for someone online to pose as someone else. It's easy for a 45-year-old man to pose as a 10-year-old girl. Even having a scanned picture should not be taken for proof.

Have Your Kids Agree to These Rules Before They Go Online

The National Center for Missing and Exploited Children and the Interactive Services Association have come up with a set of rules that kids should agree to before going online to protect their safety. Here are their rules—have your kids agree to them before going online:

➤ I will not give out personal information such as my address, telephone number, parents' work address or telephone number, or the name and location of my school without my parents' permission.

➤ I will tell my parents right away if I come across any information that makes me feel uncomfortable.

➤ I will never agree to get together with someone I "meet" online without first checking with my parents. If my parents agree to the meeting, I will make sure that it is in a public place and bring my mother or father along.

➤ I will never send a person my picture or anything else without first checking with my parents.

➤ I will not respond to any messages that are mean or in any way make me feel uncomfortable. It is not my fault if I get a message like that. If I do I will tell my parents right away so that they can contact the online service.

➤ I will talk with my parents so that we can set up rules for going online. We will decide upon the time of day that I can be online, the length of time I can be online, and appropriate areas for me to visit. I will not access other areas or break these rules without their permission.

Protecting Your Children's Privacy Online

Your children...when you look at them, you see sweetness and innocence and light—that is, when they're not arguing over who gets to use the ketchup first or whose turn it is to control the TV changer—but when direct marketers, advertisers, and sellers see them, they see big fat dollar signs. They see those dollar signs because kids spend billions of dollars a year—they're a huge consumer market. And they influence the spending of many billions of dollars more—if you don't believe that, look in your cupboard and count the boxes of cereals with names like Super-Cocoa Marshmallow Sugar Flakes or look at the toys littering your living room.

There's other reasons marketers target your children. Your kids are very susceptible to advertising and have a hard time distinguishing advertising from non-advertising. They're prime targets. And if marketers can get your kids as customers now, when their buying habits are still being formed, they'll have them as customers for life.

There are bigger dangers than being targeted by marketers. Some Web sites have posted public information about children, including their name, address, and email information, which could provide a stalker with information about your child.

Why Would an Oil Company Create a Site for Kids?

The idea, on the face of it, makes absolutely no sense. The oil giant Chevron has created a site for kids at www.chevroncars.com, and it offers games, coloring books, cartoon-like cars, and free stuff for kids. Why would they do that? When was the last time your 7-year-old filled up her car at the gas pump? (Don't answer that question—it could be held against you in court.) They, and other marketers, do it because they're trying to buy customer loyalty at the earliest possible age—if they can hook your kids on their brand when they're young, the company's got a lifetime customer.

Many Web sites take advantage of children's innocence and invade their privacy and yours. Children—and you—can end up on marketing lists where exceedingly private details of your life can be tracked. And some sites even can endanger children by publicly posting information about them, such as their names, addresses, and email addresses. Consider just a few of the facts uncovered by the Federal Trade Commission when it did a survey of Web sites designed for kids:

➤ Almost 90 percent of sites collect personal information about children.

➤ Less than 10 percent of sites that gather personal information try to notify the child's parent to get parental consent to gather the information.

➤ One site surveyed collected information including the child's full name, postal address, email address, gender, and age. It also asked for extensive personal and financial information, including whether the child had received stocks, cash, savings bonds, mutual funds, or certificates of deposit. It also asked for the entire family's financial information including whether the parents owned mutual funds.

➤ The site mentioned above also ran a contest and posted the full name, age, city, state, and ZIP code of the winner.

➤ A different Web site collected comprehensive personal information about children, including their hobbies. The site held a contest and posted the winner's full name and email addresses.

How Do They Collect the Information about Kids?

Web sites use a variety of different techniques to gather information about kids. If you know how they do it, you can warn your kids and teach them how to protect their privacy online. Here are the most common ways that Web sites gather personal information from children:

➤ **Registration.** To enter a site or use a special portion of a site, such as a games area, sites might require that your kids register and fill in personal information about themselves.

➤ **Contests.** Kids love contests—they love entering, and they love winning. Sites might require that kids fill out a form before entering contests.

➤ **Free gifts.** Sites offer giveaways, such as free screen savers or other gifts, if kids give personal information about themselves.

Just Because a Site Promises to Protect Your Kids' Privacy Doesn't Mean That It Will

Promises are easy to make, but even easier to break. Just because a site promises never to share information about your kids doesn't mean they never will. The popular site GeoCities, for example, promised never to share information that it gathered about children (and adults, as well). In fact, though, as GeoCities later admitted to the Federal Trade Commission, it turned over that information to other businesses that used it to target thousands of children (and adults) for direct email solicitations.

➤ **Message boards, pen pals, and chat areas.** To participate in discussions with other kids or to find pen pals on a site, the site might require that personal information be given out.

➤ **Surveys and polls.** Put a survey or a poll in front of a kid, and he'll fill it out. So, Web sites put them in front of kids—and might require that they supply personal information to fill them out.

How to Protect Your Children's Privacy

Now you know all the ways that sites can invade your children's privacy. Armed with that information, you can fight back—you can make sure that information about you and your children isn't gathered online. Here's how to do it:

➤ **Check out a site's privacy policies.** What information does it gather about your kids? How does the site use the info? Ideally, a site collects no information—but if it does, you want it to be absolutely minimal, and it should never be shared with any other site. And the site should send you an email to let you know that it's requesting information from your children.

➤ **Look for a special children's privacy seal on a site.** Two groups, TRUSTe at www.etrust.com and the Better Business Bureau online at www.bbbonline.com, have established programs to help protect children's privacy. When a site adheres to these standards—which are quite strict—it gets to put the seal of the group on its page. Look to see if a site has one of the seals. If it does, it adheres to the privacy rules. The nearby picture shows the TRUSTe site and its kids' privacy seal.

Look for the TRUSTe kids' seal to make sure that a site adheres to privacy standards for children.

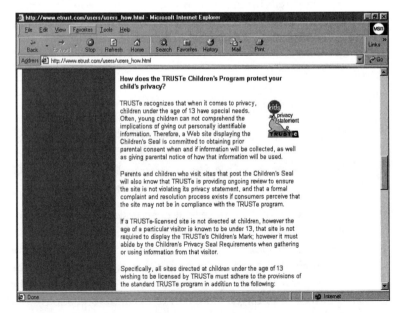

➤ **Tell your children never to give out private information about themselves.** This is one of the surest ways to protect their privacy. Make sure that they follow all the rules I detailed earlier in this chapter, such as not giving out their full name, address, and similar information in public areas.

➤ **Ask that your children check with you before registering or giving out personal information about themselves to a Web site.** That way, you can check out the site with your children before they give out their information. And it also educates them in what to look for to protect their privacy themselves.

The Least You Need to Know

➤ Apply the same common-sense rules of parenting and safety you use in the real-world to the Internet.

➤ Make sure your kids never agree to meet anyone in person that they've met online, unless checking with you first—and that you're present at the meeting and it's in a public place.

➤ Tell your kids never to give out personal information about themselves, such as their address, school, and telephone number.

➤ Know where your children spend their time online and who they're spending it with.

➤ Check out a site's privacy policy before your children register or give it any information.

➤ When visiting Web sites, check if they post child-specific privacy seals from TRUSTe and the Better Business Bureau Online.

Chapter 20

How to Keep Your Kids Safe on the Internet

In This Chapter

➤ How you can keep your kids safe on the Web

➤ What to talk with your kids about before they go onto the Internet

➤ How to keep your kids safe when they chat and use newsgroups and email

➤ What you need to know about site-blocking software—and should you use it

➤ Award-winning safe and fun sites for kids

My kids, and many others, might wake up every day and thank their lucky stars there's an Internet. They use it for homework help, playing games, hobbies, learning, making new friends, and staying in touch with current ones. Today it's as much a part of childhood as milk and chocolate chip cookies.

But you want to make sure that when your kids go online, they're safe as well. Whether browsing the Web, chatting, or using email, you want to make sure that they have fun, but that they're not in any danger. This chapter helps you make sure that your kids are safe when they head online, so you can minimize your worries about their safety.

What to Watch for on the Web—And How to Keep Kids Safe

The Web's a big place, with all kinds of great sites for kids and adults to visit. But it's also a place where kids can come across inappropriate material of many kinds, such as pornography, hate-filled sites, and commercial sites that pitch products to your kids such as alcohol. Just as you want to make sure that your kids are safe in the real world, you want to make sure that they're safe when they head out to the Web.

For general advice on how to make sure your kids are safe when heading to Internet, turn to Chapter 19, "Best Rules for Keeping Kids Safe and Protecting Their Privacy." Here, we take a look at more specific advice on how to keep them safe on the Web.

First Things First: Talk with Your Kids

Yes, you've heard this kind of advice before. Time and time again. That doesn't make it any less true. But the first thing you can do to keep your kids safe when surfing the Web is to talk to them. And make sure that you don't do all the talking—listen to what they have to say as well. These are the kinds of things you should discuss when having a talk with them:

> ➤ **Warn them about the kinds of sites they should stay away from.**
> Make clear that you don't want them visiting pornographic sites, hate sites, or other kinds of sites you don't want them to visit. Don't merely issue a command—explain why you don't want them visiting those sites and listen to what they say in response.

> ➤ **Explain to them that sites might not be what they seem.** The many hate groups that create Web sites have gotten increasingly sophisticated about disguising their ulterior motives and who they really are. Often, a hate site doesn't at first glance appear to be one—in fact, one racist site even has photos that apparently extol Martin Luther King, until you read more closely. Teach your kids how to recognize the real thing from the phony thing.

> ➤ **Let them know that if they're in doubt about whether they should visit a specific site, they should come to you.** Make sure your kids trust you and tell them that if they have any doubt, they should come to you to see whether a site is suitable for them to visit.

Spend Time Surfing with Your Kids

If you spend time browsing the Web with your kids, they soon learn what's an appropriate site and what isn't. So guide them—but make sure to look for sites that they're interested in, or it isn't of much use. (No, your favorite license-plate collecting site or site listing the top mutual funds might not be the best places to bring them to.)

Check in regularly on your kids when they're on the Web, so you can see where they're visiting—and so they know you're close at hand.

Beware of Sellers of Alcohol and Other Inappropriate Products Targeting Your Kids Online

Remember Joe Camel? That cigarette cartoon character is widely attributed to have led to an increase in smoking among children—and many people believe that the character was created primarily to hook kids on cigarettes. Well, Joe is not alone in appealing to children. Another kids' favorite is the Budweiser Beer cartoon-like lizards. Kids can head straight to the Budweiser site and download a Budweiser lizards screen saver. They can also read the Budweiser "Beer School Yearbook" at the site, can sign up for a free NASCAR racing fantasy league game, and more. To come in to the site, they only have to fill in a form saying that they're over 21—but of course, there's no checking, so kids of any age can enter.

Lead Them to Kid-Friendly Search Sites

Kids spend a lot of time looking for stuff on the Web—for hints about playing the Pokemon video game, information about Furbies, pictures of animals…just about anything you can name. The best way to find things on the Web is to go to a search site like Yahoo!. The only problem with those kinds of sites is that they're for adults as well as kids—kids can come across inappropriate material when searching on them.

There are, however, a number of kid-friendly search sites you can lead your kids to. They can find what they want fast on these sites—and they don't come across any inappropriate material, unless you consider information about Barbies and Power Rangers inappropriate. (Where I live, in Cambridge, Massachusetts, you can find a load of parents who think that.)

The best search site (and the favorite of my kids) is Yahooligans! at www.yahooligans.com. My kids have been using it for years and always keep returning to it. There are others, as

Have Your Kids Try a Kid-Friendly Browser

How's this for an idea: A browser that's kid-friendly, easy-to-use, guides them to safe Web sites, and includes safe email? That's the idea behind the free Web browser SurfMonkey. Get it for free for your kids at www.surfmonkey.com.

well, though, so check them out too. You should consider making that page your kids' Start page, so that whenever they run their browser, that's the first page they come to. Check your browser's Help menu for information on how to do that. And check out the listing of kid-friendly sites at the end of the chapter for more ideas on where to send your kids.

Just Because a Site Claims It's Kid-Friendly Doesn't Make It So

Sites might claim to be kid-friendly, but you shouldn't believe them unless you check them out yourself. For example, the search site www.magellan.excite.com claimed to have an area where kids could search for sites, and all search results would be screened, to make sure that they didn't come across any inappropriate content. The only problem was the site forgot to check out the ads, and kids doing searches on the site were subjected to viewing ads for pornographic sites. The moral of the story: Check out the sites yourself.

How to Check What Sites Your Kids Visit

Here's a touchy issue. What if you suspect that your kids are visiting inappropriate sites, but they tell you they aren't? What can you do?

There are, in fact, ways that you can check up on what they're doing. These don't always work, but sometimes they do. I suggest being careful when doing this, because your kids might feel that you're doing something behind their backs—in fact, you *are* doing something behind their backs. Still, if you suspect your kids are visiting sites they shouldn't, there are ways to see what they've been up to:

➤ **Check the history list in the browser.** Netscape Navigator and Microsoft Internet Explorer both keep a list of sites that have been recently visited with the browser. In Internet Explorer, to see this list, click the **History** button. A pane opens up in the right side of the browser, with a scrollable list of all the recently visited sites. You can see the history list pictured nearby. You can see the recently visited sites. Click any site to go to there, so you can see what's on the site yourself.

In Netscape Navigator, to see the history list, select **Window** and then choose **History**. A separate window opens up with a list of all recent sites visited. Double-click any site to go there.

Here's how you can see the recently visited sites using Microsoft's Internet Explorer.

➤ **Check the Web's disk cache.** When you browse the Web, the elements on Web pages are downloaded to your computer and stored there for a while. They're in an area called a *disk cache*. If you look in this cache, it looks like nothing at all. But special cache reader software can look into the cache and make sense of it, even reconstructing entire Web pages for you. In this way, you can see what pages have been recently visited. A good one is Microsoft Internet Cache Explorer and Netscape Navigator Cache Explorer. You can find both on download sites on the Internet, such as ZDNet's Software Library at www.hotfiles.com.

➤ **Check the favorites list.** To see what sites your kids frequently go to, check the favorites list. In Microsoft Internet Explorer, click **Favorites**. In Netscape Navigator, click **Bookmarks**.

Keep in Mind That It's Easy to Delete History Lists and Caches

History lists and caches aren't a foolproof way to see where your kids have been surfing, because it's so easy to delete those records. Turn to Chapter 15, "Holy Cow! My Browser Shows All That Information About Me?"

You Can Check Cookies

Even if the history list and cache have been deleted, you might be able to find out what Web sites are being visited on a computer. Many Web sites put little pieces of data, called *cookies*, on a computer that visits it. You can use special software, such as one called Cookie Pal, to see what sites have put cookies on the computer. You can get Cookie Pal and similar software on download sites on the Internet, such as ZDNet's Software Library at www.hotfiles.com. For more information about cookies, turn to Chapter 13, "No, They're Not Oreos: What You Can Do About Cookies."

A Collective Mission

Vice President Al Gore and 15 companies, including America Online, Yahoo!, and Lycos, announced their mission to keep pornography, hatred, violence, and evil at bay. For starters, the online companies will offer links to tools and guides for parents to use to monitor and filter Internet use.

Use Site-Blocking Software

The final way to make sure your kids are visiting safe sites is to install and use site-blocking software. This is software you install on your PC that blocks your kids from visiting sites that aren't appropriate for them. However, this technology isn't perfect, and it can restrict visits to other sites, too. For details on how to use this software and how it works, check out the section later in this chapter.

Should They Talk? What to Watch for in Chat

For many kids, chat is the whole reason to go online. Teens, in particular, are hooked on chat—as the parent of a teen, some days I think they all live in a parallel universe, hooked together by chat rooms and telephones. (In fact, my daughter frequently talks on the phone at the same time that she chats in chat rooms—often to the same people simultaneously!)

The main danger that kids face in chat rooms is that they might be targeted by adults. In the worst cases, children have been sexually abused by adults they met online and initially thought were kids. This is rare, but it can still happen if your kids aren't cybersavvy when they chat. Kids can also come across inappropriate language and discussions.

General Advice for Keeping Kids Safe When They Chat

There are some general rules you can follow the make sure your kids stay safe when they chat. To keep your kids safe when they chat, have them follow this advice (also check out Chapter 16, "How to Keep Safe and Protect Your Privacy When Chatting," and Chapter 21, "Keeping Kids Safe on America Online," for more advice):

➤ **Recognize that people might not be who they say they are.** The person saying she's a 14-year-old girl might, in fact, be a 45-year-old man.

➤ **Never give out personal information about yourself in chat rooms.** Real names, addresses, and telephone numbers are no-nos, along with any other information that can be used to identify your child.

➤ **Never agree to meet someone in real life that you've met online unless you've gotten permission from a parent.** Even then, the parent should be present at the meeting. Furthermore, the meeting should be in a public place and should not be near your home.

Site-Blocking Software Can Block Chat

There's a way that you can block your kids from chatting at all—use site-blocking software. Some site-blocking software blocks your kids from chatting at all. I don't recommend doing that, because chat seems to be such a vital part of kids' lives; but if you want to block it, technology allows it. For more information on site-blocking software, see the section later in this chapter.

➤ **If you're in a chat area and the talk makes you feel uncomfortable, leave and tell your parents about it.** If you have an uncomfortable feeling, it's for a good reason, so listen to your instincts.

➤ **If anyone exhibits abusive behavior, tell your parents about it.** Your parent should then report the behavior to the online service or Web site where the chat is taking place or to their Internet service provider.

What You and Your Kids Should Know About the Different Kinds of Chat

There are many different ways to chat online. Some are safer for kids than others. Here's the rundown of the different ways and what you should know about each to keep your kids safe.

➤ **Chats on America Online.** AOL's the place where most kids want to hang out and chat. From my point of view, it's the best place for them to chat as well. That's because many of the chat areas are moderated, which means that there's an adult present, watching to make sure that the chat stays safe. The moderated areas are in the Kids Only area (keyword Kids Only) of America Online. You can also control the way that your kids can chat on America Online. Turn to Chapter 21 for details.

➤ **Web-based chats.** Many Web sites have chat areas where hundreds or thousands of people chat. These may or may not be suitable for your children, depending on the site. Spend time in a chat room there to see what they're like. The best advice is to try to find moderated chats for kids and guide your kids there. The best place to find these sites is at the www.yahooligans.com kid site.

➤ **Internet Relay Chat (IRC).** This is the oldest form of chat on the Internet. From my point of view, it's not at all appropriate for children. Most IRC areas that I've seen aren't suitable for kids, and there are a variety of security holes in IRC that can easily be exploited. I'm very free with what I let my kids do online, but I don't let them chat in IRC. For more information about IRC, turn to Chapter 16.

➤ **ICQ (pronounced "I Seek You").** This is a special piece of chatting software that's become extremely popular on the Net in recent years. There's no kind of security filters to speak of, so I don't think it's great software for kids to use. On the other hand, they probably won't want to use it—it's aimed at adults and I haven't seen many kids hanging out with it.

Have Your Kids Try Out Freezone's Chatbox at http://chat.freezone.com/

It's a chat area for kids that's busy and lively, but is moderated so that it's safe as well.

➤ **Private chat rooms.** America Online and some Web sites allow for the creation of private chat rooms—chat areas not open to public view. Tell your kids never to go to a private chat room unless it's been created by them or a friend and they know everyone in the room.

➤ **Instant Messages and pagers.** This kind of software lets kids communicate one-on-one with others. It's built in to America Online and is fine for use there. When used by kids on the Internet, I'd be leery.

Teach Your Kids How to Use Bozo Filters

Often, chat software has a feature that allows you to ignore certain people in a chat room. For obvious reasons, this feature is often called a Bozo filter. Teach your kids how to use it so that they can block out people who might be bothering them.

How About Kids and Email?

Oh, yeah, kids like to communicate in other ways than chat online. They also like to send and receive email. Lots of it. Lots and lots and *lots* of it.

Email is great for kids, but kids should also be careful how they use it. They could get inappropriate messages, pictures, and files sent via email; they could be harassed or stalked via email; and they could pick up viruses from email. Here's how to make sure that they stay safe:

➤ **Your kids should never open file attachments from people they don't know.** File attachments can be anything—a nice picture of a pet cat, pornography, or a file containing a computer virus. So they should never open file attachments from strangers—they should delete them instead.

➤ **If your kids are made uncomfortable by a message, they should tell you about it and show you the message.** You should then contact your Internet service provider and ask them to track down the sender and take action.

➤ **You should set up email filters to filter out junk email, adult email, and email from anyone who might be harassing your kids.** Pretty much all email software lets you set these filters. America Online lets you set filters as well. Pictured here is how to set them using Microsoft Outlook. For more information on how to set email filters, turn to Chapter 10, "What Is Spam and How Can You Protect Yourself from It?" and Chapter 21, "Keeping Kids Safe on America Online."

How I Handled Someone Who Was Harassing My Daughter Via Email

One day when my daughter was 12 years old she came to me, upset, because someone had been sending her messages—dozens and dozens of them, all from the same person, all the same message, and sent one after another. Although the message didn't directly threaten her, it did call her names and was harassing in nature. The first thing I did was use America Online's email filter to block all mail from that address from getting to her again, which immediately halted the problem. Then I checked through the email itself to make sure that the true email address wasn't being hidden—and it wasn't. The mail came from the Microsoft Network, and so I sent the mail to the proper people on the Microsoft Network. My daughter hasn't heard from the harasser again.

Here's how you can set filters to keep your kids from seeing junk mail and mail with adult content in Microsoft Outlook.

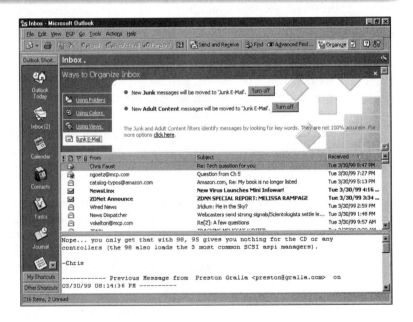

Should Your Kids View Newsgroups?

Newsgroups are Internet discussion areas in which anyone can participate. They're wide-ranging discussions about anything under the sun, moon, and stars—and judging from the oddballs you sometimes come across in them, from well beyond space as well.

There are a number of dangers for kids on newsgroups. A major issue is that many newsgroups—even those not connected with adult topics—can contain pornographic pictures and videos that can be downloaded and viewed. Another issue is that many newsgroups use language that I'd rate well beyond PG-13.

So what to do? If your kids are on America Online, there are a number of useful filters you can use to limit your kids' use of newsgroups—for example, to not allow them to visit newsgroups that have pictures in them. You can also buy site-blocking software (explained later in this chapter) that doesn't allow them to visit certain newsgroups. Finally, you can simply not allow them to visit newsgroups at all. I recommend limiting their use of newsgroups in some way, though.

How About Site-Blocking Software?

If you're looking for an all-in-one solution to keeping your kids safe on the Internet, you should look into site-blocking software such as NetNanny, CyberPatrol, CyberSitter, and SurfWatch. This software all works in a similar way. It limits your kids' use of the Internet. You can block them from using certain parts of the Internet entirely, such as newsgroups. Or you can limit their use of certain parts of the Internet, such as only allowing them to visit certain Web sites. Often, you'll get to mix and match the controls so that you can customize your kids' use of the Internet.

Before using this kind of software, there are a few things to keep in mind. Not all parents want to use this kind of software, for a number of reasons that I outline below. I've never used it for my kids, for example, but I know a lot of parents who have used it and feel it's useful. Before using site-blocking software, here are two things to think about:

➤ **Site-blocking software might block useful sites as well as inappropriate sites.** One thing to realize about site-blocking software is that it might block useful sites as well as inappropriate ones. For example, it might block sites concerned with breast cancer, because the word breast is found on the site. And it might block out sites that provide information as AIDS and other important topics as well.

➤ **Will it affect the sense of trust you have with your kids?** Putting site-blocking software on your kids' computer might say to them that you don't trust them. And the ultimate way to keep your kids safe online is if they trust you enough to ask for help and advice. Think first about whether putting site-blocking software on your computer affects that sense of trust.

Where to Get Site-Blocking Software

If you've decided that you're interested in trying out site-blocking software, you'll see that it's easy to find. Better yet, most site-blocking software lets you try-before-you-buy. You can often download them from the Internet, try them out, and if you like them, pay for them and keep using them. If not, simply stop using them and don't pay. There's a lot of site-blocking software available, but here's what I think are the best, along with their Web sites, where you can get more information, download them, and try them out:

➤ **SurfWatch**   Get it at www.surfwatch.com.

➤ **CyberPatrol**   Get it at www.cyberpatrol.com.

➤ **NetNanny**   Get it at www.netnanny.com.

➤ **CyberSitter**   Get it at www.cybersitter.com.

I think by now you're starting to see a pattern emerge.

Award-Winning Safe and Fun Sites for Kids

There are thousands of safe sites online for kids—and thousands of sites where they can have fun and learn. How to get to them all? As I recommended earlier in the chapter, have your kids start off at Yahooligans! at www.yahooligans.com, the best guide for kids to kid-friendly sites on the Internet.

If you want your kids to learn more about online safety, head them to the SafeTeens site at www.safeteens.com and the SafeKids site at www.safekids.com. In addition to teaching your kids about online safety, the sites also lead them to helpful sites.

And Cyberangels, an "Internet neighborhood watch group" that looks to keep kids safe online, has given out awards for sites that are safe, fun, and follow excellent privacy practices. The Cyberangels site can be found at www.cyberangels.org and is an offshoot of the well-known Guardian Angels anti-crime group. Here are their award-winning sites.

FreeZone

www.freezone.com

This great site, pictured here, lets kids play games, chat with other kids in closely monitored chat rooms, send postcards, make friends, create their own home pages, learn, and have fun, all while staying safe. What's not to like?

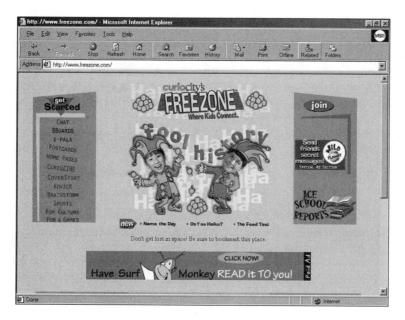

FreeZone: A place for kids to have fun, while staying safe.

Sports Illustrated for Kids

www.sikids.com

If you have kids who love sports, you'll have kids who love this site. There's articles, pictures, jokes, quizzes, and trivia contests. Kids can join in fantasy sports leagues. And they do it in a safe place with their privacy respected.

Nickelodeon

www.nickelodeon.com

You have kids, you know Nickelodeon. Shows like *Rug Rats, Animorphs, Alex Mack, Shelby Woo,* and many others—they're all here online as well as being on TV. There are games, quizzes, downloads, contests, and a very good safety guide.

Bonus.com

www.bonus.com

Definition of a kid: a game-playing machine. Games, games, and more games. That's what your kids find here. Yes, there are also educational articles and opinion polls. But the whole point of this site is to play games. Unique about this site is that it, in essence, creates its own safe surfing area when your kids visit, so it's very secure.

The Least You Need to Know

➤ More important than technology is to make sure that your kids trust you and seek your guidance when they go online, so have a heart-to-heart talk with them about their use of the Net.

➤ Yahooligans! at www.yahooligans.com is a good place for kids to go when looking for kid-friendly sites.

➤ It's best if your kids participate in moderated chats rather than freewheeling ones.

➤ Kids should never give out personal information about themselves in chat rooms or agree to meet in the real world friends they've made in chat unless you're present and it's a public place.

➤ Site-blocking software can keep your kids from visiting unsafe sites, but it can block them from useful sites as well. Think hard before deciding whether to use it.

Chapter 21

Keeping Kids Safe on America Online

America Online is a kid's paradise. It has everything kids want: zillions of other kids chatting at all hours of the day and night, cool areas to visit, easy email, and instant access to the Internet. What else could they want? (Well, that is, aside from a bigger allowance, a later bedtime, a faster computer, a new video game system, and more ice cream.)

But it also has something that you don't want: potential dangers. Because so many kids hang out there, because it's so easy to chat and send email, and because it's so easy for people to disguise their identities, America Online poses dangers to kids. This chapter clues you in on what you need to know about the dangers—and more importantly, shows you how to make sure that your kids stay safe there.

What Kinds of Dangers Are There on America Online?

America Online is generally a safe place for kids. It has grown so big, mainly due to its use by so many families. Still, there are potential dangers there. Here's the rundown of what you need to be worried about:

➤ **Your kids could be targeted in chat areas.** Kids love to chat...and chat...and chat... Adults can hang out in chat areas, disguising their identities and looking for vulnerable kids to target.

Check This Out

Some Chat Areas Are Monitored on America Online

On America Online, some chat areas are monitored by adults, who are careful to make sure that no bad language is used and that no kids are targeted. The chat areas that are monitored are found in the Kids Only area of the service—keyword Kids Only.

➤ **Your kids can be targeted or harassed via email.** In the same way that adults can disguise themselves when they chat, they can do the same via email. And they can send harassing messages.

➤ **Your kids can be sent inappropriate material via email.** It's easy on America Online to send and receive pictures. Adults—or even other kids—could send your children pornography or other inappropriate material. Often, a picture's filename can be misleading or obscure, so you don't know what you're looking at until it's too late. Your kids can also be sent junk email asking them to visit pornographic or other inappropriate sites.

➤ **Your kids can have their passwords stolen.** A common ruse on America Online is for a hacker to send someone an email or Instant Message claiming they're employees of America Online, asking for passwords. These messages are invariably false; no legitimate employee ever asks for your password.

➤ **Your kids can visit Internet sites and areas that are inappropriate.** America Online makes it easy for kids to use the Internet—which means they might come across areas that you consider inappropriate, such as pornographic or hate sites.

➤ **Your kids can have their privacy invaded.** It's easy for people to gather personal information about kids on America Online, so your kids might have their privacy invaded.

Computer Viruses Can Be Spread Via America Online Email

Just as computer viruses can be spread using other kinds of email, they can also be spread on America Online. If your kid opens up a file attachment and that attachment has a virus in it, the virus is spread to his computer. Tell your kids never to open up file attachments from strangers. And they should always virus-check attachments sent from people they know. For information on virus-checking software, turn to Chapter 26, "How to Keep Your Computer Safe from Viruses."

Luckily, there's good news here because America Online gives you a whole host of tools that you can use to make sure your kids stay safe online. Read on to see what they are and how to use them.

Taking Control with Parental Controls

To keep your kids safe on America Online, you can use the service called Parental Controls. From this one area on America Online, you can decide how your kids can use the service. For example, you can block them from viewing Web sites that might be inappropriate for them or limit the way they can use chat or email. And for once in your life, you actually *are* in charge of what your kids can and can't do, because you're the boss—using America Online's software, you get to set the rules. (Coming from a parent of two kids, I know just how much of a novel idea *this* is for parents, especially of adolescents, and computer users to boot.)

To get to the Parental Control area of America Online, use the keyword Parental Controls. (Uh, oh! A keyword that makes sense. What's wrong here?)

Before you do anything, you need to create a separate screen name for each of your children. A screen name is the name that each kid uses to get onto America Online. It gives them each a separate account, including a separate email address, and enables you to set different levels of control for each.

Never Share Your Screen Names with Your Children

You might not want to go to the trouble of creating separate screen names for your children, but it's something that's well worth doing. It's the only way you can decide what your kids can and can't see and do on America Online—and if you don't create separate screen names for them, they have access to your email, something you certainly don't want. And, you get their email, which means endless chain letters, jokes of the day, and general goofiness.

To create a screen name from the Parental Control area, click **Set Parental Controls Now**. Then, just follow the directions. As you'll see, it's pretty simple to do.

You can set different parental controls for each screen name. So if you have a 5-year-old girl and a 14-year-old boy, you can give the 14-year-old boy more freedom on what to do online than you do the 5-year-old girl. (On second thought, considering what 14-year-old boys are like, maybe you want to let your 5-year-old have more freedom.)

When you set parental controls, you block kids from going to certain parts of the Internet and America Online, and you restrict their access to certain services like chat and downloading software that could lead to problems. Internet sites are blocked by special site-blocking software built into America Online that's much like the site-blocking software people buy to block kids from visiting certain Internet sites. On America Online, because the software is built into the service, it's free.

Setting Basic Parental Controls

You have two choices when you use Parental Controls: You can use a set of built-in controls, or you can mix and match and create customized controls based on what you want each of your kids to be able to do online. It's much simpler to use the built-in ones, but they're less flexible.

To use the built-in ones, click **Set Parental Controls Now**. You come to a screen like the one pictured nearby that lists all of the screen names in your account and lets you set the Parental Controls for each one.

Parental Controls					
Set Parental Controls	The screen names you have created are listed below. For each screen name, pick a category by clicking on the appropriate circle. Then click "Go to Custom Controls" to fine-tune your settings. Categories cannot be changed for Master Screen Names. All Master Screen Names have 18+ level access.				
18+ Allows unrestricted access to AOL and Internet features.		**Parental Control Categories**			
Mature Teen (ages 16-17) Blocks access to Web sites which may be inappropriate.		18+	Mature Teen	Young Teen	Kids Only
Young Teen (13-15) Blocks access to areas of AOL and the Web which may be inappropriate for young teens.	* PGralla	⦿			
	CoolLizard	○	⦿	○	○
	LRGralla	○	○	○	⦿
Kids Only (12 & under) Restricts access to the Kids Only channel and limits chat and other features.	GIGriffey9	○	○	⦿	○
	TinkrBel5v	○	⦿	○	○
	* Master Screen Name				
	Go to Custom Controls			OK	Cancel

For once, you're in control: Here's how you can set basic parental controls on America Online.

For each screen name, click the controls you want to set. You get a choice of Kids Only, Young Teen, and Mature Teen. America Online recommends that Kids Only be set for kids 12 and under, Young Teen be set for kids 13 through 15, and Mature Teen be set for kids 16 to 17.

It's not immediately apparent what these controls actually do—you get only a very brief description, as you can see from the picture. The description is a little bit of help, but not a whole lot. Here's the rundown on exactly what each of them do:

➤ **Kids Only**   Lets kids visit only one area of America Online: the Kids Only channel. It only lets them visit Web sites that are selected for age-appropriate content for kids up to 12 years old). Everything else is blocked. It doesn't allow them to send or receive Instant Messages. They cannot join member-created or private chat rooms—although they can visit public chat rooms in the Kids Only area. They can't send or receive file attachments or pictures in their email. They are blocked from Internet newsgroups that allow file attachments. That's because objectionable pictures and other material can sometimes be found in newsgroups that allow file attachments, regardless of the newsgroup's subject.

Techno Talk

What's a Newsgroup File Attachment?

Newsgroups aren't used only for public discussions. They're also used to trade and download pictures and other file attachments. Newsgroup reading software lets you download and view file attachments to messages in newsgroups. There are many newsgroups that are used to post pornography, which is why it's a good idea to block kids from those newsgroups.

Unfortunately, even newsgroups having nothing to do with pornography aren't always safe. Because it's just as easy to send a message to one hundred newsgroups as one, people often post pornographic pictures to every newsgroup they can think of.

➤ **Young Teen**   Lets teens visit some chat rooms—but they can't visit member-created chat rooms or private chat rooms. They can only visit Web sites that have been judged appropriate for kids under 15. They're also blocked from Internet newsgroups that allow file attachments.

➤ **Mature Teen**   Restricts teens' access to certain Web sites—they can only visit sites that have been judged appropriate for kids under 17. They're also blocked from Internet newsgroups that allow file attachments.

Parental Controls Also Block Access to Premium Services

Parts of America Online charge money in addition to your normal monthly fee. For example, some online gaming areas charge a per-hour fee. Parental Controls blocks access to these Premium Services—a good idea, if you're worried about the state of your pocketbook.

Have It Your Way: Customizing Parental Controls

Maybe you trust your kids to visit only appropriate Web sites, but you're worried about their use of chat or email. Or maybe you're not worried about chat, but don't want them to visit certain newsgroups. In that case, you're in luck, because America Online offers a Chinese menu (or is that a Swedish smorgasbord?) of choices. You can mix and match controls any way you'd like.

To do that, from the Parental Control area, click **Fine tune with Custom Controls**. You can customize how your kids can use chat, Instant Messages, email, the Web, newsgroups, and download files. For example, you can allow them full access to Instant Messages, but restrict their use of newsgroups.

To set controls for any of these services, just click the control and then click the button at the bottom of the screen—for example, click **Chat Controls** to set controls for chat. When you do that, you see a screen like the one pictured nearby. You can set controls for each screen name just by clicking on the control you want to set.

	Block Public Rooms	Block Member Rooms	Block Conference Rooms	Block Hyperlinks in Chat
Parental Control Chat				
Block Public Rooms				
Blocks access to all chat rooms on AOL.				
Block Member Rooms The screen names you have created are listed below. To restrict or block a screen name from using a feature, click on the appropriate box.				
Blocks access to chat rooms created by other members on AOL.				
Block Conference Rooms				
Blocks access to the larger chat rooms throughout AOL.				
Block Hyperlinks in Chat				
Disables the use of hyperlinks in all chat rooms.				

The screen names you have created are listed below. To restrict or block a screen name from using a feature, click on the appropriate box.

Screen Name	Block Public Rooms	Block Member Rooms	Block Conference Rooms	Block Hyperlinks In Chat
* PGralla	☐	☐	☐	☐
CoolLizard	☑	☐	☐	☑
LRGralla	☐	☑	☐	☑
GlGriffey9	☐	☐	☑	☑
TinkrBel5v	☐	☑	☐	☑

* Master screen name

Previous OK Cancel Next

Pick one from each appropriate box: How to customize Parental Controls on America Online.

What do all these choices mean? Here's the rundown on each:

➤ **Chat**   You get several ways to block different parts of chat. You can block chat hyperlinks—that way, if someone sends your kid a link to a Web site, inappropriate or not, he cannot click the link and go there. You can also block kids' access to chats in the People Connection, which is aimed at an older audience than kids. You also can block access to member-created chat rooms in the People Connection and to access to conference rooms—large chat rooms on America Online. You get to choose which of these to block and which to let them use.

Check This Out

You Have to Close America Online Software for Parental Controls to Take Effect

When you set Parental Controls, they don't go into immediate effect. You have to first sign off the service and then close down the America Online software. Until you do both those things, they don't go into effect. So, if one of your children uses America Online after you've set the controls, but you didn't close down the America Online software, the controls aren't in effect and won't be until the software is closed down and then started up again.

➤ **Instant Messages**   Instant Messages are private, live, one-on-one conversations. You can choose to block your kids from using Instant Messages.

➤ **Downloading**   Worried that your kids might download inappropriate pictures, programs, or a file with a computer virus in it? You can block their ability to download files. You can block them from downloading files directly on America Online or via an Internet service called FTP, a very popular way to download files.

➤ **The Web**   If you're worried that your kids are viewing inappropriate sites on the Web, here's where to go. You can limit them to sites appropriate for kids 12 and under, or ages up to 16, or ages up to 17.

➤ **Mail**   This one's no Chinese menu—it's a veritable banquet! You have an incredible amount of control over how your kids can send and receive mail. You can block your kids from exchanging email with anyone. You can also allow them to get email only from America Online members or only from specific Internet email addresses. And you can block them from getting email from specific America Online members and addresses. You can also block them from getting pictures or attachments in any email messages.

➤ **Newsgroups**   As with mail, you have a whole lot of control over how your kids access newsgroups. You can block all access to any newsgroups. You can instead block their access to specific newsgroups. Alternately, you can only allow them to go to certain newsgroups. You can even block your kids' access to newsgroups that contain specific words in their description. And you can block them from getting any of the graphics, sounds, animations, and photographs found on newsgroups by not allowing them to download files from newsgroups.

What Can You Do If You Find That America Online Didn't Block Your Kids from Visiting an Inappropriate Site?

The software that America Online uses isn't perfect—it can't know about every single site on the Internet that might not be good for your kids to visit. If you come across a site that you think should be blocked, go to the Parental Controls area, click **Fine tune with Custom Controls**, **Web**, and then **Report a Site**. You fill out a form that lets you put the site location in as well as a description of the site and why it should be blocked. You can also ask that a certain site *not* be blocked —for example, a site about breast cancer that the software might have inadvertently blocked. In both cases, your request goes to the company that does the site blocking, and they make the final determination about what should be blocked and what shouldn't.

Kids Safety Tips on America Online

Technology can help keep your kids safe on America Online—but technology can go only so far. Better than technology is to teach your kids how to stay safe.

America Online has put together a good set of simple safety tips. Here they are. Give it to your kids and have them read it and follow it:

1. Don't give your AOL password to anyone, even your best friend.
2. Never tell someone your home address, telephone number, or school name without your parent's permission first.
3. If someone says something that makes you feel unsafe or funny, don't respond. Take charge—keyword: Kid Help.
4. Never say you'll meet someone in person without asking your parent's permission first, and your parent should accompany you to the first meeting, which should be in public.
5. Always tell a parent about any threatening or bad language you see online.
6. Don't accept things from strangers (for example, email, files, or Web page addresses).

Have Your Kids—and You—Take a Safety Test

How much do you and your kids really know about online safety? Find out in a special America Online area. Head to the Safe Surfin' Challenge area at keyword Safe Surfin, and you find a site full of safety information, tips, and quizzes to make learning about online safety fun. This is one online game that is safe to have your kids play.

Some Final Words to Parents

Remember, the best way to keep your kids safe anywhere online, including America Online, is to be a good parent and follow safety tips. For more information on general safety tips, see Chapter 19, "Best Rules for Keeping Kids Safe and Protecting Their Privacy," and Chapter 20, "How to Keep Your Kids Safe on the Internet."

To protect your kids' privacy, make sure that they don't create an America Online member profile or, if they do, that they don't give out any personal information in it. To do that, have them use the keyword Profile and click **Create** or **Modify My Profile**. Check the profile they create so that you can be sure that they're not giving out personal information.

And for an excellent central place to go for advice of all kinds on safety on America Online, use the keyword Safety and head to the Neighborhood Watch area.

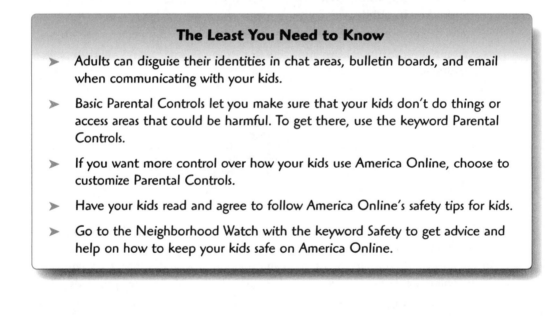

The Least You Need to Know

➤ Adults can disguise their identities in chat areas, bulletin boards, and email when communicating with your kids.

➤ Basic Parental Controls let you make sure that your kids don't do things or access areas that could be harmful. To get there, use the keyword Parental Controls.

➤ If you want more control over how your kids use America Online, choose to customize Parental Controls.

➤ Have your kids read and agree to follow America Online's safety tips for kids.

➤ Go to the Neighborhood Watch with the keyword Safety to get advice and help on how to keep your kids safe on America Online.

Part 7

Let's Go CyberShopping: How to Buy Online Safely

Take out your credit card and let's go! There are bargains to be had! The Internet is a shopper's paradise. It's convenient, you'll find amazing deals and free offers, and just about anything available for sale anywhere in the world, you'll find online. (Roast suckling pig for 20 bucks? No problem.)

But before you take out that piece of plastic and start sending it over the wires, there are precautions you ought to be taking. This part shows you how to be safe when buying online. You'll find out how to protect your credit card, how to make sure sites you buy from are legitimate and won't invade your privacy, and how to avoid common Internet shopping scams. You'll also get directed to consumer and anti-fraud sites to make you a smarter online consumer.

And you'll also learn how to get amazing deals at auction sites, without worrying that anyone will take your money and run.

So whether you live to shop, or shop to live (huh? run that by me again), this part will teach you how to be safe and secure when you shop.

Chapter 22

Show Me the Money! How Do You Buy Online—And What Dangers Are There?

In This Chapter

➤ How to shop online

➤ What you need to know about shopping before going online

➤ What you need to know about shopping carts and one-click shopping

➤ Best tips for protecting yourself when you shop online

➤ How to make sure you don't get burned when buying stocks on the Internet

I hate malls. I hate stores. I hate everything to do with having to trudge to some god-forsaken place in the middle of a huge parking lot, plunk down my filthy lucre, and trudge back home with what I've bought. I've got better things to do with my life. Like collecting fingernail clippings.

But I love to buy things online. It's simple, it's easy, I can do it in my pajamas at home, and I can get great deals on things. I've bought everything from computers to scanners to software, CDs, and more.

And I'm not alone. Millions of people spend billions of dollars a year shopping online. They're shopping online for its convenience; because you can get great deals; and yes, because it's even fun. (I never thought I would ever include the words shopping and fun in the same sentence. Live long enough, I guess, and *anything* can happen.)

But you don't want to head willy-nilly into shopping online without taking note of the dangers, and without making sure that someone doesn't abscond with your credit card or scam you out of your life savings. So read on to see how to stay safe when you shop online.

How Do You Shop Till You Drop in Cyberspace?

Shopping online is about as easy as things get. Just point your browser at a shopping site, click around until you find what you want, and pay—always with your credit card, as I explain later in this chapter.

You usually pay for shipping charges, and then whatever you've bought is delivered to you via mail or a delivery service within a few days of buying it.

The Complete Idiot's Guide to Online Shopping Gives You the Complete Rundown on How to Shop Online

Pitch alert! If you want to know everything there is to know about shopping online, get *The Complete Idiot's Guide to Online Shopping*, written by yours truly. Whether you're looking for great deals, free stuff, advice, or great sites, you can find it all there. I promise. Believe me.

You can find a lot of different kinds of buying sites online. Here's the rundown on the major kinds:

➤ You can buy directly from the manufacturer of a product, such as from computer maker Dell at www.dell.com.

➤ You can buy from the online version of a retail store or mail-order outlet, such as The Gap at www.gap.com.

➤ You can buy from a store that specializes in a specific product and that exists only in cyberspace, such as the online toy store eToys at www.etoys.com.

➤ You can buy from an online mall that sells hundreds of different kinds of products, much like a real-life mall, such as at the Internet Mall at www.shopnow.com. (The good news here is that you don't have to visit the food court. Virtual food is never very tasty, anyway.)

➤ You can buy from online auctions such as at www.ebay.com. These work much like real-life auctions, except that you bid online. Turn to Chapter 24, "How to Stay Safe When Buying at Auctions," for more information on how to buy at auction sites.

Be Careful When Buying at Auctions

The biggest scams on the Internet, according to the anti-fraud group the National Fraud Information Center at www.fraud.org, are done at auctions—scams such as not delivering the goods after they've been paid for. So you have to take extra care when buying or selling at auctions. That's why there's a whole chapter about it in this book, Chapter 24. And for more information, you can turn to *The Complete Idiot's Guide to Online Auctions*, by Michael Miller.

➤ You can buy stocks and financial services from investment sites, such as eTrade at www.etrade.com. Be careful when buying stocks online—there's a lot of fraud out there. Turn to the section later in this chapter to see how to stay safe.

So How Exactly Do I Buy Online?

After you visit a site and find what you want to buy, you go to a special secure area of the site and pay using your credit card. You fill out a form asking for your name, address, credit card information, and sometimes more information. Click again (yes, there's usually a lot of clicking when you buy online, but it's better than waiting in lines) and you get some kind of verification about what you've bought. Some sites also send you email verifying your order.

That's it. Now sit back and wait for the goodies to arrive.

To make shopping easier for you, most sites let you establish a standing account. (After all, the easier it is for you to shop, the more money they take in.) So when you want to shop again, you don't have to type in your name, credit card information, and other things—that is already on record. In fact, some sites require that you establish an account before shopping there. Often, for you to access your account, you need to type in a username and password, or possibly just a password. Sometimes, the site creates the username and password for you, but more often than not, you get to create both.

When Selecting Your Password for a Shopping Site, Make Sure It's One That Can't Be Guessed

If you have a shopping account, you don't want anyone breaking into it by using your password. So, make sure that when you choose a password, it's not a common one that can be easily guessed. In general, hackers get people's passwords by using their computer to try many common passwords, to see if they can break into an account. A recent survey found that the most common password is—yes, you guessed it—*password*. For more information on how to create hacker-proof passwords, turn to Chapter 4, "How to Create Hacker-Proof Passwords."

Many sites let you use virtual shopping carts—a place where you put things you're thinking of buying. You can stack your shopping cart high with items you want and then proceed to a virtual checkout where you fork over the moolah. It works like a real-life shopping cart, except that the wheels don't rattle. As you go through a site, you click items, putting them into the cart. At some point, your cart fills up with whatever you want to buy. Then you fill out a form with your credit card, unless the site already has your account information, and you buy. Pictured here is a shopping cart at the popular toy site eToys at www.etoys.com.

Get ready to buy! A virtual shopping cart at www.etoys.com.

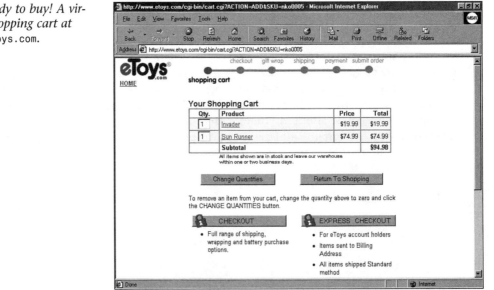

Many sites also offer Express Shopping or one-click shopping in which you don't need to fill out a form or put anything in a shopping cart. Just click that you want to buy and bingo!—it's charged to your credit card, and it's winging its way to you.

What Dangers There Are in Online Shopping— And How to Protect Yourself

There are all kinds of dangers you might face when you shop online. Your credit card might be stolen, or someone might take your money and run. You could be the victim of a scam, or your privacy might be invaded. But yes, you guessed it: Help is on the way. Follow my advice and you should never go wrong:

➤ **Always pay with your credit card.** When you pay with a credit card, you're given a great deal of consumer protection—and your credit card company stands behind you. If you've been subject to a scam, at most, you'll be out $50; and the truth is, if you push your card company hard enough, you won't even have to pay that.

➤ **Know the site you're buying from.** You want to make sure that it's a creditable site that won't take your money and head to Bermuda. So check out a site before buying. Turn to Chapter 23, "How to Protect Your Credit Card and Buy at a Secure Site," for information on how to check out a site.

Check This Out

Never Give Out Your Social Security Number to a Shopping Site

If someone has your Social Security number, he can do almost anything—steal your identity, get into your bank account, and more. Never give out your Social Security number when filling out a shopping form. There's no reason any site should ever ask you for it.

➤ **Only shop at secure sites.** When you send your credit card information, you want to make sure that it's scrambled so hackers can't look at it in transit. For how to know you're shopping at a secure site, turn to Chapter 23.

➤ **Always print out your order form and keep a copy of it.** If you don't have evidence of what you've bought, what you've agreed to pay, and when you did the buying, it is tough to prove that you've been ripped off. Print out all order forms and keep them in a safe place.

➤ **If other people can gain easy access to your computer, be leery of signing up for one-click shopping.** When you sign up for one-click shopping, when you click to buy something, you don't go to a checkout area or a virtual shopping cart. Instead, your credit card is charged, and the goods are shipped to you. If other people can gain access to your computer—such as at work or if your kids use your computer—be leery of setting up any one-click shopping accounts. They can charge things to your credit card just by surfing to a site and clicking.

What's an Ewallet?

In the not-so-distant future, expect that you'll be shopping with an ewallet—an electronic wallet on your computer that has information about you such as your credit card. Then, when you visit a shopping site, you don't need to input any information—the site can get it from your ewallet when you tell it to. But if others can get easy access to your computer, be careful about using an ewallet, because others would be able to charge things to your account.

➤ **Check out hidden costs before buying.** Remember, there are shipping and handling costs when you buy, so make sure that you know the true cost of a product before turning over your plastic. And, depending on where you live, you might have to pay sales taxes at some sites. Look around a site to see where these costs are spelled out—often in the Help or FAQ areas. If you can't find information about the costs, buy at another site.

➤ **Know what the return policies and warranties are.** How long do you have to return something you buy? If the goods arrive damaged and you have to return them, who pays shipping costs? Who covers the warranty—the manufacturer of the goods or the site you buy from? Know all this information before buying.

➤ **Watch out for Internet scams.** There are all kinds of buying scams you'll run into on the Internet—get-rich-quick schemes (although only the scammer ends up getting rich), stock fraud, and more. To protect yourself against them, turn to Chapter 6, "How to Protect Yourself Against the Most Common Internet Scams."

➤ **If you've been scammed, you can fight back.** In Massachusetts, where I live, where politics is a contact sport, there's a saying: Don't get mad, get even. If you've been scammed, you can still fight back. Turn to Chapter 6 to see how.

Never Buy at a Site That Charges a Restocking Fee

When you buy computer products at some sites, you might notice in small type something called a restocking fee. That means that if you decide to return something you buy there, you are charged a fee. This restocking fee can be shockingly high, sometimes as high as 25 percent—for example, if you return a $2,000 computer, you might have to pay $500 merely to return it. Never pay restocking fees, and look closely at any sites that sell hardware to make sure they don't charge one.

Taking Stock: How to Make Sure You Don't Get Burned When Buying Stock Online

With the stock market skyrocketing to amazing heights, it's hard not to get caught up in stock fever. Everyone wants to make a fast killing.

Unfortunately, a lot of the people making quick killings on stocks these days are scamsters of all kinds, who prey on our desire to get an inside deal. Online stock scams and schemes have become so frequent that they're now one of the top scams on the Internet. The Security and Exchange Commission (SEC) has targeted the problem, recently rounding up and charging nearly four dozen people in a national anti-stock-scam sweep. But there are many others waiting in the wings to take the scamsters' places.

However, forearmed is forewarned. With the right information, you can make sure that you don't get scammed when buying stocks online. Here's what you need to know:

➤ **Watch out for pump and dump schemes.** It's one of the oldest stock scams in the book—an individual or a group of people claim they're disinterested parties giving out advice about a previously unknown stock that's about to go through the roof. You buy the stock at a high price, it instead heads for the cellar, and you're out a lot of money. The disinterested parties were, in fact, the stock owners trying to get the price on their stock bid up so they could sell at a high price and get out. On the Internet, people sometimes send out free newsletters touting great stock deals, not telling you that they're the owners of the stock. Unsolicited email and messages in bulletin boards can tout stock as well. The general rule: Don't believe anything anyone says online about stocks unless you know for an absolute fact that you can trust them.

How Much Stock Fraud Is There Online?

No one really knows how much money is wasted on online stock fraud. But consider this: Marc Beauchamp of the North American Securities Administrators Association (www.nasaa.org) believes that "investors are losing about $1 million an hour from stock fraud," a fairly astounding number.

➤ **Check out the SEC Web site for advice on how to avoid scams and be a savvier online investor.** The SEC Web site at www.sec.gov, pictured here, is a great source of information on how to avoid scams. Check it out regularly to make sure you don't get burned.

Great advice from the Feds: Check out the SEC Web site at www.sec.gov *for advice on avoiding online stock scams.*

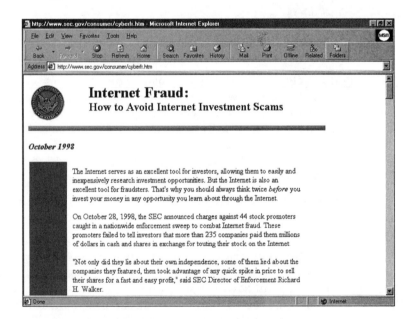

➤ **Watch out for people who don't use their real names online.** People online often use handles, or aliases, instead of their real names. Only deal with someone who gives you his real name, address, phone number, and other contact information.

➤ **If anyone offers a guarantee on a high rate of return, run the other way.** All investment entails risk, and the higher the rate of return, the greater the potential risk. The SEC warns that language such as "guarantee," "high return," "limited offer," or "as safe as a C.D." might be a sign of a scamster.

➤ **Be leery of offshore investments.** When you send your money overseas, it's hard to track what happens to it, and you don't have the same protections as when you invest in the United States. Be very careful about directly investing overseas.

➤ **Watch out for those who offer inside information or try to pressure you to invest before you can check out the offer.** That's often a sign that a scamster is at work.

Do a Background Check on Your Stockbroker

You can find out your broker's employment history, whether there's been disciplinary action taken against him, and much more at the National Association of Security Dealers (NASD) Web site at www.nasdr.com.

➤ **Check into the Stock Detective site at www.stockdetective.com.** It's a great site that tracks online stock scams and gives hordes of useful advice. It's pictured here.

Anyone can be a stock detective at the www.stockdetective.com *site.*

The Least You Need to Know

➤ Always pay with your credit card when you shop online, because it offers complete consumer protection.

➤ Check out a site before buying—make sure it's reputable and that it's a secure site that scrambles credit card information so hackers can't steal your information.

➤ Look for hidden costs and understand warranties and return policies before buying.

➤ Always print out your order form and keep it in a safe place.

➤ Beware of pump and dump online stock scams—people who claim to be giving objective advice, but are trying to get a stock bid up so they can sell at a profit.

➤ Head to www.stockdetective.com for the latest information about stock scams.

DID WE BUY A BOAT?

Chapter 23

How to Protect Your Credit Card and Buy at a Secure Site

In This Chapter

➤ How to make sure that your credit card information can't be stolen

➤ Figuring out whether a site uses a secure connection for protecting your credit card

➤ How to check out a site before buying to make sure it's a reputable one

➤ Where to get the lowdown on shopping sites online

➤ Things you should never buy online

Before you put your plastic on the line and shop till you drop in cyberspace, you want to know that your credit card information won't be stolen. And you'd like to make sure that the site you're buying from is a legitimate one and won't take your money and run.

Luckily, it's easy to protect your credit card from being stolen—and it's simple as well to check out a site before you buy to make sure it's a legitimate one.

How do you do that? I thought you'd never ask. Check out this chapter and you'll never go wrong.

How to Know You're Buying Through a Secure Site

The biggest fear many people have about buying online is whether their credit card will be stolen. What's to stop a hacker from intercepting your credit card information as it makes its way across the Internet? Will some 16-year-old cracker capture your credit card information and then use it to buy Megadeth CDs, life-sized posters of Pamela Anderson, a five-year supply of pepperoni pizza (and a five-year-supply of pimple cream), and round-trip tickets to Tahiti for him and his adolescent friends?

These things won't happen if you buy at what's called a secure site. When you buy at a secure site, your credit card information is scrambled as it's sent across the Internet so that no one can read it except the site you're sending it to. At a secure site, you're safe from hackers, crackers, and other assorted ne'er-do-wells reading your information as it travels through cyberspace.

What's Encryption?

To keep information private, it can be encrypted. That means a kind of super-secret code is used to scramble the information as it's sent across the Internet so that only the receiver can read the information.

All well and good, you're no doubt thinking. But how can you know when you're shopping at a secure site?

It's exceedingly easy to know. When you've put everything you want into your shopping cart (don't forget the tea caddy with the knitted figurine of Bob Dole and the Pope on top, please) and it's time to pay with plastic, you are sent to a page where you're supposed to enter your credit card information. Before you get to that page, a window pops up, like the one you see here, alerting you that you're about to enter a secure site. (It shows the message you get in Microsoft Internet Explorer. The one for Netscape Navigator is slightly different.) Click **OK**, and you get sent to the secure site where you can go ahead and buy.

Here's how to know you're entering a secure site. If you don't see this dialog box, it's not a safe place.

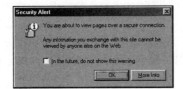

Now, here's something peculiar. See the little check box in the window? If you want, you can use that check box to tell your browser *not* to alert you each time you visit a secure site. Why would you *not* want to be alerted? I haven't a clue. But this is the Internet, after all, and it sometimes seems to be a looking glass world. My strong advice is to make sure that you tell the browser to alert you every time you're about to visit a secure site. And never, even in your wildest imagination, enter credit card information in a site that isn't secure.

By the way, if things aren't confusing enough for you, think about this one: If you want to always be alerted when you visit a secure site, you make sure the box is checked in Netscape Navigator, but in Microsoft Internet Explorer, make sure the box is *unchecked*. It must be just Netscape and Microsoft's way of making sure you're paying attention. Ain't the Internet grand?

Checking for the Locked Lock

That pop-up window is one clue that you're entering a secure site. But there's another way to check as well. Look for the little icon of a lock on the bottom bar of your browser. In Netscape Navigator, if the little lock is unlocked, it means that the site is not a secure one. If the lock is locked, it means the site is secure.

In Microsoft Internet Explorer, if there is no lock at the bottom of the browser, it means the site is not secure. If there is a lock there, it means the site is a secure one. See the picture on this page to see the secure icon in Microsoft Internet Explorer.

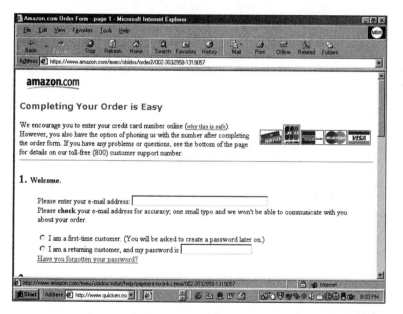

To make sure you're at a secure site, look for the locked lock icon in Microsoft Internet Explorer, like this.

What Is SET?

No, it's not a portion of a tennis match. SET stands for Secured Electronic Transaction, and it's the electronic encryption and payment standard that a group of big companies, including Microsoft, Netscape, VISA, MasterCard, and others, are pushing to become the standard for doing electronic commerce on the Internet. Some sites are already using it; soon every site might be using SET.

How to Check Out a Site Before Buying

Making sure a site is a secure one ensures that no hackers steal your credit card when you send it to a site. But what about the site itself? What if the Web site you're buying on is a scam? The truth is it doesn't take a whole lot of skill or money to put together a professional-looking Web site (although considering all the crud you come across when surfing the Web, that might come as a surprise to you). In a real-life store, by checking out how well a store is maintained, seeing what the merchandise is like, talking to the staff, and other means, you can often tell if the store is an honest one. But just because a Web site has a pretty face doesn't mean much—lurking behind that pretty face could be a scam artist, just itching to get his hands on your money.

But fear not, dear reader, there are ways you can check out a site before buying so that you can tell whether the site's on the up-and-up or is a lowdown crook. Here's what you need to know:

➤ **Does the site make available contact information?** You want to know things such as the address (or at least the city) of the site's main headquarters. Better yet, does it list the names of the company's officers (not many sites do this, by the way). Is it a publicly traded company (if it is, it'll tell you so)? How about a contact telephone number—does it list any? The more of this kind of information a site is willing to post, the more likely it is that it's an honest one. If you can't find any of this kind of information about the site, be leery.

➤ **Does it prominently post important information, such as its shipping and return policies and warranties?** Make sure this kind of information is posted—if it isn't, it could be a sign that there's a shady character in there somewhere. If it isn't posted, when you send an email to the site, does it respond quickly and with the specific information you've asked for? If you can't find out this kind of information, take a hike—because the site might take a hike with your money if you buy through it.

➤ **If the site has message boards, check them out.** Busy message boards often means a lot of active users and can be a sign that the site has return visitors. If people keep returning, the site can usually be trusted. But check out what kinds of messages are being posted—if it's loads of complaints, that's a bad sign. Be careful not to rely too heavily on message boards, though. The site can forge messages and weed out complaints.

➤ **Have you heard of the site before?** A site associated with a well-known bricks-and-mortar store can usually be trusted. If the site has shelled out big bucks for a national advertising campaign, it often means it's well-funded and so should be around a while.

Know Your Rights about Shipping Times

You have the force of the law behind you when it comes to knowing when the goods you've ordered will be delivered to you. Internet shopping is covered by the Federal Trade Commission's Mail Order Rule. That rule says companies must ship orders to you within the time they've promised—if they haven't promised a time, they must ship them within 30 days of when you've ordered them. If there's a delay, they have to notify you and ask whether you agree to the delay or let you cancel the order. You then get a full refund within seven days or one billing cycle of your credit card account. If they don't notify you of a delay and the goods still aren't shipped, you have the right to cancel the order and get a refund.

Where You Can Get the Lowdown on Shopping Sites

Tips help you check out a site, but there are even more tricks at your disposal. There are a variety of ways to get the inside scoop on online shopping sites to see whether they're honest. Here's where to go.

Check Out the Better Business Bureau

Better Business Bureaus are local, not-for-profit corporations that can give you the inside skinny on any businesses that have a less-than-savory reputation. And they tell you if businesses have any outstanding complaints lodged against them.

You can get a free report from the Better Business Bureau about any company they have a record of. It tells you how long the company has been in business, whether there have been complaints with the Better Business Bureau about the company, and how the complaints were resolved—if they were resolved at all. If a government agency, such as the Federal Trade Commission or a state Attorney General, has taken actions against the company, the Better Business Bureau also tells you that. The reports usually cover the past three years and also tell you if the company is a member of the Better Business Bureau.

Keep in mind that the bureau doesn't have reports on every business. If it doesn't have a report, it generally means that either the company is a new one or there have been no complaints against it.

What Should You Never Buy Online?

There are some things that you should never buy online because the possibilities for fraud are simply too great. Don't buy collectible Beanie Babies. As any 10-year-old child or toy collector can tell you, collectible Beanie Babies are big business and commonly sell for hundreds or even thousands of dollars. Although buying garden-variety Beanie Babies online for $5 and $10 is fine, buying expensive collectibles is a very bad idea—it's too easy for scamsters to sell counterfeit goods. I wouldn't buy sports memorabilia, either. As with Beanie Babies, you cannot examine the goods before you buy. In a recent case, baseballs were being offered that were supposedly signed by baseball great Roberto Clemente. The only problem— the baseballs were manufactured five years after Clemente had died.

Better Business Bureaus are all local. So a Better Business Bureau in Peoria, Iowa, for example, can't tell you about a business based in Hackensack, New Jersey. (To all you New Jerseyites: Quick, what exit is that?) So before checking in with a Better Business Bureau, you need to find out where the Web site's main offices are. If you can't find it out, you've answered the question already—stay away.

To find contact information for a Better Business Bureau near you, check the Yellow Pages or call directory assistance. If you're like me and would rather do things on the Web, go to the bureau's Web site at www.bbb.com to find contact information. You can also search for reports on the Web site.

You Have Credit Card Rights Under the Fair Credit Billing Act

The Federal Fair Credit Billing Act covers credit card transactions over the Internet and gives you legal rights if there's an error on your credit card bill because of a transaction you made over the Internet, or if you're disputing a credit card bill because of a transaction over the Internet. If you find that you've been billed incorrectly for some reason, such as for goods and services you haven't received, an error in the amount charged, or unauthorized charges, the law covers you. Under it, you must write a letter to the company that made the incorrect charge, describing the error and including your name, address, or charge card number. When you send the notice, the company must, by law, send you a written acknowledgment of your claim within 30 days and must resolve the problem within 90 days.

Head to the BBBOnline Site

So much business is being conducted on the Internet that the Better Business Bureau has hung out its shingle online—it's put together a program for checking out online sites in the same way that it checks out bricks-and-mortar businesses. The program is called BBB*Online* and you can get information about it at the BBB*Online* site at www.bbbonline.com.

Here's how it works: A Web site agrees to participate in the program and so must abide by BBB*Online* standards. These standards mean that the company:

➤ Agrees to resolve complaints quickly and fairly

➤ Has a satisfactory record with the Better Business Bureau

➤ Has been in business at least a year

➤ Agrees to correct or withdraw misleading Internet advertising

➤ Provides contact information such as addresses, phone numbers, and company officials

The company also agrees to binding arbitration with a consumer if there's been a complaint. All in all, it's a pretty good deal for consumers.

Companies who participate can also place a *BBBOnline* seal on their site—so when you see that seal, you know the site is willing to abide by strict standards. Even better, you can click the seal, and when you do, you get a full rundown about the company. You can find address, phone number, contact information, and the like, and you also are shown how long the company has been in business. If there have been any complaints against the company, you are shown that as well.

Last time I moseyed over there, many, many stores had signed up for the program. Not all of them, though, display the seal on their sites, so you don't always know whether a particular company is part of the program. To find out, head to www.bbbonline.com. From there, you can search for any company to see if it is a member. If it is, you can see the full *BBBOnline* report on the company.

Take a Close Look at the PublicEye

Here's a great idea for a site: Have the people who actually shop at sites rate the sites for reliability, customer satisfaction, and sensitivity to privacy issues. That's what the PublicEye at www.thepubliceye.com does. The PublicEye, pictured here, gathers information from consumers about their experiences at sites and uses the information to rate sites. It does more than merely rate sites—it also publishes comprehensive information about the sites, including ratings for reliability, safety, privacy practices, customer support, and more. You can even see individual comments that people make about a site. It's a great way to get a true picture of a shopping site.

Take a close, close look at a site at www.thepubliceye.com. You get comprehensive consumer ratings of buying sites.

Check Out the Money Guys at CPA WebTrust

If you want to find out whether it's safe to spend your money, what better place to go than to accountants? To see whether an online shopping site can be trusted with your hard-earned cash, head to CPA WebTrust at www.cpawebtrust.com, run by an association of certified public accountants (party guys and girls, like all accountants, I'm sure). The organization gives CPA WebTrust seals to companies that adhere to a set of online selling principles. These include posting warranty and return information, not using information gained about customers in a way that would invade the customers' privacy, and running a Web site that has secure transactions. If you see the seal on a site, you know it adheres to those principles.

Head to Usenet Newsgroups

One of the best places to find out the goods on an online merchant is in newsgroups and online discussion boards. There are a number of newsgroups you can head to, but I've found that for information about which online sites to stay away from, misc.consumer is the best by far. In a single day, for example, there were three messages posted warning people to stay away from buying at certain Web sites. Head there, read the messages, and post questions of your own. You'll most probably get answers—and honest ones. Before you go, though, check out Chapter 17, "Protecting Your Privacy on Internet Newsgroups and Discussion Areas," on protecting yourself in Usenet newsgroups.

You Need a Newsgroup Reader to Read Newsgroups

To read newsgroups, you need a special piece of software called a newsgroup reader. Netscape Navigator and Microsoft Internet Explorer include them. You can also read newsgroups at the Deja.com Web site at www.deja.com.

The Least You Need to Know

➤ Only buy through sites that feature secure transactions—you can tell if they're secure by looking for the locked lock at the bottom of your browser.

➤ Check out sites you buy from with the Better Business Bureau and other consumer sites.

➤ Make sure that the site you buy from lists contact information, including address and phone numbers.

➤ Check out return policies and warranties online before buying—and don't buy from a site that doesn't tell you of its policies.

➤ Beware of buying collectibles online, such as "retired" Beanie Babies and sports memorabilia.

How to Stay Safe When Buying at Auctions

Where can you get the best deals on the Web? At online auctions.

Where are the most common scams committed on the Web? At online auctions.

It's no accident that auctions offer you the best deals and also are where the most scams are committed. They're incredibly popular sites, drawing many thousands of people bidding on millions and millions of items a day. The vast majority of them are safe—but before bidding, you want to make sure you know what's up so you don't get scammed.

Read this chapter, and you can be a bidder, too—knowing you won't get burned. I let you know everything there is about how to stay safe and not get scammed while you're pursuing great deals.

Sold American! What Are Online Auctions?

An auction done online? How is that possible? How can a smooth, fast-talking auctioneer rattle off bids and bargains rat-a-tat tat style over the wires and modems that make up the Internet?

Not only are online auctions possible, but they're also about the hottest things going these days. The basic idea of an online auction is the same as a traditional auction: You bid against others, trying to buy something at the lowest price possible. But there's no live auctioneer, there's less pressure, and you don't need to show up a certain time and place—auctions take place 24 hours a day, seven days a week, at sites all over the Internet. Many hundreds of thousands—and possibly millions—of items are being auctioned off online right now as you read these words.

Keep in mind that auctions aren't just for buyers. You can also make a pretty penny by cleaning out your attic and putting up things for sale. Don't look down your nose at those odd items you have laying around your house. (And if your house is like mine, those items can be very odd, indeed. As I write this, I'm looking at a goat skull hanging on my wall, a telescope on the floor, and an old ant farm near the window. Wonder how much they'd sell for?) Realtors say that every house, no matter how eccentric, has its buyers. Any old junk may have a buyer as well.

Check Retail Prices Before You Buy at an Auction

It's easy to get carried away at an auction, assuming that you're getting the best deal possible...but are you? Before bidding on an item, make sure to find out its true retail price; otherwise, you can end up paying more than you would in a store.

Bidding Your Time: How Do Online Auctions Work?

The basics of buying at an auction are pretty simple. You bid by going to an auction site, browsing for things you're interested in buying, and then making bids. To make a bid, you first register, for free, at the site. In some instances, you have to enter your credit card number and information, if you're buying the item directly from the site itself. (More on this circumstance later in this chapter.) In other instances, you don't have to enter your credit card number, because you don't buy the item from the site, but rather from a private person who put the item up for bid. (Again, more on this later.)

Every auction lasts for a certain amount of time. Most auctions last for several days and often up to a week or more. If you're making a bid, you should check in regularly to see how the bidding is going, because you're probably not the only person who absolutely has to have those wind chimes that play the theme to *Love Story* every time a breeze blows by. You can see the history of the bidding so that you can see how many other people are bidding and what they've bid. Pictured here is a typical auction on the popular eBay auction site at www.ebay.com.

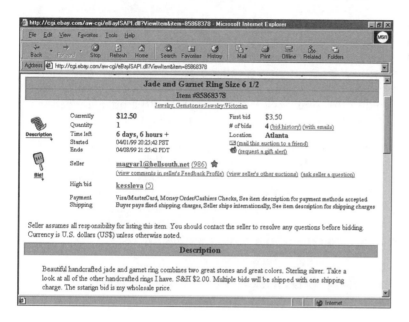

Get ready to bid! Bidding on jewelry at the www.ebay.com *auction site.*

At the end of the auction, if you're not the highest bidder, you've only spent your time—although you might never forgive yourself for not spending an extra $5 for those *Love Story* wind chimes.

However, let's say that your dream came true, and you snagged the wind chimes for a mere $27.50. (A bargain at twice the price!) You are told by email that you're the winning bidder. If the auction site is directly selling the item, you pay the auction site through your credit card. If instead you're buying it from a private seller at the auction site, you make arrangements with that private seller.

What Kinds of Auction Sites Are There?

Auctions might look the same, but very often, they're quite different from one another. The first step to making sure that you don't get burned at an auction is knowing at what kind of auction you're buying because there are different dangers you face depending on the kind of auction you buy at.

How Rare Is Scamming on Auction Sites?

Numbers are hard to come by, but the eBay auction site says that fraud is exceedingly rare, occurring in only about 27 in every one million transactions. Of course, if you're one of those 27, it doesn't seem rare at all. It feels more like well-done.

In general, there are two types of auctions. Here they are and what you need to know about each.

Auctions Where You Buy Directly from the Site

At some auction sites, such as OnSale at www.onsale.com, you buy directly from the site itself. You don't deal with a different private seller each time you buy. The transaction is usually done via credit card, and so when you pay, you get the normal consumer protections that credit cards offer you. When you deal with a private seller, you don't get that protection, because you don't pay via credit card.

But you have to be careful when buying at these sites to make sure that the site itself is on the up-and-up, that they'll actually deliver the goods at the price you agreed on, and that the goods aren't damaged in any way. You also want to make sure that the site protects your privacy. Because these sites can gather an incredible amount of information about you—not just your credit card, but also what products you buy and bid on—and that information is quite valuable to marketers and sellers. Later in the chapter, I show you how to safeguard your privacy at sites like these.

Auctions Where You Buy Directly from Individuals

At many other sites, such as the popular www.ebay.com and the computer auction site auctions.zdnet.com, the site doesn't sell anything—it's just there to help buyers and sellers get together.

Take into Account Shipping Charges When Figuring Out Your Buying Price

The price you pay at an auction might seem like a good deal, but make sure when comparing prices to what you'd pay retail that you take into account shipping charges. When you're buying a large item, shipping charges can add up—they can even be $50 or more.

A big draw at these kinds of auctions is the incredible variety of stuff you can buy there. On the monstrous eBays site, for example, on any given day there two million or more different items for sale. "Groovy drinking birds," Pentium PCs, potato peelers, Martin 0042 guitars, glass pigs—pretty much anything you can imagine, and a whole lot of things you've never imagined (and may never want to), are for sale here.

But because you buy directly from individuals at these sites, there's also more danger in getting burned at them. After all, you're buying from someone, sight unseen—how can you know the goods will ever be delivered? And often you don't pay with your credit card, so you might lack basic consumer protections. As you see in this chapter, though, there's a lot you can do to make sure that you don't get burned when you buy at auctions.

First Things First: Checking Out the Auction Site Before Bidding

The best way to make sure you don't get burned at an auction is to check out the site first. It's important to check out an auction site even if you aren't buying from the site itself, because there's a lot an auction site can do to make sure that there are no scams being done there. For added safety, some sites have even begun to offer free or low-cost insurance to reimburse you if you get burned. Here's what to know about a site before bidding:

➤ **Check out their privacy policies.**
Auction sites of any kind can track what you buy—and if you're buying from the site, you're giving them your credit card information. Make sure that what they do with the information doesn't invade your privacy. Look for privacy seals, such as the TRUSTe seal, which indicates that they adhere to strict privacy guidelines. For more information about checking privacy and the Web, turn to Part 4, "Protecting Your Privacy and Security on the World Wide Web."

➤ **Look for insurance and guarantees.**
Auction sites have recognized that if they don't stamp out scams, they'll put themselves out of business. So some of them, such as www.amazon.com and www.ebay.com, have put insurance and

Insurance and Guarantees Often Don't Cover Everything for Sale on an Auction Site

Read the fine print about insurance and guarantees, because they don't always cover all the items up for sale, even if those items cost less than $200 or $250. Some sites put a label of some kind next to items that are covered.

guarantees into effect. These anti-scam features guarantee that the site reimburses your money if you've been scammed. Typically, they cover items that cost up to a certain amount of money, as in $200 or $250. In some instances, for example at eBay, you have to pay the first $25. Sometimes, you have to pay some kind of annual fee for them. But they're helpful, they help protect you against scams, and they're a sign that the site is a reliable one that takes scams seriously.

➤ **Find out if they police the site for scam artists.** Some sites take a laissez-faire attitude towards scamsters, saying that essentially the site only acts as a middleman, not a policeman, and so it has no responsibility for policing the site. Other sites, though, have begun to crack down by actively looking for scamsters and then ejecting them. eBay, for example, looks for and ejects shillers who artificially bid up the costs of items. It ejects sellers for other reasons as well. Click around the auction site to see if it provides information on how it polices itself.

➤ **If you buy from the site**, **does it post warranty, shipping, and return policies?** You want to make sure that you can return things, that what you buy is covered by a warranty, and you know what the shipping costs are. If you can't find that information, head to an auction elsewhere.

➤ **Is there a comprehensive help section detailing safety, privacy, and consumer issues?** Auction sites can be confusing places, and if you have a problem, it's often hard to know where to go and how to solve it. You want a site that spells out all its policies in explicit detail and is easy to find. Pictured here is the Safe Harbor section of eBay that details all that.

Staying safe at eBay: Here's the Safe Harbor section detailing all its consumer, safety, privacy, and related issues.

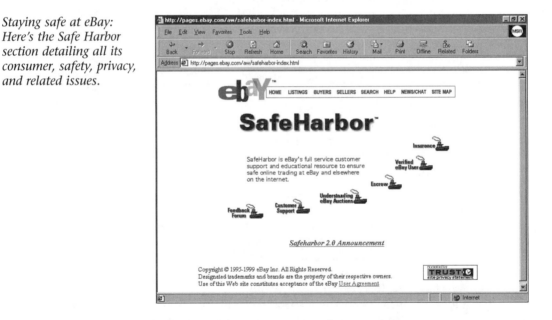

➤ **Can you view information about how reputable the sellers and buyers are?** A good way to make sure you don't get burned is to make sure you buy from someone reputable. But if you're buying from someone sight unseen, how can you check on them? Some auction sites let buyers and sellers rate others for reputability. That way, you can see how clean a record someone has. Look for sites that allow these kinds of ratings, because at them, you have better ways to make sure you don't get burned.

➤ **Does the site have rules about not allowing illegal or other inappropriate items to be sold?** Some auction sites have been used to sell a variety of items that are either illegal or inappropriate to sell online, such as handguns and firearms. Sites have begun to crack down on this, and some have formulated specific policies against it. A site that has policies against selling this kind of thing is a site that's more likely to be reputable.

Here's Part of the Banned List at eBay

eBay has banned a variety of illegal or inappropriate items from being sold on the site. The list is long, but here's a small selection of what can't be sold: firearms; bazookas; explosives; beta or pre-release software; pirated movies and music; illegal animal parts; Federal, New York, and Seattle police badges; live animals; Cuban cigars; skulls; and human remains. Talk about a mixed bag!

How to Make Sure You Don't Get Scammed at Auctions

Checking out an auction site before bidding can help make sure you don't get burned—but it only takes you so far. There are many thousands of people who bid on auctions, so how can you make sure that when you buy that matched set of salt and pepper shakers in the shape of Minnesota that you'll really get the goods?

If you've bought it at an auction where you buy directly from the site, you're all right, because you're paying by credit card and you've checked out the site first. But what do you do if you've bought it at a site where you buy from a private seller? How can you make sure the seller doesn't just take the money and run? It's actually not that hard to do. Follow these tips and you should be just fine.

Research the Seller

How trustworthy is the person who's doing the selling? Some sites, such as eBay and the computer auction site at ZDNet at `auctions.zdnet.com`, allow you to get detailed information about how the seller has treated other buyers. At eBay, for example, you can see a profile detailing how other sellers have rated the buyer—you can see a tally of the total number of positive, neutral, and negative comments, and you can read the individual comments. If someone has several negative comments, stay away. (In fact, if someone has too many negative comments, and eBay confirms they're accurate, that person is kicked off the service.)

The auction site provides you with the email address of the seller. Send an email to the seller asking a question and see how fast you get a response. If you don't get a response, or get a slow one, that's a bad signal. And certainly stay away if you can't get an address and phone number.

If the site has a message board or chat area, head there and ask if any other people have had dealings with the seller. If they have, they'll be happy to share them with you—both good and bad.

Understand How the Site Works Before Buying

Auctions can be a confusing place, and you should know how they work before you buy—you don't want to face the equivalent of a situation in a real-life auction when you swat at a mosquito buzzing around your face, only to find out that you've just made the winning bid on a $25 million Picasso up for sale. You want to know details such as whether you pay for an item before the seller ships it or after you receive it.

Be Careful When Bidding at Flash or Express Auctions

Flash or "express" auctions are auctions that are done very quickly—often, they take an hour or less. In that way, they're similar to real-life auctions. These kinds of auctions get your adrenaline flowing, because you're in pitched battle against other bidders. When your adrenaline is flowing at one of these auctions, it's easy to get carried away—especially because some of them allow you to chat online with other bidders, which means a bit of taunting can take place. In a hothouse atmosphere like this, macho posturing sometimes takes over, and you can find yourself bidding very high prices on an item just to prove you can win. But when the bidding is over, you might find yourself paying well over top-dollar for an item that isn't worth a plug nickel. So make sure before you bid at one of these to set a top price over which you won't go.

Get Contact Information from the Seller

You want to get the seller's real-life mailing address and phone number as well as his email address. If the seller won't provide that information, don't trust that person. Most sites only provide email addresses, so you have to contact the seller via email.

Find Out About Warranties, Returns, and Deliveries

How long before the goods are shipped to you? Who pays for shipping? What kind of warranty do you get? How do you get service if there is a warranty? Sometimes this information is covered in the auction listing itself, but it isn't always. Get all the details—in writing—before closing the deal.

Don't Buy Expensive Collectibles

One of the biggest scams going is the sale of collectibles online. Don't trust buying retired Beanie Babies, sports memorabilia, and other expensive collectibles—they're all very common scams. In one particularly noteworthy scam, someone was offered for sale a signed baseball by baseball great Roberto Clemente. The only problem is that the ball was manufactured five years after the ballplayer's death!

eBay Offers Authentication Services

The eBay auction site, recognizing the possibility for fraud in buying products such as rare coins and trading cards, has made a deal with a service that authenticates that the items being sold are real. The service, Collector's Universe, also offers a financial guarantee that backs the authenticity of the products.

Never Pay by Cash or Money Order

Send cash or a money order and you have absolutely no recourse when someone takes the money and runs. If someone demands cash, it's a possible sign that you're about to be scammed.

Ask That Shipping Be Done Cash on Delivery (C.O.D.)

Here's a simple way to ensure that someone can't just cash your check and then not send you the goods—ask that they ship it cash on delivery. When something is shipped C.O.D., it means that you pay for the item only when you receive it. It costs a few dollars extra, compared to regular shipping, but if it's the first time you're dealing with a seller, it might be worth the cost. And you can always try to get the seller to pay for the extra C.O.D. charge, or to at least split the charge with you.

Make Sure That You Don't Buy Fraudulent or Copyright-Infringing Goods

When you buy something sight unseen, such as a CD, it's hard to know whether what you're buying is illegal—that it hasn't been pirated, for example. There are signs of pirated items, though. Some warning signs: If the documentation is photo-copied, if a CD is sent only in a jewel case, if you're asked to send money to a Post Office box instead of a street address, and if you're asked to send cash.

Use an Internet Escrow Service

If it's the first time you're buying or you're spending serious money, more than $100 or so, you might want to use what's called an Internet escrow service. These services act as a good-faith go-between between the buyer and the seller. Generally, here's how it works. You make your payment to the escrow service, but the service doesn't immediately turn the money over to the seller. Instead, it keeps the money in escrow. The seller sends you the goods. You inspect them, then tell the escrow service you've gotten what you paid for. The escrow service then releases the money to the seller.

There are several escrow services that do this kind of thing: TradeSafe at www.tradesafe.com, I-Escrow at www.iescrow.com, and Trade-direct at www.trade-direct.com. Fees vary. The minimum fee is $5, and a typical fee is five percent of the selling cost of the product. Again, haggle with the seller to get him to eat the cost, or at least to split it with you. Some Web sites have specific escrow services associated with them.

The Least You Need to Know

➤ Before bidding at an auction, know whether you'll buy from the site or a private individual.

➤ Shop at auction sites that offer insurance and guarantee against fraud and scams.

➤ It's best to shop at auction sites that actively police themselves against shills and scamsters.

➤ Before sending money to sellers, check their background. For big-ticket items, use an Internet escrow company.

➤ Never pay by cash or money order.

➤ Don't buy expensive collectibles online—they're too easy to counterfeit, and you can't examine the goods before buying.

Part 8

Protecting Yourself Against Viruses, Trojan Horses, and Other Nasty Creatures

There are beasties out there. Nasties that want to trash your hard disk. Viruses, Trojan horses, time bombs, evil ActiveX controls, and worms. (Worms? Yes, worms.) And there's more nastiness out there as well. Only recently a new virus called Melissa wreaked hurricane-like havoc on the Internet.

Any time you download something from the Internet, you could be downloading a virus of some sort. And even when you just go to a Web site, there's a possibility it could do you damage.

But fear not, dear reader. You have your trusty anti-virus fighter here to help. You'll learn in this part that it's exceedingly easy to protect yourself against most of the viruses and other beasties and nasty creatures you might come across online. You'll see steps you can take to reduce your risk of getting a virus or having your computer damaged or privacy invaded by oddball things called Java applets or ActiveX controls. (Do ActiveX controls have something to do with The X-Files? Check out this part to find out.)

Chapter 25

What Are Viruses and How Do They Work?

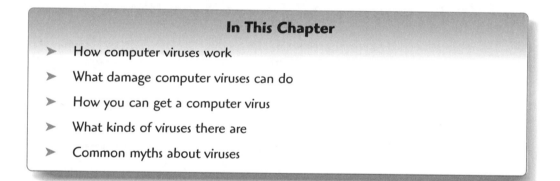

In This Chapter

➤ How computer viruses work

➤ What damage computer viruses can do

➤ How you can get a computer virus

➤ What kinds of viruses there are

➤ Common myths about viruses

Malevolent programs that delete every file on your hard disk. Nasty programs that lie in wait until a certain date and then spring into action, doing evil on your computer. Files attached to email programs that can steal your America Online password. These are a few examples of the malicious programs called viruses that can harm the data and software on your computer.

In this chapter, you get a good understanding of what computer viruses and other malicious programs are, how they work, and what damage they do. For information about how to fight viruses and other destructive programs, turn to Chapter 26, "How to Keep Your Computer Safe from Viruses," and Chapter 27, "Keeping Safe from Java, JavaScript, and ActiveX Applets."

What's a Computer Virus?

You're running your computer, and all is normal. Except you notice that your files start acting funny—for some odd reason, they keep growing in size. Or one day you try and run your computer, and whammo!, it won't start. Or files start vanishing, your hard disk crashes, or you get odd messages on your screen from time to time.

Unfortunately, I've got bad news for you. You've most likely been hit by a computer virus.

Computer viruses can do all kinds of damage to your computer. They can be as harmless as merely displaying a silly message on your screen or be as destructive as wiping out your hard disk or deleting your operating system. And as more and more computers hook up to the Internet, there are greater and greater chances that viruses will be spread from computer to computer.

Why Would Someone Create a Computer Virus?

That's one of life's great mysteries. It's hard to fathom why someone would do something destructive like that. Sometimes, someone is out for revenge or wants to attack a company or group and writes the virus to put it directly onto someone's computer or network. Other times, they're looking for some kind of odd fame as a virus creator. Sometimes, it's to see if they can do it. And often, it's just plain maliciousness.

There are many different kinds of computer viruses, as you see later in this chapter. But they all have one thing in common—they do something that you don't want them to do, and they do it stealthily, hiding their action, possibly until it's too late for you to do anything about it. Usually, they're destructive, but they don't have to be; sometimes, they just display a message on your screen. And viruses can be very...well, eccentric is a nice way to put it. Take the Smiley virus, for example. When it's active, smiley faces suddenly appear and start bouncing around your screen—kind of like a horrifying flashback to the 1970s. You almost expect polyester-suited John Travolta to start discoing around the screen beneath a big, glittering mirrored ball. Now *that* would be a virus to stay away from!

So How Do Computer Viruses Work?

There are literally thousands and thousands of different computer viruses out there, with more created every day, and they often work differently. But there are some general types of viruses, and all have similarities.

In some ways, a computer virus is very much like the biological kind. When you get a biological virus, it burrows into cells, takes over those cells, and in essence turns them into little virus factories. Each infected cell manufactures copies of the virus; then the cell dies and releases all the new viruses; each of these new viruses in turn infects a cell and turns *it* into a little virus factory; and so on.

Computer viruses work in much the same way. They don't exist by themselves. Rather, they burrow their way into a file on your hard disk—usually a program file that ends in the extension .exe or .com, such as WORD.EXE. But they can infect other kinds of files as well, such as Word documents and files needed to start up your computer.

After the virus infects a file, you need to run that file for it to do its dirty deeds. It can't run by itself. When you run the infected file, it starts on its nefarious work. In one kind of virus, one of the things it does is look for another program file to infect, and after it infects that one, looks for another file to infect, and so on. No matter how the virus works, though, after you run an infected program, it does whatever damage the virus programmer instructed it to do. (Oh, no! Not the Polyester Travolta virus, please!)

How Prevalent Are Computer Viruses?

Computer viruses get a great deal of news coverage and publicity, but the truth is, they're pretty rare. I've been using computers for 15 years and have downloaded thousands of files from the Internet, and I've only gotten a single virus in all that time. The virus I got wasn't even from a downloaded file—it was in a Word document sent over a corporate network to me, attached to a memo (many other people got the virus as well). Killing the virus was a simple matter—I deleted the file and ran a virus scanner that tracked down the virus and found it in a Word macro. The scanner killed the virus, and my computer was none the worse for wear.

By the way, I'd like to emphasize something important here. (So you in the back row, stop talking and start paying attention!) *You can't get infected by a virus unless you run or open a file that's been infected!* You can't get a virus any other way. Even if you put an infected file on your computer, if you don't run it, you won't get infected. (OK, you in the back row, you can go back to slouching and chatting now.)

What Kinds of Viruses Are There?

There's a whole lot of different kinds of nasty virus things. Although there are many different kinds of viruses, here are some common types:

➤ **Time bombs**   These are viruses that are programmed to do their damage at a certain date, or after a certain amount of time has elapsed. For example, the infamous Michelangelo virus was programmed to lie dormant until March 6, when it was supposed to spring into action. (This might have been the most overhyped virus of all time, with news stories around the world warning about it just before March 6, 1992. In fact, very few computers ended up being infected.)

➤ **Trojan horses**   These kinds of viruses take their name from the Trojan horse of Greek legend, which appeared to be a gift, but in fact harbored the Greek army within, which sacked the city of Troy. In the same way, a Trojan horse virus appears to be an innocuous or helpful program, such as a piece of personal finance software, when in fact, when you run the program, it damages your computer. Probably the most infamous Trojan horse of all time is a program called Back Orifice. When you install this piece of software, it allows someone to completely take over your computer—they can delete files, copy files, and even remotely control your computer by issuing it commands.

➤ **Self-replicating viruses**   This is the kind most like a biological virus. When you run an infected file, it looks for other files to infect, and when those are run, it looks for files to infect, and so on. Sometimes, these kinds of viruses make each file they infect larger—and can end up clogging your hard disk. Other times, they lie dormant until a critical mass of them is reached, and then they spring into action.

Techno Talk

The Worm That Ate the Internet

There's a kind of virus designed to infect networks called a worm—called that because it worms its way through a network, infecting network computers along the way. The most famous worm of all time was released into the Internet by Robert Morris, Jr., in 1988. He had written it hoping to cause mild consternation, but he had made a mistake in programming it, and it replicated out of control at a break-neck pace. In short order, it, in essence, closed down the entire Internet. (Of course, the Internet was much smaller in those days, but still, it was quite a feat.) Morris, who ironically was the son of the world-famous computer security expert Robert Morris, Sr., was convicted of violating the Federal Computer Fraud and Abuse Act and was sentenced to probation, 400 hours of community service, and a fine.

➤ **Boot viruses** These viruses infect the boot sector of your PC—the files that start up your PC. These can be deadly, because they can make your computer unable to start, and because they start before other programs, can also easily infect other programs.

➤ **Memory resident viruses** These are viruses that, when run, stay in your computer's memory. When there, they can infect other programs that you run.

➤ **Document viruses** At one time, it was thought that viruses could only infect programs and could not infect data files, such as Word or Excel documents. In fact, though, viruses can infect Word and Excel documents. That's because Word and Excel allow you to run things called *macros* that are like little programs embedded in the documents. So, viruses can run in macros and, in that way, can infect document files. The Melissa virus that recently caused so much concern was a document virus.

➤ **Dangerous Java applets and ActiveX controls** Java applets and ActiveX controls are technologies used to make World Wide Web pages more interactive and useful. In essence, they're kinds of programs. Although the Java applets and ActiveX controls can't actually be infected by viruses, the applets and controls can be programmed to do damage to your computer when you visit a page and run them. For more information on what to watch out for, turn to Chapter 27.

How Do You Get One of These Nasty Things?

For your computer to be infected by a virus, one has to get onto your system, and you have to run it. But how can you get a virus? More ways than you can imagine. Here are the most common:

➤ **By downloading an infected file from the Internet.** Some files on the Internet are infected with viruses. If you download one that's infected and you run it, you get the virus.

➤ **From software you buy in the store.** Yes, there have been instances where software you buy from a store has been infected by a virus.

➤ **By using a disk a friend gave to you.** A friend gives you a copy of the latest MegaKiller SuperDeath Shoot'em'up game. It has a virus on it. You run the program. You get the virus.

➤ **By loading a document file that someone gives to you.** Someone—maybe someone at work, maybe a friend—gives you a Word file. If it has a virus on it, your computer could get infected.

Techno Talk

What's an Email Attachment?

When someone sends a picture, graphic, program, or other file via email, that file is called an *attachment*. To use it, you have to detach it from the email with your email software.

➤ **By opening and running an email attachment.** Contrary to common belief, you can't get a virus from reading a piece of email. But if you open up and run an email attachment—a file attached to the email message—you could get a virus. In fact, a very common kind of virus is aimed at America Online users—when you open and run the attached file, it finds your username and password and sends it to someone, so they can use your America Online account.

How Can I Make Sure I Never Get Infected?

Want to make sure that the dreaded PolyesterTravolta virus never damages your computer? It's not that hard to make sure that you never get hit.

There's a whole host of things you should do to make sure that an infected file never makes its way onto your system—things such as never opening an email file attachment from someone you don't know. Turn to Chapter 26 to see how.

You should use anti-virus software and make sure it runs all the time on your computer. When used properly, anti-virus software detects infected files before you run them, so that to kill the virus all you need to do is kill the infected file. You should also regularly scan your hard disk for infected files with anti-virus software. Here you can see Norton AntiVirus, my favorite virus killer, checking my computer for viruses. Luckily, it found none.

Keep your machine clean: Scanning for viruses with Norton AntiVirus.

When anti-virus software finds a virus, it can kill the virus as well. Sometimes it can kill the virus and repair the file the virus infected, which makes life easy. Other times, it cannot repair the file, and you have to delete whatever file was infected.

Virus Myths, Hoaxes, and Urban Myths

Consider these horrifying stories:

➤ The Federal Communications Commission has uncovered a virus that you can get if you read an email message with the subject of "Good Times" in it—and if you read the message, your computer's processor will be sent up in smoke because it will be set to an "n^{th} complexity infinite binary loop."

➤ If you read an email greeting card sent to you over the Internet from a certain card company, a virus will infect your computer.

➤ Companies that sell anti-virus software also create viruses and set them loose, as a way of scaring people so that they can sell more anti-virus software.

➤ If you receive an email message with the subject "It Takes Guts To Say 'Jesus'" and then read that message, every file on your hard disk will be deleted.

Yes, you should consider those horrifying stories all you want. Because they're all untrue. Every last one of them. And there are hundreds of more hoaxes and myths like them. Viruses are surrounded by more fear, hype, and hoax than just about any computer technology you can name. To get the lowdown on the latest hoaxes and myths (and old ones as well) and to get great information on the truth about viruses, visit the Computer Virus Myths home page, pictured here. It's run by security expert and old friend Rob Rosenberger and is a great place to get the rundown on the truth about viruses. Visit it at `http://www.kumite.com/myths/`.

Good Times virus? Email messages that blow up your computer? Read about these myths and many others at the Computer Virus Myths home page.

Why Virus Hoaxes?

Why would someone create a bogus virus threat? It's easier than writing a virus. As you've seen, anti-virus software can hunt down and kill a virus program. But well-intentioned but gullible email readers can help ensure a hoax like Good Times can stay alive for years.

The Least You Need to Know

➤ A computer virus can't damage your computer unless you run a program that contains the virus.

➤ You can get a virus by downloading an infected file, having one given to you on disk, or even from commercial software.

➤ You can get viruses by opening files attached to email messages—but you can't get them by merely reading the email itself.

➤ Always run anti-virus software on your computer to make sure that you don't get infected.

➤ For every genuine virus prowling the Internet, there's at least one virus hoax designed to cause unnecessary worry.

Chapter 26

How to Keep Your Computer Safe from Viruses

In This Chapter

➤ Top tips for making sure you don't get hit by a virus

➤ How anti-virus software works

➤ How to use anti-virus software to protect your computer

➤ What you can do if you've been infected

As you saw in the last chapter, there's all kinds of viruses loose on the Internet and other places as well, such as your business's network, disks your friends give you, and other places. The potential dangers are no doubt overblown—isn't that why we have newspapers and magazines, after all?—but they're very real. And it is small comfort to you to know that there aren't *that* many viruses online, if one is eating your computer and spitting it out right now.

Luckily, it's easy to protect your computer from viruses. You find out how in this chapter. So read on, and you don't need to worry about anything chomping on your programs or data.

Top Tips for Avoiding Viruses

As you see later in this chapter, one of the best ways to make sure you don't get attacked by a virus is to use anti-virus software. But that, on its own, shouldn't be enough. There's a lot more you can do to make sure you don't get attacked by a virus. Here's what to do:

➤ **Only download files from Internet sites that virus check their software.** There's a whole lot of sites on the Internet where you can download software—hundreds, if not thousands of them. But the vast majority of those sites don't check their files to see if they've been infected with a virus. That means that you stand more of a chance getting a virus on that site than on one that does virus checking. To be safe, only download from sites that virus check the files on their site. Check the Help or FAQ area of a site to see if they do virus checking. The ZDNet Software Library at www.hotfiles.com, for example, virus checks all the software it carries.

Check If a Site Uses Multiple Virus Scanners

When it comes to virus scanners, two are better than one, and three are better than two. Ideally, you'd like a download site to check its files with more than one virus scanner to make it even less likely that a file it carries has a virus.

➤ **If someone gives you a floppy disk with files on it, virus scan the files on it before you copy it to your computer.** You want to know whatever you're being given is safe, so that you don't infect your computer. Keep in mind that even document files such as Word files (that end in a .doc extension) and Excel files (that end in an .xls extension) can carry viruses, so check them as well.

➤ **If someone sends you a file over your business network, virus scan it before using it.** A common way of getting a virus is from someone at work giving you file that contains one. In fact, in all the years I've been downloading files from the Internet and using a computer, the only time I've gotten a virus is from someone at work sending me a Word file that had a virus in it.

➤ **Never open a file sent to you via email from someone you don't know.** This is a common way of spreading viruses. The stranger might tell you that it's a screen saver or some other program, but it might in fact be a virus. This is also a way some hackers use to steal your password. They send out a file that appears to be a useful program, but in fact, behind the scenes it's stealing passwords and sending them off to the hacker, who now has access to them. Even when someone you know sends you a file, you should virus scan it before opening it. To do that, save the file to your hard disk, but don't open it. Then run your virus scanner on it to see if it's infected.

➤ **If possible, copy files you download to a floppy disk and virus scan them there.** For absolute safety, virus scan a program on a floppy disk before running it on your system. This isn't always possible, though, because many files you download are too large to fit onto a floppy disk.

What Does FTP Mean?

Spend any time online downloading files and you'll come across the term FTP. FTP stands for File Transfer Protocol, and it's a way of downloading files from the Internet that's been around since before there was even a World Wide Web. Most of the download sites you visit are on the Web, but there are many that are based on FTP as well. To download files via FTP, you need to know the location of the FTP site, as well as an FTP client—a piece of software that lets you download via FTP. (You can use your Web browser for this, but it's much harder to do, and the downloads are slower.) To make things more confusing, some Web download sites actually use FTP as the underlying technology, but you only need a Web browser to download software from them.

➤ **Copy down the size and date of your system files, such as command.com, and check if there's been a change if you suspect a virus.** Some viruses do their dirty deeds by attacking system files. When they do this, they often change the size and date of system files. Write down the size and date of system files such as command.com. You can usually find command.com and other system files in the C:\ directory. If you notice your system behaving oddly, check those file sizes and dates. If they've changed, you might have a virus.

➤ **Consider disabling macros in Word and Excel documents.** The reason that Word and Excel files can be infected with viruses is that they contain macros, which are like little programs inside the files that can automate certain tasks and give you extra features. To be safe, you can disable the macros in any Word or Excel file before you open it. Viruses can only be spread if the macro is run; so a virus inside the file cannot spread, because you're disabling the macro. When you open a Word or Excel file that has a macro in it, you get a note asking you if you want to disable the macros in the file. Say yes. If for some reason, you cannot use the file because the macro has been disabled, close the file and check with a virus scanner to see if it contains a virus. If it's clean, open it back up and enable the macros.

How to Enable Word's Built-In Macro Guards

It's easy to have Word to warn you every time it opens a file with macros in it—giving you the option to disable the macros and so protect yourself against viruses. In Word 97, choose **Options** from the **Tools** menu, then click the **General** tab. Click **Macro Virus Protection**, and you are set. In Word 2000, choose **Options** from the **Tools** menu, then click **Macro and Security**, and make sure the Security Level is set to **Medium** or **High**. A dialog box explains what each setting means.

➤ **Always run a virus scanner.** The way to make sure you stay safest is to always run a virus scanner and to keep it in Auto-Protect mode so that it's checking for viruses all the time, not just when you remember to run it. For more details on how to use virus scanners, read the rest of this chapter. The picture below shows the virus scanner Norton AntiVirus in action.

Checking that your machine is clean: Norton AntiVirus looking for viruses.

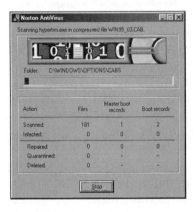

How Does Anti-Virus Software Work?

The best way to guarantee that a virus does not harm you is to run anti-virus software. This software looks for viruses on your system and kills them if you tell it to. It detects viruses in several ways. It looks for tell-tale signatures—information embedded in virus files or information that viruses leave behind that are sure signs a virus is present. It can also check your computer for odd behavior that indicates a virus is present. (On the other hand, it can't check *you* for odd behavior; for that, you have to rely on your doctor.)

Anti-virus software can help protect your system in these ways:

➤ **It checks the files on your system to see if they've been infected.** Just run the software, and it does the rest. It reports if it finds any infected files.

Techno Talk

What Does Zip Mean?

When you download a file from the Internet, it's usually been compressed—that is, shrunk in size. It's been shrunk so that you can download it to your computer faster. When you get it on your computer, you have to uncompress it to run the program. The most common way that files are compressed is using a compression standard called Zip. Uncompressing a file that has been zipped is called unzipping it. There are many programs that unzip programs that you download. The most popular is called WinZip, and it's available at many download sites on the Internet, including the ZDNet Software Library at `www.hotfiles.com` and the WinZip site at `www.winzip.com`.

➤ **It can check files before you run them to see if they're infected.** You can tell anti-virus software to automatically scan files before they're run.

➤ **It can check system files to make sure they haven't been infected.** The software can keep a constant vigil, watching your system files to make sure nothing nasty is happening to them.

➤ **It can remove viruses from your system.** After it finds a virus, it can kill it.

➤ **It can repair files that viruses have damaged.** When viruses do their dirty work, they typically damage the files they infect. Anti-virus software can not only kill viruses, it can also repair the damaged files so that you can still use them. Keep in mind, however, that this isn't always the case. Sometimes anti-virus software cannot repair the damaged file, and you have to delete it entirely.

What Is Heuristic Virus Checking?

Virus scanners detect viruses by looking for the presence of unique signatures that each virus contains. But what happens if there's a new virus just released with no known signature? Does that mean anti-virus software can't detect it? Anti-virus software can often detect viruses for which it has no signature. It does this by *heuristic scanning*—checking a computer for certain behaviors and conditions that viruses might cause. You should make sure your virus scanner detects viruses both ways: by looking for signatures and by doing heuristic scanning. Norton AntiVirus, among others, does both.

How to Use Anti-Virus Software to Keep Your Computer Safe

There's a simple first step you need to take before running anti-virus software—get a copy of one. Any one. Any anti-virus software is better than none. You can buy the software in a retail store or on the Web. And if you want, you can try out a copy for free—you can download and use all major anti-virus software for free for a certain amount of time. Head to any of the major download sites such as the ZDNet Software Library at www.hotfiles.com.

I have to be clear about my prejudices here, though. From my point of view, the best anti-virus software is Norton AntiVirus from Symantec Corp. It's the most comprehensive, the easiest to use, has the best features, and, I believe, is the most reliable. I've tried them all, and it's the one that I use. Another popular piece of anti-virus software is VirusScan.

OK. Time to get down from my soapbox. Let's move on.

Using anti-virus software is fairly simple. Start off by reading the manual. (Well, read it as much as you can stand it—it's usually written in a language that only occasionally resembles English.)

When you're familiar with how your anti-virus software works, follow this advice:

> ➤ **Set your virus scanner to Autodetect.** Most anti-virus software lets you keep it running permanently on your system, scanning files for viruses before they're run, or while they're copied or moved. Always use the Autodetect option. It's the best way to make sure you never get infected. You might also be

given various options on how to use Autodetect—in other words, whether to use the feature only when you run files, only when you copy them, or only when you download them from the Web. Use Autodetect all the time. Here you can see how you set the Autodetect options in Norton AntiVirus.

All virus checking, all the time: How to use the Autodetect feature in Norton AntiVirus.

You Have to Disable Your Virus Scanner Before You Download and Install Certain Programs

Some programs require that you disable your virus scanner while you download and install them. The most notable example is Microsoft Internet Explorer. It's fine to disable your virus scanner temporarily when downloading Explorer. But only do this for a file from a well-known source that you know does virus scanning. And as soon as you install the file, turn your virus scanner back on.

➤ **Inoculate your system.** Many anti-virus programs include an inoculation feature. It basically takes a snapshot of your system files and then regularly compares that snapshot to the current state of your files. If it notices a difference, this could mean you've been hit with a virus, and it alerts you.

➤ **Set your virus scanner to automatically check files as they're downloaded from the Web.** Virus scanners can check files for viruses before you save them on your system. Make sure to set yours to do this, for maximum safety. The nearby picture shows Norton AntiVirus checking a file for a virus as it's downloaded from the Web.

*Better safe than sorry: Set
your virus scanner to look
for viruses automatically
when you download from
the Web, like Norton
AntiVirus does.*

➤ **Even if you virus-scan a file downloaded from the Web, virus-scan it
again after you install it.** Often, when you download a program from the
Web, it comes as a single, compressed file. Your virus scanner checks that file for
viruses. But after you install the program, it expands into many files, and the
scanner might not have been able to check them all for viruses during the
download. So whenever you install a new program from the Web, do a virus
check.

➤ **Scan regularly for viruses, even if you use Autodetect.** Yes, Autodetect
scans all the time for viruses, so in theory, you don't need to tell your virus
scanner to look for viruses. On the other hand, it can't hurt. I do it all the time,
just for safety's sake.

➤ **Regularly visit the Web site of the company that makes your anti-
virus software.** Companies continually release new versions of anti-virus software, and to be safe, you should always have the newest version. To make sure
you have the newest version and to get any other news about viruses, regularly
visit the Web site of the company that makes your anti-virus software.

➤ **Download new virus definitions every month.** New viruses are coming
out all the time. If your anti-virus software doesn't know about them—and their
unique signatures—it might not be able to protect you against them. Make it a
habit to download new virus definitions every month. You get them from the
Web site of the company that makes your anti-virus software. Most anti-virus
software has a built-in feature that lets you download and install these virus definitions easily. Pictured here is the LiveUpdate feature that Norton AntiVirus
uses for getting new definitions.

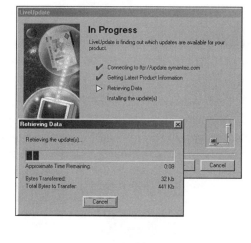

Be a good boy (or girl) and get new virus definitions every month. Here's how to do it in Norton AntiVirus.

Techno Talk

Can My Anti-Virus Software Report a False Virus Reading?

Yes. It's possible to get a report that you have a virus when in fact you don't. There can be a number of causes for this, including an error in the program's virus definition file. Still, though, it's a good idea to listen to your program's advice when it tells you that you have a virus.

Uh, Oh! I Have a Virus. Now What Do I Do?

You've got a virus. What to do? Take two aspirin, get plenty of bed rest, and...OK, let's get serious here. Computer viruses, after all, are a serious matter.

If you get a virus, I have only one piece of advice for you: Follow the directions that your virus scanner gives to you. If it detects a virus, it usually asks whether it should try to get rid of the virus—and yes, that's certainly a good idea. It kills the virus and tries to repair the file. If it can't repair the file, it instead deletes it. Bite the bullet and go ahead. It's good for you.

Backup, Backup, and Backup. Oh, and Did I Mention Backup?

You might one day get a virus that kills your hard disk. That deletes all your data and records. That eats all of the past three years of hard work. And if you don't back up your hard disk, there's nothing you can do about it.

Backing up your hard disk means making a copy of the programs and files on it. You can back up to a zip disk, to another hard disk, to a tape drive, to floppy disks, to your company's network, and even, these days, to a backup service on the Internet. I can't stress how important it is to do this. Yes, it's annoying to do. Yes, it can be time-consuming—although only the first backup takes a long time. And yes, you don't want to do it.

But do it. Believe me. It saves your rear-end if you do it and you get hit by a virus some day.

The Least You Need to Know

➤ Try to download files only from Internet sites that virus-check their files.

➤ Virus-scan any file that someone gives to you, whether it be on disk, over your company's network, or via email.

➤ Never open a file attachment sent via email by someone you don't know.

➤ Set your virus scanner to Autodetect so it's always checking for viruses—even files as they download from the Web.

➤ Get new virus definitions once a month from the anti-virus maker's Web site.

➤ Back up your hard disk at regular intervals.

Keeping Safe from Java, JavaScript, and ActiveX Applets

The Web has become a dynamic, interactive place in large part because of technologies that let you do more than just read pages and look at pictures. Three technologies—Java, JavaScript, and ActiveX—let you do some pretty amazing things on the Web. They let you play games, track stock quotes and issue warnings when a certain price is reached, help you navigate, and a lot more.

But these technologies can present some dangers as well. In this chapter, you take a look at what you need to know about the dangers and how to make sure that they don't damage your computer or invade your privacy.

Java...Does That Have Something to Do with Coffee?

Has the coffee culture gone crazy? Isn't it enough that Starbucks (a chain otherwise known to me as McCoffee) has a caffeine stand on every urban, suburban, and rural corner in this country? I mean, there's a limit to things, isn't there? (Don't get me wrong. I'm a big fan of cappuccino. In fact, as I write this I'm sitting in a café in Boston's South End with a big double cup of it steaming right in front of me—decaf, of course, otherwise I won't sleep for the next two weeks.)

But does the coffee culture have to invade our *computers* as well? And how in the world do they get Java coffee into our computers, anyway? Won't it gum up the hard disk?

Rest easy, the Java in this case isn't the common slang term for a caffeine-laced drink. Instead, it's a kind of computer technology—and it can, in fact, jazz up your computer in the same way that a strong cup of Java can set your head buzzing.

What's a Computer Language?

Your computer runs programs that have been written by someone. But how are those programs written? A computer programmer uses a computer language, which has a set of commands and instructions that can tell a computer what to do. There are many different kinds of computer languages. Java is one of them.

Java is a computer language used to create programs that can be run by your browser when you're on the Web. When you visit a Web page, instead of you merely reading text, you can do all kinds of things. You can track your investments as stock tickers and other gizmos run on your screen, for example. You can play interactive games. You can create charts and graphs and change them as you go. There are all kinds of gee-whiz things you can do. In short, Java can make the Web come alive in a way not possible before.

These programs are called applets. (Kind of sounds like cute little baby apples, doesn't it?) Tech-types often call programs applications, and so Java programs are called applets because they're generally small and not as big, for example, as Office 2000. (Which is about as big as the state of Montana, give or take a few acres.)

So far, all this sounds good. The Web becomes more interactive, you can play games and track your stocks, and everyone is happy. What could be wrong?

Sorry. There's some bad news. (You knew there had to be some of that, didn't you? Seems to be the way of the world—for every piece of good news, there's one bad.) Java can also potentially be used to create destructive programs that can do nasty things to your computer and invade your privacy as well.

What Does Platform Independent Mean?

In general, when a programmer writes a program, it's written for a specific computer—a PC, for example, or a Macintosh. This can be a pain, because it's difficult to write a program that can run on different kinds of PCs—you have to do all kinds of work to make it run properly. Java is what techies call platform independent, which means that when you write the program, it can run on any kind of computer—a PC, a Macintosh, and other kinds of computers. This is important because you never know what kind of computer visitors to your Web site use.

To understand how that can happen, you have to venture into tech-talk for a minute or two. Don't worry, though. You'll come back into the real world after a short while.

How Does Java Work—And How Can It Harm Your Computer?

It all starts when a programmer creates a Java applet and puts it on a Web page. The applet sits there, doing nothing, until visitors come along. When you visit the Web page, your computer downloads the Java applet to your computer. Your browser then starts something called a byte-code interpreter that runs the applet. The applet then runs in your browser window, and you zap the aliens or watch your Internet stock go through the roof or do whatever else the applet was designed to do.

The people who created Java recognized that this could cause trouble. They didn't want people writing Java applets that could maraud through your hard disk, deleting everything in sight. So they built security into Java. The security is fairly complicated, but the short version is this: the Java applets were designed to be restricted into what techies call a sandbox. And from that sandbox, they're not supposed to be able to look at your files or change them or invade your privacy in any way.

Sounds nice in theory, doesn't it. Ah, but in practice…that's another matter. Security experts have found all kinds of holes in the theory and point out that rogue Java applets can potentially do nasty things. They say that the applets can figure out ways to jump out of the sandbox and delete files on your computer or invade your privacy. An applet can figure out a way to crash your computer when you visit a Web page. The risks are generally small, because a lot of this stuff is tough to do—and in fact, to date, Java applets haven't wreaked destruction anywhere on the Net. Still, the possibility is there, and you should know about it and how to keep yourself safe.

How to Protect Yourself Against Rogue Java Applets

The possibility is small that you'll get harmed by a rogue Java applet, but still the possibility is there. If you're visiting a Web site you know is safe or a well-known, popular one, you most likely won't have any trouble. But you might be concerned that you could get harmed if you find yourself in one of the many out-of-the-way dark corners of the Internet.

Both Microsoft Internet Explorer and Netscape Navigator include ways that you can decide whether to run Java applets on your computer. It's fairly straightforward to do it in each. Here's how.

If You Disable Java Applets Completely, You Cannot Fully Use Some Web Pages

Keep in mind that if you completely disable Java applets you'll be locked out from using some parts of the Web. Decide whether the theoretical possibility of danger is worth not getting access to these parts. Your best option is to ask to be informed before a Java applet is run, so you can gauge the risk on a case-by-case basis.

How to Handle Java Applets in Netscape Navigator

If you're worried about Java applets, you can stop them from running when you use Netscape Navigator. It's easy to do. Here's how to do it in Netscape 4.0 and later: Choose **Preferences** from the **Edit** menu and then click **Advanced**. You see a dialog box like the one pictured here. To make sure that Java applets can't run, uncheck the box next to **Enable Java**. From now on, when you visit a Web page with a Java applet on it, it doesn't download to your computer.

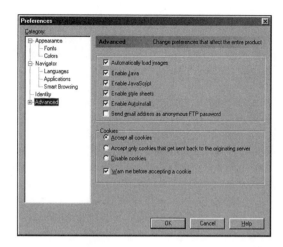

Here's how to stop Java applets from running when you use Netscape Navigator.

The problem with this method, of course, is that you cannot do any of the neat things that Java lets you do. So how are you going to kill those aliens in that game you want to play? Here's my suggestion: If you're worried about Java applets, disable them, as I've discussed here. But then when you visit a Web site you know you can trust, turn them back on. You'll have the best of both worlds.

How to Handle Java Applets in Microsoft Internet Explorer

Microsoft Internet Explorer 5.0 and later gives you more ways to handle Java applets than does Netscape Navigator. Internet Explorer lets you set a variety of security settings for Java, so that you can still run Java, but the program does some security checks for you. And you have several levels of security to choose from.

Here's how to do it. Choose **Internet Options** from the **Tools** menu and click **Security**. You see several Security Zones listed, and the Internet one is highlighted. That's what you want to customize. Now click **Custom Level**. A new window called Security Settings pops up. Scroll down until you come to the section titled Java. Here's where you can customize how to run Java on your computer.

If you want to disable Java completely, click **Disable Java**. If you don't want to disable it, but are a little leery of running just any applet that comes your way, you have three levels of security to choose from, as you see pictured nearby: High Safety, Low Safety, and Medium Safety. I'm not going to go into all the technical details of what each of those levels mean, because it's full of mind-numbing jargon and technical detail that could even cause a seasoned computer geek to run out of the room, tearing his hair and shrieking. But choosing a higher level of safety means you might not be able to run as many Java applets. I've opted to keep mine at High Safety and haven't yet run into Java applets that don't run, so I suggest you keep yours at that as well.

Microsoft Internet Explorer gives you more flexibility than Netscape Navigator in protecting against Java applets.

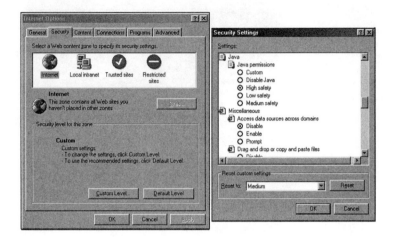

Java Jockeys Can Customize Their Security Levels

If you're a Java jockey, you can customize how Internet Explorer runs Java programs. Click **Custom** in the Java section of Security Settings and then fill out the screens of information you see. You have to know about things like File I/O, Reflections, Threads, and Client Storage. But if you're a true Java jockey, all that stuff is second nature to you.

Now I Have to Worry About JavaScript, Too? I Thought We Just Covered That in Java

Get ready to get confused. You just learned about the dangers of Java, and now it's time to learn about JavaScript. Guess what? They have nothing in common. That's right, nothing, apart from the letters J-a-v-a, that is. But aside from that, the technologies have nothing to do with one another. Go figure. Because I sure the heck can't.

JavaScript can't do things that a true program does, so in that way it's not like a Java applet, which is a true program. But it can add all kinds of interactivity and animations to Web pages. It's used all over the place on Web pages and has become ubiquitous. For example, when you move your cursor over text and it changes color, or over a graphic and it changes to something else, JavaScript might be working behind the scenes. It's a way for non-programmers to better control Web pages.

But JavaScript can do some malicious things as well, such as send information about your computer back to a Web site.

As with Java, there are ways to control how it's run in both Microsoft Internet Explorer and Netscape Navigator. Here's how.

Controlling JavaScript in Netscape Navigator

If you're worried about the dangers of JavaScript, you can tell Netscape Navigator not to run it. You do it in the same way as telling Navigator not to run Java. In Netscape 4.0 and later, choose **Preferences** from the **Edit** menu and click **Advanced**. You come to a dialog box like the one you saw previously. To make sure that JavaScript doesn't run, uncheck the box next to **Enable JavaScript**. From now on, when you visit a Web page with a JavaScript on it, Netscape doesn't run it.

The problem is that when you do this, you lose out on a good part of the Web. A workaround is to always run JavaScript except when you visit an unfamiliar page and turn it off for that page. But everywhere else, run JavaScript.

How to Handle JavaScript in Microsoft Internet Explorer

Microsoft Internet Explorer 5.0 and later gives you more ways to customize running JavaScript than does Netscape Navigator. You can turn JavaScript on or off, or instead you can be prompted before deciding whether to run it.

Make Sure to Download the Latest Browser Patches

Computer guys and gals are always finding security holes in browsers—ways to use Java applets or JavaScript and similar technologies to invade your privacy or do nasty work to your computer. In response, Microsoft and Netscape came up with browser patches—files you download to your computer and run that fix the newly discovered security hole. It's always a good idea to have the latest patches for your browser. Get them from www.microsoft.com and www.netscape.com.

You do it a lot like you customized Java. Choose **Internet Options** from the **Tools** menu and click **Security**. You'll see several Security Zones listed, and the Internet one is highlighted. That's what you want to customize. Now click **Custom Level**. A new window called Security Settings pops up. Scroll down until you come to the Scripting section and look for Scripting of Java Applets. You have three choices: Disable, Enable, and Prompt. If you're worried about running JavaScript, choose either **Disable** or **Prompt**. When you choose **Prompt**, you get a message every time JavaScript attempts to run, asking you if you want to run it.

Does ActiveX Have Something to Do with *The X-Files?*

Sorry, conspiracy fans. ActiveX doesn't have anything to do with *The X-Files*. Instead, it's a kind of technology developed by Microsoft that allows programs to be downloaded to your computer and run on Web pages. I know that this sounds a lot like Java. But it's very different than Java in technical ways (I can assure you that you don't want to know about these ways). In ActiveX, the kinds of things that get downloaded to your computer are called ActiveX controls.

There are a lot of potential security problems with ActiveX. It can potentially delete files from your computer and invade your privacy in a number of ways. Microsoft recognized this and built some security into ActiveX. The main security feature has to do with what are called certificates. When someone creates an ActiveX control, he's supposed to go to a company called Verisign and get a certificate that proves who created the ActiveX control. The idea is that people wouldn't create a dangerous control and then sign their name, address, and other information to it. When they get that certification, the control is referred to as signed.

Netscape Navigator Can't Run ActiveX Controls

If you're using Netscape Navigator, you don't have to worry about security when it comes to ActiveX. That's because Navigator can't run ActiveX controls.

By default, in Microsoft Internet Explorer, your security settings are set to high for ActiveX controls. That means that when you go to a Web page with a signed ActiveX control on it, you get a warning like the one pictured here. The warning tells you who created the ActiveX control and gives you the option of downloading it or not. Depending on whether you trust the control or not, you can decide whether to download it. If there's a control that hasn't been signed with a certificate, Internet Explorer automatically rejects it.

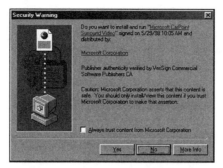

Microsoft Internet Explorer can warn you when you're about to run an ActiveX control.

If you want, you can change these security settings—in the same way that you can change Java and JavaScript settings—so that they're less stringent. But don't do it. You want to be safe, so don't take any chances.

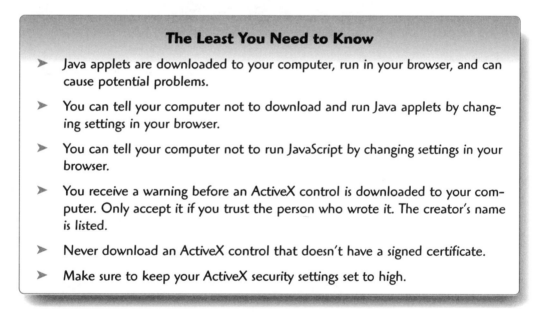

The Least You Need to Know

➤ Java applets are downloaded to your computer, run in your browser, and can cause potential problems.

➤ You can tell your computer not to download and run Java applets by changing settings in your browser.

➤ You can tell your computer not to run JavaScript by changing settings in your browser.

➤ You receive a warning before an ActiveX control is downloaded to your computer. Only accept it if you trust the person who wrote it. The creator's name is listed.

➤ Never download an ActiveX control that doesn't have a signed certificate.

➤ Make sure to keep your ActiveX security settings set to high.

Part 9

Protecting Your PC and Other Privacy Issues

Yes, strange but true: There's a world beyond the Internet. I spend so much time online that sometimes I forget. But there are dangers to your computer security and privacy even when you're not online. Someone could steal your computer's password or could snoop into your computer, for example—and they can even read files that you thought you had deleted.

This final part shows you how to protect your PC—and it also shows you how you can use the Internet to fight back and get information about privacy and security online as well as in the real world. So then you can follow the cardinal rule of Massachusetts's politics: Don't get mad, get even.

Keeping Your PC Safe from Prying Eyes

In This Chapter

➤ How to use a screen saver to password-protect your PC when it's on

➤ How to password-protect a PC so that you're the only person who can turn it on and use it

➤ Making sure that others at work can't read your files across your company's computer network

➤ Ways you can encrypt your files so that only you can read them

➤ How to permanently erase files from your hard disk

The Internet isn't the only place where your privacy can be invaded. It can also be invaded at the office where you work, or even your home. You might not want your children to be able to get at certain sensitive files on your computer, such as your tax returns, and there are probably many files that you don't want co-workers to see.

In this chapter, I show you how you can keep your PC from prying eyes, so that you are the only person who can get access to it and all your data.

How About Password-Protecting Your PC?

If you work in an office, or any place where other people might have access to your PC, the greatest danger to your privacy might not come from hackers, crackers, spammers, scammers, or other assorted slimeballs. Instead, it might come from your co-workers or other people who have access to your computer.

It's not something pleasant to think about, but it's true. A co-worker might want to snoop on you by looking at what's on your PC. (Office rivals, take note: There's nothing on my PC worth looking at—unless you think the complete lineup of the 1989 Red Sox is an industrial secret.)

It's not only co-workers who can invade your privacy at work. In most offices, many people pass through—visitors, maintenance people, and others—and it is easy for them to sit down at your PC and begin snooping around.

If you're a member of the great army of cubicle dwellers in corporations all across the country, you know how many people pass by your little piece of the universe on a given day. Every one of them can look into your PC and invade your privacy.

And you, you with the smug look on your face, yes, that's right—you over there! You have an office, so you think you're immune from this kind of invasion of privacy? Well, think again. Do you lock it every time you leave it? And even if you do, there might be cleaning and maintenance people who walk in every night and can discover all your secrets just by flipping a switch.

Here's just a few of the things people can do by turning on your computer when you're not there:

➤ They can make copies of all the files on your computer, including sensitive data, personal financial information, and more.

Check This Out

It's Easy for an Intruder to See What Web Sites You Visit, What Newsgroups You Visit, and What Messages You Post

If someone you don't know gains access to your computer, they also can find out in great detail what you do when you're on the Internet. Simply by checking your browser's History list and Favorites list, they can see where you commonly go and where you've recently been. And by looking into your newsgroup reader, they can see what newsgroups you visit and what messages your post and read when you're there.

➤ They can copy down all your passwords and any other information you have on your computer that can give them access to your bank account, Web accounts, and other sensitive information.

➤ They can pose as you and send email messages.

➤ They can delete any files on your computer that they want.

There's a lot of other bad stuff they can do—just use your imagination, and you get some idea.

There's a simple way to secure your system against prying eyes, though. Read on, and you'll see how you can do it in about three minutes.

The Three-Minute Cure for Privacy Woes: Password-Protect Your PC with a Screen Saver

It's easy to protect your PC so that when it's turned on and you're not using it, no one else can use it either. You do it by telling your PC to run a screen saver—and then password-protect the screen saver.

To do it, right-click your desktop and choose **Properties**. Now click **Screen Saver**. You see the screen pictured here.

On the road to privacy: Here's the screen that lets you password-protect your PC.

Click the arrow underneath the box that says Screen Saver and choose the screen saver you want to use. (Myself, I'm partial to the Dangerous Creates screen saver. It reminds me that there might be sharks on my screen, but they're nothing compared to the sharks out there in the business world.) You can see a small picture of what the screen saver really looks like, but to get the full effect, click **Preview**. Now it launches full screen and gives you the full screen saver effect. Warning to refugees from the 1960s: Do not choose The 1960s USA screen saver! You'll get serious flash-backs, and you'll find yourself looking for old love beads, flag-bedecked bell-bottom jeans—and you'll wonder what happened to all that lovely long hair you used to have!

Now, to password-protect the screen saver, click the **Password Protected** box. You see the screen pictured here. Type the password you want to use—preferably not a password you already have. You have to type it in twice to confirm it. That's it! Your

PC is now password protected. When your screen saver is running, the only way to get at your PC is to type your password. For information about creating the best passwords that can't be guessed, turn to Chapter 4, "How to Create Hacker-Proof Passwords."

Enter the secret word here and no one else can use your computer.

Have Your Screen Saver Start Very Soon After You Stop Using Your PC

When you use a screen saver, it automatically starts by itself a certain amount of time after you use your PC—usually about 14 minutes or so. But you can change that so it starts as little as one minute after you stop using your computer. To do that, change the number in the **Wait** box in the Screen Saver tab—for example, to one minute.

Of course, if you use your computer intermittently—let's say you're on the phone a lot—you might want to provide a longer delay so you can take a five-minute call without the screen saver—and password—kicking in.

Another Three-Minute Cure for Privacy Woes: Password-Protect Your PC

Using a screen saver to password-protect your PC works well when your computer is running and you're away from it. But how about when your computer is turned off? All someone has to do is turn it on, and your life is an open book—because a screen saver doesn't start when your computer turns on.

Rest easy, because it's simple to password-protect your computer. That way, when your computer turns on, no one can use it unless they have your password.

To do it, click the **Start** button and choose **Settings, Control Panel**. Double-click the **Passwords** icon. You see the dialog box pictured here. Click **Change Windows Password**. Type your password and then type it again to confirm it. Now, whenever you start your computer, a password appears when Windows starts to load—and no one can use your computer unless they enter the password.

Here's how to password-protect your PC so that no one but you can start it.

Surprise! People at Work Might Be Able to Read Your Files—Right from Their Own PCs

Strange fact number one: You might not realize it, but your co-workers might be able to see all the files on your computer and read them and copy them to their own computers—without you ever knowing about it!

This bit of frightening magic is brought to you by Windows 95 and Windows 98. There's a little-known feature in it called File and Printer Sharing, and if it's enabled on your computer, anyone on your company's computer network might be able to get at the files on your computer.

You Can Download Software That Will Protect Your Computer

If you want more sophisticated protection for your computer than password protection can provide, there are many programs you can download from the Internet and use. Win-Secure-It, The Lock 98, File Protector, and BookLocker Professional are just a few of the programs you can use. Many of them are shareware, which means that you can download and try them for free and pay for them only if you continue using them. You can find them at popular download sites, such as the ZDNet Software Library at www.hotfiles.com.

Luckily, it's easy to turn that feature off. Here's how. Click the **Start** button, choose **Settings**, and then click **Control Panel**. Double-click the **Network** icon and then click **File and Print Sharing**. You see the screen shown here. If nothing is checked on the screen, you're safe—no one can get at the files on your computer. If anything is checked there, uncheck it. *Now* you're safe.

Good news: No one in your company's network can read your files from their computer.

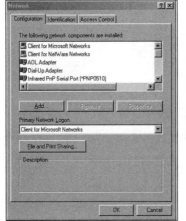

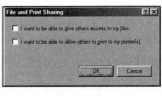

How to Encrypt Your Files so That Snoopers Can't Get at Them

Passwords are good at protecting garden-variety snoopers like your co-workers and the maintenance people from looking into your computer. But a professional hacker might be able to circumvent password protection. And maybe you don't feel the need

314

to password-protect your entire PC, but there are certain files that you want to keep from prying eyes.

In those cases, you can encrypt certain files so that no one—not even the most determined hacker—can read them. To encrypt a file means to scramble it using secret codes so that no one except you can read it.

There are many encryption programs you can try out and use to do this. My favorite is Pretty Good Privacy, more commonly called PGP. It has super-strength encryption—so powerful that the government doesn't allow it to be exported.

There's even more good news—you can use a version of PGP for free if you plan to use it for your personal use and not in a business. It's called PGPFreeware, and it's available from the PGP Web site at www.pgp.com. Just go to the Web site, download it to your computer, install it, and use it for free, forever. For information on installing it, turn to Chapter 9, "Keeping Your Email Private with Encryption." As you'll see, it's great for encrypting email as well.

After it's installed, in Windows Explorer, just right-click the file you want to encrypt and choose **Encrypt** from the **PGP** menu. You see a screen like the one that appears here. It has a group of keys on it. (I don't go into the whole key-thing here; turn to Chapter 9 for the full rundown on keys.) From here, drag your name to the bottom part of the screen. Check the box next to **Conventional Encryption** to encrypt the file. When you do that, you create an encrypted file that only you can read, but it still leaves your original file on your hard disk. Check the box next to **Wipe Original** if you want to also delete the original file so that only the encrypted file is on your hard disk.

Here's how to use PGP to encrypt any file so that only you can read it.

After you do all this, you are prompted for a password. Now you hold the key to the file—only someone who has that password can get at the file.

There Are Other Encryption Programs

PGP isn't the only encryption program out there. There are many dozens of others—and some of them are easier to use. Cryptext, Neocrypt, and Crypto are all good ones. They're either free or are shareware and are available at many download sites on the Internet, including the ZDNet Software Library at www.hotfiles.com.

How to Permanently Erase Data from Your PC

When you delete a file from your computer, you can feel pretty safe that it's deleted, can't you? You delete it, it gets sent to the Recycle Bin, and then you clean out your Recycle Bin. After it's gone from there, it's history, right? Gone forever? *Sayonara*? I have some bad news for you. The answer is no. When you delete a file from your hard disk and then empty it from the Recycle Bin, you don't actually delete it. It lives on. Yes, you heard me right, delete doesn't really mean delete.

Ah, technology. Isn't it grand?

When you delete a file from your computer, you aren't really erasing the data. All you do is eliminate the first character of the filename. Because nothing exists where the first character used to be, the computer doesn't bother looking for the rest of the file-name. As a result, your computer loses track of the file, and it *looks* as if the file is deleted. Over time, other files might overwrite your original file, and so eventually it goes away. But you don't know how. And you don't know when.

The trouble is that some sophisticated programs can examine your hard disk directly. They might, for example, find the remnants of an important contract and be able to read the names or figures it contained.

If you're one of the super-paranoid types, or have good reason to make sure that you completely erase files from your hard disk, there are ways you can do that. You need some extra software to do it.

You can use PGP to kill the data from files. After you've installed PGP, right-click a file in Windows Explorer, and choose **Wipe** from the **File** menu. That wipes the file off your hard disk, and you can bid it good-bye. There are other good programs for delet-ing files, such as Mutilate File Wiper, Download It, and other similar programs, from the ZDNet Software Library at www.hotfiles.com.

316

The Least You Need to Know

➤ A good way to protect your PC from others is to password-protect it with Windows' built-in screen savers.

➤ Make sure to set the kind of password protection that doesn't let anyone but you turn on and use your computer.

➤ Check your file and printer sharing to make sure it's turned off so that no one on your company's computer network can read your files.

➤ Use Pretty Good Privacy or a similar encryption program to encrypt individual files on your computer so that only you can read them.

➤ When you empty your Recycle Bin, the files aren't permanently deleted—there are ways they can still be read by someone.

➤ Use Pretty Good Privacy or a similar file-wiping program to permanently delete files from your hard disk.

Chapter 29

Using the Internet to Get Information About Privacy and Security

In This Chapter

➤ How to get your credit report online—and correct it

➤ How to use the Web to get your name off of telemarketing and junk mail lists

➤ How to get your name out of Lexis-Nexis P-Tracker Database

➤ Best privacy-related sites on the Internet

If you've read much of this book, you know that there's a whole lot of ways your privacy can be invaded online. (And if you haven't read much of this book, and you're reading this now, you're clearly one of those people who jumps to the end of a mystery novel to find out whodunnit before you even discover what they dun. Shame on you!)

You've also learned that there's a whole lot you can do to make sure you protect your privacy and security online. Here's even better news—you can use the Internet to fight back and uncover what private information is being gathered about you by credit bureaus, databases, and other companies. And in many cases, you can use the Web to delete that information or at least make sure that the information is correct. This chapter shows you how—and gives you the rundown on the best privacy-related sites on the Internet.

How You Can Use the Internet to Protect Your Privacy and Security

The Internet can be used to invade your privacy and endanger your security. But it can also be used to protect your privacy and security. You can use the vast resources of the Web to help you. Here are some of the things you can uncover on the Web:

➤ You can get copies of your credit ratings and history from the top credit bureaus—and you can correct any information if it isn't right.

➤ You can find out some of the information that the database giant Lexis-Nexis gathers about you—and you can ask that certain information not be provided about you.

➤ You can learn how to stop the major credit bureaus Equifax, Experian, and Trans Union Corporation from sharing information about you with direct marketers and others.

➤ You can find out how to get your name off of telemarketing and junk mail lists.

➤ You can discover an enormous amount of information about protecting your privacy and security by visiting any of the many sites devoted to privacy and security.

So come along. It's time to protect yourself and seek revenge!

Credit Where It's Due: How to Get Your Credit Ratings Online—And Correct Them

These days, without a good credit rating, you practically can't be part of the national economy. Have a good rating, and you're on top of the world—you can get a mortgage, a car loan, a college loan, and do any of the other myriad things that good credit can bring your way. But if you have a bad rating...bad news. Don't be expecting to buy that dream house any time soon.

Who compiles these mysterious credit ratings? Three big companies—Experian, Trans Union Corporation, and Equifax. (Interesting how you can't possibly tell from their names that any of those companies are in the credit business—think maybe they don't want people to know that?)

These companies compile a good deal of personal information about you and your credit history—and sell that information to companies. So a bank, for example, checks your credit ratings with one of them before extending you a loan. They also provide that information to other businesses, such as your landlord.

Here's some of the information in your credit report:

➤ Identifying information, such as your name, address, previous address, date of birth, telephone number, and Social Security number

➤ Your current and previous employer

➤ Your credit history of paying bills with stores, banks, finance companies, and mortgage companies

➤ Public records about you, such as tax liens, bankruptcies, and similar information

Beware of Credit Repair Schemes

One of the most common scams on the Internet is the credit repair scheme—someone promises that if you have bad credit he can repair it. If you hear a promise like that, run the other way—it's almost certainly a scam. Often, you end up paying a good deal of money for nothing or something you could easily do yourself. People have even given out personal information such as credit card numbers and been the subject of fraud.

Clearly, you want to know what's in your credit report—and you want to be able to correct the report if it's wrong. Here's how to get your credit report from each of the big credit bureaus. After you get your credit report, follow the instructions on each of the credit bureau's Web sites on what to do if you find errors.

Getting Your Credit Information from Trans Union Corporation

Getting your credit report from Trans Union is about as simple as it comes. Head to the company's site at www.transunion.com, click **Order Your Credit Report** and follow the directions. How much you pay depends on the state you live in. For most states, you are charged $8—although in some states, you pay less. State law governs how much you are charged for your credit reports, so whether you get yours from Trans Union, Equifax, or Experian, the cost is the same.

If You Live in Colorado, Georgia, Maryland, Massachusetts, New Jersey, or Vermont, You Can Get Your Credit Report for Free

If you live in these states, you don't have to pay to get your credit report—it's free. You can't get them for free over the Web, however. Instead, you have to call by telephone (how low-tech!). For your Trans Union credit report, call (800) 888-4213. For your Equifax credit report, call (800) 997-2493.

You can order your reports over the Web, using a secure connection, so your credit card information can't be stolen. (If that happened, who knows *what* would happen to your credit?)

Trans Union also has a good deal of helpful information about your rights concerning credit: Click **Consumer Products & Information** and start reading.

Getting Your Credit Information from Equifax

At Equifax, as at Trans Union, it's easy to get your credit report. Head to www.equifax.com, click **Consumers**, and then follow the links for ordering your credit report.

Stop Getting Junk Mail from Credit Card Companies That Get Information About You from the Major Credit Bureaus

Is your mailbox (your postal one, that is) inundated with offers for credit cards? It could be that credit card companies have checked your credit rating with credit bureaus, figured that you were a good bet, and hope you're an easy mark for their cards. If you want, you can stop getting junk mail based on information garnered from your credit reports at Equifax, Trans Union, and Experian. You can visit their Web sites and look for an opt-out policy. (Although last I checked, none could be found at Experian.) Or, you can call 888-5OPTOUT (888-567-8688) and ask to be removed from the lists of all three.

There's also a great deal of helpful information about credit at the site, and you can even see a sample credit report, shown nearby.

Hope your credit is better than this guy's! An example of a credit report from Equifax.

Good Luck Trying to Get Your Credit Report at Experian

Want to get your credit report online from Experian? Good luck. The last few times I checked, they took that option down. Go to the Web site, and you find nothing to let you do it. In fact, the last few times I visited the site, you couldn't even tell what *business* the site conducted. Again, maybe they don't want you to know.

One-Stop Shopping: Get All Your Credit Reports from ICredit.com

It can be a bit annoying, surfing all over the Web to get your credit reports, filling out different forms at different sites. So ICredit.com has a better idea: You can order your reports online from one place—through it. Head to the site at www.icreditreport.com and you can order all your reports (yes, including even the ever-elusive Experian credit report) from one place. You have two choices: You can order a single report and view it online for $8, or you can order all three and get them delivered to you via mail for $29.95. Pictured here is a sample of their single sample report delivered via the Web.

Doesn't anyone around here have any good credit? A sample credit report delivered on the Web by ICredit.com.

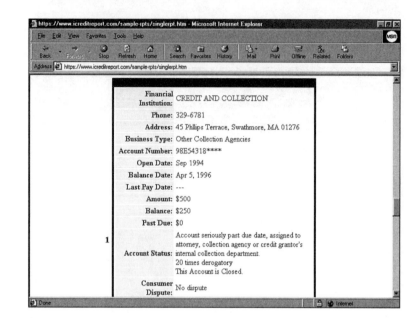

I'm Talking to You in My Underwear...How to Get Your Name Off Telemarketing and Junk Mail Lists

It's 7 p.m., and you're at home after a long, hard day at work. Finally, for the first time all day, you, your spouse, and your kids are all together, having a quiet family dinner. The phone rings. Could be your mother, calling about vacation plans, so you pick it up.

"Hello, Mr. Gralla, I'm calling from the Slimeball Bank of Outer Mongolia, and we have a new credit card with your name on it! Just ask for it now and..."

You slam down the phone. Another dinner ruined. You could have used your favorite technique for getting rid of telemarketers. ("I'm so glad you called," you say. "Because I'm talking to you in my underwear." And for once *they* slam down the phone.) Instead, you just wanted to get off the phone fast. Isn't there anything you can do?

In fact, there is something you can do. You can visit the Direct Marketing Association Web site at www.the-dma.org and ask that you be taken off telemarketing and junk mail (the postal kind) lists. Just head to the site, click Consumers and follow the directions. It doesn't eliminate every call or piece of junk mail, but it gets rid of many. By the way, you cannot file the form right on the Web. Instead, you print out a page from the Web and then mail it in. After all, they don't want to make it *too* easy for you to get off the lists, because then they'd be out of business.

Get Your Name Out of the Lexis-Nexis's P-Track Database

Lexis-Nexis is a huge database company with an enormous amount of personal information compiled about people. Businesses and others can get that information on the company's Web site at www.lexis.com—by paying a fee. If you want to get your name out of Lexis Nexis's P-Track database, which is designed for attorneys trying to track down people involved in lawsuits and law-enforcement personnel, send an email to remove@prod.lexis-nexis.com, asking that your name be removed, or mail the request to Lexis-Nexis Name Removal, P.O. Box 933, Dayton, OH 45401. You can also fax the request to (800) 732-7672.

Best Privacy-Related Sites on the Internet

The Internet is chocked full of sites that can provide you with information about privacy issues. Here's a list of the best.

American Civil Liberties Union

www.aclu.org

The privacy area of this well-known civil liberties group is a very good resource for finding out information about privacy online. Especially useful is the Data Defense Kit page, where you can report privacy violations and talk with others about privacy. There are also updates on privacy- and security-related laws and lawsuits.

The Center for Democracy and Technology

www.cdt.com

An excellent site that focuses primarily on providing information about government legislation having to do with online privacy issues.

Computer Professionals for Social Responsibility

www.cpsr.com

This group focuses on the overall impact of technology on society as whole. As you might expect, they devote a good deal of their time and energy to privacy issues.

Their home on the Web is a great place to get privacy-related information and join the group if you want.

Electronic Frontier Foundation

www.eff.org

Probably the best site in all of cyberspace for getting information on online privacy issues. You get news, government information, the latest doings inside the industry, and much more. You can also subscribe to a free email-privacy email alert—and they don't give your email address away.

Federal Trade Commission

www.ftc.gov

The government agency charged with regulating interstate commerce has an incredible amount of helpful information about protecting your privacy and safety online. Click around to the many parts of the site for help. But the best page is www.ftc.gov/privacy/protect.htm, which gives great information about your privacy rights concerning credit bureaus, direct marketers, and the way that your state Department of Motor Vehicles can release information about you to direct marketers.

The Privacy Page

www.privacy.org

Great comprehensive site for keeping up with the latest news about how to protect your privacy online and in the real world as well. In addition to news, there's lobbying efforts and advice on how to protect your privacy.

Privacy Rights Clearinghouse

www.privacyrights.org

This one provides useful information and articles about privacy, including some good ones for what to do in the event of identity theft. There's also a good set of links to other privacy-related sites.

The Least You Need to Know

➤ Instead of requesting credit reports from each individual credit bureau, you can get all of them from one source at www.icreditreports.com.

➤ If you live in Colorado, Georgia, Maryland, Massachusetts, New Jersey, or Vermont, you can get your credit report for free by calling (800) 888-4213 for your Trans Union credit report and 800-997-2493 for your Equifax report.

➤ Get your name out of the Lexis-Nexis's P-Track database by sending email to remove@prod.lexis-nexis.com.

➤ To get your name off of telemarketing and junk mail lists, visit the Direct Marketing Association Web site at www.the-dma.org and ask that you be taken off telemarketing and junk mail (the postal kind) lists.

Glossary

Speak Like a Geek

ActiveX   A technology for Microsoft Internet Explorer that allows programs to be downloaded and run in your browser.

Anonymous email   A way of sending email so that no one can tell the true identity of the sender.

Anonymous posting   A way to send messages on Usenet newsgroups so that no one can tell the true identity of the sender.

Anonymous remailer   A program or Web site that lets you send anonymous email or post anonymously to a newsgroup.

Anonymous surfing   A way to browse the World Wide Web so that no information can be gathered about you from your Web browser.

Applet   A Java program. See *Java*.

Bozo filter   A feature of some chat programs that lets you block messages from individuals who annoy you.

Browser cache   A directory on your hard disk that temporarily keeps files such as Web pages and graphics that have been downloaded to your computer when you visit a Web site.

Cable modem   A device that hooks you up to the Internet through your cable television system.

Chat   A way in which people can communicate with each other in real time, by typing messages on their keyboards.

Chat channel   A place where you chat, particularly when using IRC. See *IRC*.

Chat room   A place where you chat, particularly on America Online.

Cipher   A code used to encrypt information.

Communications protocol   A kind of language that allows computers to talk to one another over a network such as the Internet.

Cookies   A bit of data, put on your computer by a Web server, which can be used to track what you do when you are on the Web.

Deja.com   A Web site that lets you post and read newsgroup messages.

Digital certificate   A key used to encrypt and decrypt information that can be used to guarantee that you're the sender of a message or to verify the authenticity of a person sending you a message.

Digital signature   An encrypted electronic signature that identifies you as the sender of a message—and that can't be forged.

Download   To transfer information or files from the Internet to your computer.

Dumpster diver   Someone who sifts through garbage and trash cans, looking for paper with identifying information about people or their passwords.

Email filter   A way of automatically sorting incoming email so that some are automatically routed to certain folders or deleted, based on the sender and the content of the message. Email filters can be used to cut down on spam sent to you.

Email spoofing   A way of forging the From address in an email message so that it appears that the message came from someone other than the real sender.

Encryption   A method of scrambling information as it's sent across the Internet so that no one can read it.

Ewallet   An electronic wallet that contains your credit card information or electronic money so that you can use it to easily shop at many online shopping sites.

File attachment   A file attached to an email message or a newsgroup posting. Any kind of file can be attached to email or newsgroup postings.

File extension   The three letters on the end of a filename that are used to identify the kind of file it is. For example, files with .doc extensions are typically Microsoft Word files.

Finger   An Internet service that allows people to find out information about you by typing in your email address.

Flame   To vociferously attack someone in a newsgroup or other discussion area, often for no clear reason.

FTP (File Transfer Protocol)   A way of downloading files on the Internet. See *Download*.

History list   A list, kept by your Web browser, of all the recent Web sites you've visited.

ICQ   Software that lets you chat and communicate with others over the Internet.

Infomediary   A site or a piece of software that protects your privacy and lets you determine what information should be made public about you on the Internet.

Instant message   A message sent privately to an individual when both the sender and receiver are online at the same time.

Internet mailing list   See *Listserv*.

Internet service provider (ISP)   A company that provides you with access to the Internet for a monthly fee.

IP address   The numerical address of something on the Internet—the address that computers can understand. It's a series of four numbers separated by periods like this: 147.23.0.124.

IRC (Internet Relay Chat)   A way of chatting on the Internet. To chat this way, you need special IRC software.

Java   A programming language that can be used to run programs in your browser that you get from the Web.

JavaScript   A technology that allows Web designers to use a variety of interactive features on Web pages.

Key   A piece of data used to encrypt or decrypt information.

Listserv   A public discussion, similar to a newsgroup, carried on via email.

Macro   An automated set of commands in a file such as a word processing file or a spreadsheet. Macros can be infected with viruses.

Mail bomb   The automatic sending of dozens, or even hundreds or thousands, of email messages to a single email box or mail server so that the server or computer crashes.

Mail header   The part of an email message that contains the subject line, the sender, the receiver, and similar information.

Message board   A public area online where people can read and send messages.

Moderated chat   A chat in which a monitor can kick people out of the chat room if their behavior is inappropriate. See *Chat*.

331

Munge   A way of posting a message to a newsgroup so that the identity of the sender appears different from the true sender. Unlike true anonymous posting, there are ways to discover the true identity of the sender.

Newsgroup   A discussion area on the Internet.

Newsgroup reader   A piece of software used to read newsgroups.

Online auction   Just like a real-life auction, except that it's done online.

Opt out   A policy that lets you say that you don't want to receive junk mail or similar information.

Parental Controls   A feature of America Online that lets parents decide where kids can go on America Online and the Internet, and how they can use America Online and the Internet.

Password   A set of private letters and numbers or words you type in to give you access to a service or site.

PIN (Personal Information Number)   A set of private letters and numbers or words you type in to give you access to a service or site. Often used interchangeably with the term password.

POP3 server   A kind of Internet computer that lets you receive email. You usually have to put the name of your POP3 server into your email program to receive mail.

Pretty Good Privacy (PGP)   A program used to encrypt and decrypt information. It's especially useful for sending out private email that only the sender and recipient can understand.

Private key   Someone's key in an encryption scheme that only one person can use. It's used in concert with that individual's public key to encrypt and decrypt information. See *Key* and *Public key*.

Pseudonymous emailer   A kind of anonymous remailer in which the sender is given a false email address. Someone can respond to that email address, and it is sent to the true sender. See *Anonymous remailer*.

Public key   Someone's key in an encryption scheme that anyone can use. It's used in concert with that individual's private key to encrypt and decrypt information. See *Key* and *Private key*.

Registration form   A form on the Web you fill out to enter a special area of the Web site or to get special services.

Screen name   A person's name as it appears on America Online in chat areas and discussion areas. It's also that person's email address on America Online.

Secure site   A site that encrypts your credit card information as it's sent across the Internet so that the credit card number can't be stolen.

SET (Secure Electronic Transactions)   The electronic encryption and payment standard that a group of companies, including Microsoft, Netscape, VISA, and MasterCard, are pushing to become the standard for doing electronic commerce on the Internet.

Shareware   Software you can download from the Internet and try out for free, paying for it only if you decide to keep it.

Site-blocking software   Software that can block children from accessing certain sites or resources on the Internet.

SMTP (Simple Mail Transfer Protocol)   A kind of communications protocol that lets you send email. You usually have to put the name of your SMTP server into your email program to send mail.

Spam   Email sent to you that you've never asked for, trying to sell you a product or visit a Web site.

Spamoflauge   A method by which senders of spam hide their addresses by faking information such as who is sending the message.

SSL (Secure Sockets Layer)   A technology that scrambles information as it's sent across the Internet so that hackers can't read it.

SYSOP (System Operator)   Someone who moderates a chat room or is in charge of a message board.

TCP/IP (Transmission Control Protocol/Internet Protocol)   The two basic communications protocols that let you connect to and use the Internet.

Trojan horse   A malicious program that appears to be benign, but in fact is doing damage to your computer.

TRUSTe   A company that sets voluntary standards for privacy on the Internet and gives out seals that companies can post on their Web sites if the companies adhere to those privacy rules.

Unmoderated chat   A chat in which there is no monitor or moderator present.

Usenet newsgroup   See *Newsgroup*.

Virus   A malicious program that can do damage to your computer.

Web browser   A piece of software, such as Netscape Navigator or Microsoft Internet Explorer, that lets you visit Web sites.

333

Web database   A Web site that contains information that can be searched through, such as email addresses.

Web white pages   Web sites that contain information that can be searched through for identifying information such as email addresses, phone numbers, and addresses.

WebTV   A product that lets you get access to the Web on your television set.

Wipe   To permanently erase a file from your hard disk so that it cannot be re-created.

Index

337